Private Enterprise and the State
in Modern Nepal

Private Enterprise and the State in Modern Nepal

Laurie Zivetz

Madras
OXFORD UNIVERSITY PRESS
Delhi Bombay Calcutta
1992

Oxford University Press, Walton Street, Oxford OX2 6DP
New York Toronto
Delhi Bombay Calcutta Madras Karachi
Petaling Jaya Singapore Hong Kong Tokyo
Nairobi Dar es Salaam
Melbourne Auckland

and associates in
Berlin Ibadan

© Oxford University Press 1992

ISBN 0 19 562872 1

Phototypeset in Garamond by Mudra Typesetters
2-A, First Floor, First Cross, Mohan Nagar, Pondicherry 605 005
Printed by All India Press, Pondicherry 605 001
and published by S.K. Mookerjee, Oxford University Press
219, Anna Salai, Madras 600 006

Contents

List of Illustrations	vii
List of Tables	ix
Preface	xi
Introduction	1

Chapter One: The Determinants of Entrepreneurship   7
   Social Marginality / 10
   Social Organization / 20
   Factors of Production / 36
   National Policy Issues / 40
   Conclusions / 43

Chapter Two: Entrepreneurship in Nepal:
  An Overview   47
   Portraits from Nepal / 47
   An Historical Overview / 50
   The Growth of Modern Industry and
     Entrepreneurship: India and Nepal / 61
   The Ethnic Distribution of Entrepreneurship
     in Nepal / 64

Chapter Three: Entrepreneurial Communities
  in Nepal: Some Case Studies   73
   The Newars / 73
   The Marwaris / 83
   The Thakalis / 96
   The Sherpas / 103
   The Tibetans / 112
   The Gurungs and the Managis / 121

Chapter Four: Private Enterprise and
  the Public Sector   133
   Nepal's Industrial Sector: a Review / 135
   The Public : Private Sector Relationship:
     Problems and Tensions / 143
   The Public : Private Sector Relationship:
     Two Case-Studies / 178
   Conclusions / 185

Chapter Five: The Entrepreneur and the
Enterprise   189
    The Entrepreneur: Choosing a Business Career / *192*
    The Enterprise / *206*

Chapter Six: Looking Back, Looking Forward:
Some Concluding Observations   225

Glossary   233
Bibliography   235
Index   243

Illustrations

Maps
1. South Asia — 4
2. The 'Homelands' of Nepal's Major Indigenous Communities — 51

Figures
2.1 Ethnicity of Nepali Entrepreneurs by Number and Size of Industry — 66
2.2 Population and Industrial Ownership according to Ethnicity — 67
2.3 Owners of Business by Ethnic Group in West–Central Nepal — 68
2.4 Ethnic Distribution in Different Businesses in West–Central Nepal — 69
2.5 Members of Pokhara Chamber of Commerce by Ethnic Group — 69
2.6 Members of Nepal Trans-Himalayan Traders Association by Ethnic Group — 70
2.7 Distribution of Shares in Nepal's Salt-Trading Corporation by Ethnic Group — 71
2.8 Ethnic Distribution of Owners of Tourist and Trekking Agencies — 72
4.1 Nepal: Sectoral Distribution of GNP (1981/82) — 136
4.2 Public vs. Private Manufacturing Enterprises: Value Added and Employment — 166
4.3 The Performance of Public Enterprises (1982/83) — 167
4.4 Non-Nepalese Labour in Nepal by Type of Industry — 175
5.1 Reasons for Entering into Industry by Size of Industry — 194
5.2 Father's Primary Occupation by Size of Industry — 196
5.3 Grandfather's Primary Occupation by Size of Industry — 197
5.4 Other Family Members in Business — 200
5.5 Source of Skill Training for Current Industry by Size of Industry — 202
5.6 Position of Entrepreneurs in Family vis-à-vis Brothers — 207
5.7 Initial Source of Funding by Type of Industry — 215
5.8 Source of Funding for Running the Business — 217
5.9 Secondary Source of Financing by Size of Industry — 218
5.10 Market Outlet by Size of Industry — 223

Plates (following page 160)

1. and 2. At work in Nepal's labour-intensive carpet industry
3. The garment sector: an important modern arena of employment
4. Tourism: rich opportunities for the creative entrepreneur
5. A kerbside cobbler: informal sector entrepreneurship
6. An Indian immigrant hawking fruit: a commonplace sight in Nepal
7. A wayside cane furniture venture: typical of many small enterprises
8. Inside a food-processing factory: ripe for expansion?
9. Roadside repair services: what will democracy bring?

Tables

4.1	Basic Statistics Concerning Various Industries in Nepal (1981/82)	137
4.2	Classification of Industries under the Industrial Act, 1981	140
4.3	Details of Sector-wise Tax Exemption under the Industrial Act of 1981	141
4.4	Perceived Problems of Nepali Entrepreneurs	145
4.5	Problems of Industrial Entrepreneurs and Managers	146
4.6	Use of Raw Material by Types of Industries (1981/82)	147
5.1	Age of Industry by Size of Industry	208
5.2	Employment of Economically Active Population over 10 years of age according to the 1980 Census	209

Preface

The research for this book grew out of my own personal experience as a small-scale entrepreneur in Nepal. Owning and managing a small industry in the country led me into a dimension of the culture and society which aroused my curiosity about the process of industrialization, and in particular the individuals—the entrepreneurs—who were at the forefront of making that process possible. I hope that I have been able to convey something of their perspectives and dilemmas in this book.

This book would not have been possible without the help of Ashok Malla, who assisted me not only with the logistics of collecting the data for this work but also in the task of understanding and interpreting the stories, comments and insights of the entrepreneurs and civil servants we interviewed together. Mr. Om Rajbhandari, Director of Management Support Services, also provided logistical and professional assistance. I would also like to mention the special help of Jim Tomecko, Magee and Vijay Shah, Mahesh Regmi, the staff of the Small Business Promotion Project, and Abraham David. My son, Sion, now eight, also deserves thanks for his patience during those long hours in front of the computer. And my thanks, also, to my husband, John Draper, who has shared the frustrations and joys of being part of this process.

Finally, I would like to thank all of the entrepreneurs and government officials who agreed to be interviewed, and who shared their life stories and personal perspectives so willingly and freely with me.

This book is based on doctoral research carried out between 1985 and 1987. This research would not have been possible without the support of my parents, my committee, and the staff of the Union Graduate School, Ohio, U.S.A.

Some of the observations which follow may appear critical, even harsh. They are put forward in the spirit of constructive criticism. Having spent seven years living and working in Nepal, I, too, have an investment in its future. Needless to say, the opinions put forward in this document are solely my own.

Significant changes have occurred in Nepal since I researched and wrote this book. The trade and transit embargo imposed by India in March 1989 has had a tremendous impact on the supply of essential raw materials and imported commodities, export facilities, market outlets, and, presumably, access to Indian skilled labour. Related to this, the political turmoil which has rocked the country since February, 1989 promises far-reaching changes in political structures and shifts in power bases within the country. Inevitably, these events have left their mark on the private sector.

Without first-hand knowledge, I can only guess that in the short term, small entrepreneurs in particular have probably suffered significantly. My only hope is that, with a resolution in Nepal's relationship with her southern neighbour and a more democratic system of national government, these short-term difficulties will pave the way for a more open and supportive environment, one in which Nepal's tiny but diverse entrepreneurial community—from the village tailor to the large-scale industrialist—can flourish and find a more productive and accepted place in national development.

Canberra, Australia
May, 1990

Introduction

Industrialization, as a part of economic development, requires more than changes in modes of production and marketing. Without infrastructure such as roads, electricity, water, communications, technology, raw materials, technical expertise and policies which protect and support new and on-going enterprises, there would be no foundation for industrial development. Industrialization also involves changes in culture: in ways of behaviour, belief, human interaction, and attitudes towards technology. But none of these factors—alone or in tandem—is enough to catalyze or sustain the process of industrialization without the key human element: the entrepreneur. It is the individual who is able to recognize an opportunity where none has seen it before; is able to translate that vision into an operational enterprise, and is able to withstand sundry obstacles inherent in the environment; who makes the process of industrialization possible.

The emergence of industrial entrepreneurship depends in large measure on how much cultural room there is for the innovator to emerge. Equally important are the nature and degree of economic incentives in the prevailing market and policy situation which determine whether the innovator will choose industry over other investment options. In subsistence agrarian societies, which characterize most of the Third World, status and wealth are traditionally a birthright of the ruling elite. Technological change and economic innovation are often viewed with ambivalence, even suspicion. Industrialization, then, is a process of transformation. Old forms of production must be discarded or altered in favour of new ones. Old patterns of behaviour, both economic and political, must also change.

In the aftermath of World War II, emerging nations found they had to fend for themselves in a situation where much of the economic pie was already spoken for. Developed nations have assumed the role of assisting these new nations, at least insofar as global peace is maintained. In this context, new schools of thought concerned with expediting industrialization in the Third World began to crystallize. The first thinkers, most of them Western scholars, assumed that the formula was straightforward—stimulate the demand for industrial products, and the supply of entrepreneurial talent would naturally follow. This assumption, grounded in neo-classical economic thought, assumed (somewhat ethnocentrically in retrospect) that the only way to proceed from point A, the subsistence agrarian society, to point B, the diversified technological economy, was to mirror the process that had taken place 200 years before in Western Europe and later in the United States. Experience has shown that economic change is not that simple. Modernization and industrialization are far more complex processes. Third World countries which have achieved a certain level of economic development vividly demonstrate that divergent pathways can lead to similar ends. The examples of Japan, Korea, Taiwan, Hong Kong and—of special interest for the current study—India, suggest that traditional social, cultural and even economic institutions do not necessarily contradict, but can in some circumstances support the process of industrialization.

In a study of industrial entrepreneurship, several questions must be addressed. What are the economic and social preconditions for industrialization? What kind of person becomes an innovator in a society with deep-seated attitudes based in hierarchical, ascriptive values of status, affluence and power? How do governments, faced with the economic ultimatum of dwindling agricultural resources against burgeoning population growth, but sceptical about relinquishing political power to an upstart private sector, balance future imperatives with the status quo upon which their power rests? What kinds of policies encourage entrepreneurship? Do they provide enough incentives for entrepreneurs to invest in industry as opposed to other, more familiar options like trade or landholding? What kinds of cultural forms encourage the innovator to come forward, and how do they support him or her through the minefield of cultural criticism, not to mention bureaucratic, technical, manpower and raw material constraints which the industrialist inevitably faces in starting and operating a successful enterprise?

These are some of the issues to be considered in the following pages. They may be of interest to students and practitioners of economic and socio-cultural change in developing nations. They may also enlighten readers curious about some of the people who are spearheading that change. While this is a book about industrial entrepreneurs, it is especially a book about Nepal—about the struggle of a small landlocked nation to shake off its feudal past and find a place in the sun without abandoning its culture. This is a book about the actors in this drama.

Nepal is just at the beginning of the development process. Squeezed between two Asian 'superpowers', and increasingly linked with the Indian economy, the country possesses few of the natural or human resources necessary for industrialization. Geography and political history have further conspired against the economic advancement of the nation. The stunningly beautiful Himalayas, one third of the country's land mass, are virtually unproductive, save for the comparative advantage they provide Nepal in the tourist industry. The rugged terrain of the hills, and the southern alluvial plains of the country—the Terai, malarial swamp until forty years ago—served, historically, to isolate communities of subsistence farmers from one another, and from the centre of power in Kathmandu. Today, 91 per cent of the population is still engaged in subsistence agriculture.

Nepal was never colonized. As a result, it remained untouched by the external influences which set the stage for post-colonial development in other Third World nations. In 1951, when Nepal opened her doors to the world, few among the ruling élite were literate; health and other services were virtually non-existent in rural areas; the basic infrastructure necessary to build an industrial sector was extremely rudimentary, confined largely to two or three urban areas. In addition, the country was undergoing a massive reorganization of its political priorities and institutions in an effort to replace centralized, feudal control with democracy and far-ranging economic development.

In the thirty-five years since Nepal emerged from her previous isolation, the ruling regime has been preoccupied with providing basic services to its rural population. As a result, basic education is more widely available. Infant mortality had by 1978 dropped from an estimated 182/1000 live births to an estimated 104/1000 live births. This, as well as increases in longevity—from 26 for males and 21 for females in 1954 to 43 for males and 41 for females in 1975 (CBS, 1975)—has resulted in population growth, and hence pressure on precarious natural resources. In particular, deforestation and consequent soil erosion have led to the dessertification of land which provides sustenance for about 88 per cent of the population of the country.

With GDP growing at 2.3 per cent and population at 2.6 per cent per annum, the urgency of rapid economic development is highlighted. While government proclamations acknowledge the importance of

MAP 1

South Asia

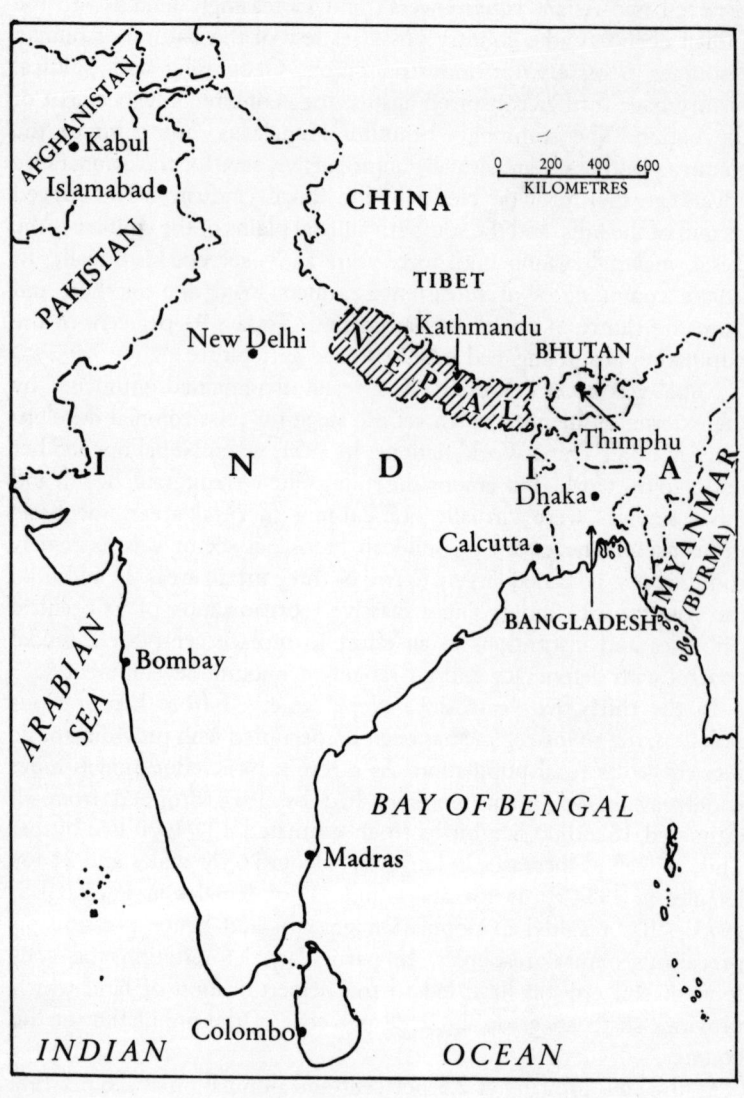

industrialization as part of national economic development priorities, there is simultaneously a marked ambivalence—reflected in the implementation of such policies—about sharing power and control over resources with the private sector. The fact that most up-and-coming industrialists are first-, second- or third-generation immigrant Indians further complicates the situation. The presence of Indian businessmen who have not assimilated is a tangible reminder for Nepalis of the economic shadow in which the country's economy functions. Like that of any satellite nation, Nepal's relationship with the Indian 'superpower' is a love-hate affair.

As a foreign observer once commented to the author, the private non-agricultural sector is still in its embryonic stages, and as such it is difficult to predict the type of child, let alone the adult, into which it will develop. According to the 1980 Census, manufacturing, both public and private, contributed 4.6 per cent to GDP. Industry employs only 0.48 per cent of the labour force. The consumer market for manufactured items is stymied by the same factors which prevent peasants from launching cottage industries: limited capital and cultural conservatism. Indigenous manufactured goods face increasing competition from imported items from India, China and South East Asia.

To unravel the complexities of entrepreneurship as a cultural and economic phenomenon, we begin with an overview of theories on entrepreneurship. Chapter I explores what the literature has to say about the impact of 'traditional' institutions such as religion (in this case Hinduism and Buddhism) and caste on the rise of industrial entrepreneurship. It also examines the impact that traditional elites and power structures, the extended family, child-rearing practices and the position of women, and agrarian forms of production may have on the process. Theories of social marginality are especially important in this examination, as they offer a framework for understanding why certain communities—which diverge in certain respects from the mainstream culture—can successfully support entrepreneurship.

Chapter II presents a broad survey of entrepreneurship in Nepal, while Chapter III considers the evolution of entrepreneurship in each community, taking into account both socio-historical factors and internal organizing principles. A common feature links these communities: they are or were culturally marginal, a factor which allowed and encouraged them to take commercial risks in order to seek to raise their cultural and economic status.

In Chapter IV, an analysis of industrial policies since 1951 and case-studies of specific private sector industries highlight the tension between the private and public sectors. In their effort to limit independent entrepreneurial activity, the forces of 'palace capitalism' still prevail in the formulation and particularly the implementation of economic policy. Corruption is explored as a medium of collusion and economic exchange: a substitute for traditional modes of patronage and reciprocity.

Chapter V takes a closer look at Nepal's industrial entrepreneurs. Who are they? Why have they chosen to enter industry? What management strategies have they adopted to survive in the highly uncertain environment in which they operate? Factors relating to the market, technology and the labour force are also examined.

The entrepreneur is viewed in this study as a product of, and an important actor in, the process of economic change. He or she is a player in the dialectic between traditional institutions and values and the social, political and economic forces that promote change.

At a superficial level, entrepreneurship may appear to express a basic capitalist tendency; the desire of the few to exploit and control the labour and resources of the many. This position assumes a political relationship between state and bourgeoisie which is not evident in Nepal. The following analysis assumes rather that private sector entrepreneurship can be a positive, even humanitarian force for redistributing control over resources to a wider segment of the population. Additionally, by strengthening and expanding indigenous economic institutions, the entrepreneur offers Nepal a means to loosen the ever-tightening grip of foreign aid, and to strengthen its hand with neighbouring nations. This book is an attempt to understand not only how and why this process is taking place, but also to give voice to those for whom the day-to-day reality of making an enterprise survive often goes unrecognized. Indeed, such individuals often face criticism, despite their role in helping to achieve the lofty goal of national prosperity.

Chapter One

The Determinants of Entrepreneurship

> *Throughout much of the world, social, religious, or ethnic distinctions often separate the merchant community from the surrounding society. In pre-dominantly pre-industrial economies, the taking of profit is considered socially illegal. Profit signifies the introduction of economic rationality into a system which is based on the rationale of kinship and family. Whatever group undertakes business and the making of profit also accepts social ostracism and develops over time social traits which allow it to withstand the slings and arrows of its non-commercial neighbours (and victims) as well as traits which maximize the production of profit which is so socially disreputable.*
> – Fox, describing a merchant community in Uttar Pradesh, India, cited in Timberg, 1978, pp. 313–14.

What makes the entrepreneur different? Why do individuals from a particular community undertake the difficult task of economic change when it usually makes them unpopular? How does the community shield the individual from conservative and critical forces in the larger society and encourage him to go against the tide in the pursuit of economic innovation? Can we define what an entrepreneur does—and what motivates him[1] to do it—in a way that is applicable across cultures? What contextual economic and policy factors stimulate or stifle entrepreneurship?

The following discussion attempts an overview of what the literature has to say about some of the socio-cultural and economic factors that determine (and are in turn influenced by) entrepreneurship. An underlying assumption of this review (which is intended as a theoretical

---

[1] The use of the male pronoun in this and the rest of the text is meant to include both male and female subjects. While there are fewer female entrepreneurs in Nepal and other countries than male, women do play a variety of roles in business and non-business spheres.

framework for the empirical analysis that follows), is that in the early stages of economic development—most relevant for our case-study of Nepal—the tension between the entrepreneur (as economic innovator and agent of change), and the larger culture (in particular as articulated by and through the ruling élite) is highly pronounced. It is the entrepreneur who activates and embodies both cultural and economic change and is thus a deviant *vis-à-vis* the status quo. Two factors seem of special interest in this regard: firstly, the internal socio-cultural and fiscal organizing formations which allow the entrepreneurial community to engage in commercial endeavour; secondly, external economic realities (for example, the relative strength of market forces) which provide incentives and disincentives for entrepreneurial activity.

It would clearly be wrong to assume that such processess are universally identical, that the phenomenon of entrepreneurship can be duplicated—in form, if not in substance—under circumstances which differ across time and space. The behaviour which we call entrepreneurship—the ability of an individual to identify and act on novel economic opportunities in a particular situation—may vary substantially from one context to another. While in one circumstance a slight improvement in technology or the introduction of a new technology may suggest a new market niche to one individual, the more efficient organization of labour in manufacturing a product already on the market may be an equally legitimate entrepreneurial activity for another. Entrepreneurship is not limited to innovation in the technical and managerial spheres either. In the developing country context the entrepreneur may differ from his non-commercial counterpart in his personal traits (for example, his degree of 'charisma') or his ethnic affiliations. These may facilitate access to the patronage networks embedded in government bureaucracies. The factors motivating entrepreneurship are likewise diverse. While industrial entrepreneurship may represent a way to achieve, or re-establish, a degree of status for one individual or community, for another it may offer a means to diversify beyond an existing economic base. This is not to imply that these factors are mutually exclusive. We should, however, consider and allow for a variety of causal and contextual factors in exploring the phenomenon of entrepreneurship.

What we *can* say is that entrepreneurship always involves change. But in order for the individual, or community, to step into the shoes of the agent of change, the benefits—perceived or real—must outweigh the risks. The factors that determine both the perception and the reality of these risks and benefits are not always based on objective economic realities. In this and the chapters that follow the compelling influence of cultural, political and historical currents on human economic behaviour is scrutinized.

A growing body of theoretical and empirical literature on entrepreneurship in developing countries has led to the evolution of some important—if sometimes contradictory—insights into the subject. As a relatively new field of research, the study of entrepreneurship inevitably reaches with one hand into the Pandora's box of basic human motives, both individual and cultural. It also probes the complex dynamic of economic and political change. This is an ambitious task. To use Peter Kilby's (1981) apt metaphor, the study of entrepreneurship is like hunting the heffalump—the search for a beast whose precise nature is not yet clearly understood in a forest wherein much of the terrain is likewise only partially familiar. This case-study of Nepalese entrepreneurship aims at least to add a little clarity to the search.

There is a tendency in the literature on entrepreneurship towards reductionism: a single independent variable is often put forward as the primary catalyst for, or determinant of, entrepreneurial activity. The need for achievement, social marginality, caste status, and experience in trade are some of the variables that have been identified. This chapter follows this shopping-list approach as a way of setting out the ingredients from which the final product, entrepreneurship in its various manifestations, is achieved. But while this approach has the merit of simplicity, it ignores the *reciprocal* relationship between the so-defined dependent and independent variables. In the final analysis, we will suggest that what determines entrepreneurship can also be determined by it. Social marginality, for instance, may be as much a cause for as an outcome of entrepreneurship. Likewise, a more complex variable like caste can delimit or catalyze entrepreneurship, but in so doing often engenders a *redefinition* of caste status—both internally and in relation to other castes.

It is important to emphasize at the outset that the conceptual terrain to be covered is vast. In one chapter the most that can be achieved is an overview of the essential issues, each of which could legitimately consume a volume. While the discussions that follow on such subjects as religion, caste, and child-rearing and their relationship to entrepreneurship may appear superficial to scholars, they aim to provide a framework for the empirical analysis which follows. Because so little has been written on Nepal in many of the areas of concern, the discussion relies heavily on the literature from the Indian experience.

SOCIAL MARGINALITY

In discussions of entrepreneurship in developing countries, it is generally agreed that entrepreneurs come from distinct social sub-groups; they are not randomly drawn from the population at large. In addition, it is virtually unheard of for the leading commercial and the leading political elements in a given society to spring from the same sub-group, though alliances may exist between the two. An entrepreneurial community is usually separate in some way or other from the prevailing culture: it may be an immigrant group; a formerly powerful group that is now out of favour; a group in religious transition; a group historically at the margin, now trying to elbow its way into power or riches; or a group of traditional traders or financiers now exploiting new investment avenues. Of course, not all such communities become entrepreneurial, nor do all members of entrepreneurial communities become entrepreneurs. However, the social organization and prevailing attitudes of the entrepreneurial community support those who do, and, if the pioneers succeed, generally encourage others to follow.

Weber (1968) was the first to put forward the concept of a 'pariah' people whose very low political and social status either promotes or results from commercial activities considered aberrant by the society at large. Hoselitz (1964) describes social deviants, or 'marginal men', as the ideal group for introducing economic change 'precisely because of their ambiguous position from a cultural, ethnic or social standpoint—peculiarly suited to make new creative adjustments in situations of change ... [they] develop genuine innovations in social behaviour.' (Park, 1950, quoted in Hoselitz, 1962). Hagen (1962) suggests that the prerequisites for entrepreneurship most commonly occur in a community which has experienced 'status withdrawal'. The initial anger which this engenders is turned inward, affecting the family dynamic, and, over several generations may be transformed into an urge to reassert and re-establish power and prestige through alternative and more accessible avenues such as business. Young (1981) contends that 'reactive sub-groups', experiencing status withdrawal, immediately begin searching for alternative opportunities for power, prestige and prosperity, which involve minimal conflict with the dominant culture. According to Young, the success of such groups depends upon a resilient, cohesifying cultural organization and an 'internal definition' which is better suited to entrepreneurial endeavour than that of other marginalized groups in the society. Geertz (1962) further suggests that intra-community homogeneity is important, and that the 'internal definition' is typically based on a self-perception that the community is morally superior to the larger society, which is regarded as wayward, unenlightened, or stagnant.

Several empirical studies have lent support to these theories of social marginality and entrepreneurship. Nandy (1973a) attributes the successful bid for prestige (in this case, through industrial entrepreneurship) by a low caste, agrarian community in West Bengal to the community's social cohesion. The community's new socio-economic status further strengthened its 'internal definition'. Geertz (1962) describes the emergence of an industrial community in Indonesia in terms of an internal re-definition, melded from simultaneous social and religious upheaval within and around the community. Change, and a new self-perception, allowed economic innovation to take place within the formerly non-entrepreneurial community. Papanek (1973), in her study of the Memons, a leading entrepreneurial community in Pakistan, describes a strong business ethic as the cultural glue of this community. Timberg (1974) attributes the entrepreneurial success of the Jews of Calcutta—as elsewhere—to their strong communal identity in both the religious and business spheres.

Immigrants and refugees. Immigrants and refugees are, by definition, outside the mainstream culture. The entrepreneurial immigrant moves because he perceives opportunities in another context for filling certain gaps. They may relate to investment and innovation opportunities or to contracting opportunities in the market-place at home (Bauer and Yamey, 1957). Migration here takes place with the motivation, skills and capital necessary to undertake the new commercial activity. Bauer and Yamey point out that when immigrants come from countries poorer than the ones to which they migrate, they have the added advantage of a more frugal lifestyle, allowing them to save and reinvest their savings.

Refugees are also a self-selected population. In times of crisis which compel people to flee their homes, not all the population which is at risk is able or willing to uproot itself. As one would expect, it is those with greater vision, wealth and/or political contacts who move. It is not uncommon for the refugee to arrive in the host country without any of the skills or capital necessary to establish an immediate foothold in the new market-place. Furthermore, the shock of exile may impede adaptation on the part of refugee populations. Refugees in a state of shock and disorientation have been known to take a generation or two to recover. Ultimately, however, the refugee community is compelled to identify income-generating opportunities in the new society, or remain dependent upon it.

The newcomer, then, whether immigrant or refugee, must adapt and survive, the combination sometimes lending itself to new forms of economic activity. Because they are foreigners, immigrant groups are typically barred from investment in land or access to administrative positions (two sources of power traditionally coveted by indigenous elites in developing societies). Additionally, because they are outsiders, immigrants are less constrained by the normative pressures which the mainstream culture exerts on domestic commercial groups. This greater cultural flexibility is a potential advantage which immigrant groups have over their indigenous counterparts, particularly when economic innovation involves a restructuring of modes of production or a shift in control over resources. The combination of marginality and internal flexibility characterizes many immigrant and refugee communities which are successful in industry and/or commerce. The degree to which immigrant or refugee groups assimilate—through intermarriage in particular—has an obvious and direct bearing upon their cultural exclusiveness. In many cases (for example, Jewish communities throughout the world, the Indians in East Africa, and the Marwaris in Nepal), endogamy and the maintenance of community-based cultural integrity appear inextricably interwoven with the community's continuity as an entrepreneurial group.

On the other hand, such cultural and social separateness renders such communities easier targets for censure, discrimination, and even expulsion in some cases. In general, the contribution of foreign entrepreneurs to economic development tends to be minimized, and often harshly criticized, when their community fails to assimilate. Criticism is commonly focused on what is construed to be foreign competition with domestic commercial elements (Bauer and Yamey, 1957).

Traders and merchants. In most traditional societies, traders, financiers, money-lenders, and merchants are drawn from specific castes, tribes or other sub-groups. Because the traders and financiers of today often become the industrialists of tomorrow they are of special interest to us here.

While mercantile status in a society may be ascriptively defined (as with the *vaisya* or commercial multi-caste category in the Hindu hierarchy), geography is clearly a key element in the emergence of trading communities. These arise at, or gravitate to, a strategic crossroads of goods and services—a seaport, the confluence of navigable rivers, the juncture between different geographic zones or nation states with reciprocal demands for one another's products, services, or capital. The economic longevity of a trading community to a large extent depends upon its ability to continuously identify new products and services that, available on one leg of the trade route, can be marketed in another.

In predominantly agrarian settings (that is, in most traditional societies) communities living on less fertile land or in inhospitable growing conditions will resort to trade to supplement their income. Trade is also an economic alternative for communities who for some reason cannot own land. Since these communities usually border counterparts in similar resource-deficit conditions, trade tends to be localized. In this case, merchants operate in a traditional bazaar economy, sometimes on a barter basis, and within a circumscribed market-place. However, a localized tradition of trade may sow the seeds for long-distance, greater volume trade.

At the village level, it is often the trader or merchant who responds to new consumer tastes and introduces new products. He forms the economic bridge to the larger market-place. In the very early stages of economic transition, it is the trading community which typically introduces the money economy (Sadie, 1964). While this offers a potentially greater market for locally produced agricultural and non-agricultural goods, it also upsets traditional barter and reciprocal exchange systems by concentrating profits in the hands of the trader or trading community. For this reason, Hagen (1962) suggests that in some traditional societies, people who trade in other people's goods are perceived to be selling the dignity or identity of the craftsperson.

This is also the case in agrarian settings where land provides the greatest degree of economic security and social prestige. The landed gentry are commonly the ruling élite (Lambert, 1964). Trade can and does introduce new forms of profit accumulation, but in so doing cuts into the traditionally ubiquitous control of the landed elite over resources. Landowners, generally hesitant to invest in trade, seek to place constraints on the trading community in order to preserve their traditional prestige and power. This is reinforced by the fact that the trading community commonly has the capital reserve to finance loans—a role also traditionally in the hands of landowners.

Several aspects of the trader mentality are inherently entrepreneurial, especially when compared with the ethos of traditional farming communities. First of all, the long-distance trader, unlike the farmer, is constantly moving about, gaining exposure to new people, places, and ideas. Not only does this give the trader a broader world-view, but it also requires him to adapt to new situations, and to make friends and alliances outside his own sub-culture. The trader therefore tends to be more flexible in his systems of belief and behaviour, whether social or economic (Papanek, 1973; von Fürer-Haimendorf, 1975). In other respects, too, trading seems far removed from the experience and lot of the subsistence farmer. The trader's arena of action is the marketplace; here, he requires skill in judging fluctuations in supply and demand, and in organizing the finances and logistics necessary to put the two together. Thus, even if trade is of a barter nature, it requires a greater degree of economic savvy than does farming (von Fürer-Haimendorf, 1975).

Whether the trader of today will become the industrialist of tomorrow depends to a large degree on the opportunities for profit in industry—both perceived and real—and the ability and willingness of the trader to take advantage of those opportunities. Industry requires long-term investment, the organization of a labour force and technological expertise which may not be easily accessible. While traders are used to risk-taking, their returns on investments are usually more immediate, linear and founded on the single deal. Industry, in contrast, requires investment in fixed assets for which the return is incremental and long-term. Geertz (1973) and Mines (1973) cite examples from India where merchant communities were unable to make this transition and were surpassed by more technically oriented communities. Harris (1971), in a study of Nigerian entrepreneurs, found that traders and craftspersons were important in creating infant industries in the country, but that traders had a harder time with technology. Other researchers likewise conclude that access to capital may be less important than technical or management expertise for the novice entrepreneur (Hoselitz, 1952).

A preliminary conclusion from these studies is that when traders become industrialists it is the long-distance trader rather than the sedentary, bazaar-based merchant who is more likely to diversify into industry. This is particularly so when trade and manufacturing complement one another and serve to expand economic returns. The long-distance trader has the advantage not only of exposure to new ideas and technologies but also of a longer term perspective on investment and its likely returns. This conclusion seems substantiated in the case of Nepal, as Chapter II attempts to demonstrate.

The money-lender. The money-lender in an agrarian community has a function analogous to that of the local merchant (and indeed they are sometimes one and the same person). As the precursor of formalized banking, the money-lender collects the village surplus (in the form of money, grain, animals, or even labour) as interest, collateral and equity itself. This he in turn sells or invests in a larger market-place. The money-lender is often the one who owns the village shop which markets items imported into the village. This shop is also the conduit through which surplus goods are bartered or exported out of the village. In Nepal, it is the money-lender who extracts labour in lieu of debt repayments (Caplan, 1972). In many parts of the country, it is common practice for the village *sahuji* (a word which means synonymously shopkeeper and money-lender, and bears a somewhat pejorative connotation) to purchase milch animals, giving them out on loan to farmers. The farmers then feed and raise the animals, making short-term use of the manure and milk they produce. When the animal is full grown, the farmer is obliged to return the animal to the *sahuji*, who resells it at a profit.

Although the *sahuji* characteristically enjoys a monopoly position which enables him to exploit the local peasantry, he does provide an infant market-place through which peasants, by 'investing' their money, goods and services, can gain access to credit. The village money-lender can be described as socially marginal in the sense that his position contradicts modes of reciprocity and equalization of wealth and threatens élite control over resources and culturally sanctioned modes of economic behaviour. As Lambert (1964) comments, 'Moneylenders, storekeepers, and traders who mediate between the village and the outside world are considered to be parasitical, since, in the view of the peasants, their work does not contribute to the agricultural process.' (p. 275) Peasant farmers, constrained by funds as well as the social stigma associated with money-lending, rarely engage in this type of economic activity. It is rather the outsider—in Nepal, the immigrant Newar or the high-caste Brahmin—whose business acumen in the first instance and superior status in the second gives him or her the cultural immunity to perform the money-lending function (Caplan, 1972). It is noteworthy that while these individuals are seen to play a parasitical economic role in the village setting, in other respects they embody the mainstream culture.

Other groups with entrepreneurial potential. Traders and merchants, immigrants and refugees are of course not the only groups with entrepreneurial potential. Hoselitz (1960) suggests that bureaucrats can put to rewarding use their expertise in long-term industrial planning—an advantage they have, he suggests, over the trader with his more limited time-frame. Noblemen, too, are not without prospects in this area. Geertz (1962) describes a group of disenfranchised nobles in Bali who used their organizational ability and tutelage role to move into the industrial sector: 'Thus in their bid to create a modern economy the aristocrats have at their disposal a quantity of cultural capital in the form of traditionalized social loyalties and expectations.' (Geertz, 1962, pp. 400–1) This Hindu group, facing domination by a Muslim majority at the national level, illustrates Hagen's point about status withdrawal: ' "We have lost control of the government," these disestablished nobles say, "so we'll capture the economy." ' (p. 401) Geertz compares this group with a Javanese Muslim trading group that has successfully entered industry in the wake of internal socio-religious reformation, and comments, 'The Japanese entrepreneurs want mainly to get rich, the Balinese to get (or remain) powerful.' (p. 404)

Technical expertise can also predispose individuals or communities to industrial entrepreneurship. In more traditional settings, occupational ascription plays a major role in determining the type and extent of skill an individual brings to a new enterprise. Caste artisans (in the Hindu context) can capitalize not only on their inherited skills but also on the absence of taboos against manual labour which may inhibit the entrance of higher caste individuals into industry (Nandy 1973b). In more technologically advanced societies, entrepreneurial communities often seek out educational opportunities which will enhance their business interests. In present-day India, for instance, where the groundwork for industrialization has already been laid, new industrialists come with better technical training than did their predecessors. In the early stages of industrialization, technical expertise—particularly among smaller entrepreneurs—is often acquired through on-the-job training. In India (and increasingly in Nepal), 'imitative' entrepreneurship acts as a multiplier in the industrial sector.

Several studies point to religious 'marginality' or minority status as an important prerequisite for community entrepreneurship. Adherence to religious beliefs which separate a community from the religion of the majority can bind it together in ways which allow it to pursue commercial endeavours shunned by the society at large. Several communities have been mentioned above (Timberg, 1978; Papanek, 1973; Geertz, 1962) for which an internal definition based on socio-religious norms is vital to entrepreneurial success.[2] While not all religious minorities use entrepreneurship as a means for self-assertion, it is not uncommon to find that entrepreneurial communities in traditional societies practise a religion different from that of the majority.

The colony. It could be argued that colonialism established a kind of 'marginality' relationship which contained within it both seeds and obstacles for entrepreneurship in the colony after independence. McClelland (1969) suggests that colonial domination can stimulate feelings of status withdrawal on a national scale; when this happens, the post-colonial culture tends to be more achievement-oriented and economically innovative. On the other hand, if a hostile or reactionary attitude to the colonial culture (including the technologies and modes of production which are equated with that culture) sets in, potentially beneficial economic modalities may be rejected in favour of a reassertion of traditional economic behaviour (Hagen, 1962).

---

[2] Timberg (1974) offers several examples of the correlation between religious minority status and entrepreneurial activity, among them the Iraqi Jewish communities along the Shanghai-Baghdad trading route, the Jewish diamond dealers of Antwerp, the Armenian and Parsee communities in Calcutta and the Marwaris of India. Papanek (1973) and Geertz (1962) provide examples of Moslem commercial communities, and Geertz (1962) of a Balinese Hindu commercial community, with an internal definition based on a combination of religious orthodoxy and business acumen. In Nepal, the Marwari community adheres to a specific interpretation of Hinduism which similarly offers a strong business-based internal definition.

If we assume (as these scholars may not) that where the economic imperatives are sufficiently strong, a culture will give way and adapt, it would be fair to predict that in the post-colonial era a country would pick and choose to its best advantage from what the colonial power had earlier introduced. For example, it is possible that even as a national culture seeks to shake off the colonial mantle in the post-colonial era, specific indigenous communities which have gained expertise under the colonial regime may begin independently asserting themselves. In India, for instance, while the Gandhian movement was engaged in rejecting technologies introduced by the British, a number of Indian Marwaris were establishing modern industries based on what they had learned under the British. (At the same time, many Marwaris supported the Gandhian cause.)

Whether the colony turns its 'marginality', or relative social, economic and political disadvantage, to commercial gain is dependent, of course, on more than cultural considerations. The economic interdependence of colony and colonial power, and the conditions prevailing in internal and international market-places at the time of independence also influence the extent to which a former colony can escape from past dependencies or exploit those dependencies in its own self interest.

Traditional Élites. Our discussion of the social marginality or minority status of entrepreneurial communities in traditional societies would not be complete without some consideration of their foils: the traditional élites who reflect and shape the mainstream culture. The political power of the ruling élite is generally established through force and/or economic control over important resources. Power is perpetuated through symbolic or institutional ascriptive forms such as religion, caste, lineage, and the monarchy (Marx, 1958a; Weber from Giddens, 1971). For this reason, ruling élites are typically conservative elements: the preservers and protectors of the prevailing cultural, religious and economic status quo.

Lambert (1964) describes what he calls 'caretaker élites' in the Asian context as 'self-styled' institutions that claim to champion democracy and an improved quality of life for the rural poor. These efforts are made and legitimated, however, through maintaining tight control over the reins of resource distribution and by keeping 'suspicious' business elements out of the ruling ranks.

> They [i.e., the 'caretaker élite'] consider that both wealth and savings in the economy as a whole will be most effectively increased and best utilized for national growth to the extent that they are controlled by government. The history of the private sector in their economies, and what they consider the anti-social acquisitiveness of both foreign and indigenous business groups, do nothing to dissuade them from this viewpoint. (Lambert, 1964, p. 271)

Viewed more cynically, the business community threatens not only to upset the balance of control over resources, but also to undermine popular faith in the legitimacy of the power of ruling élites.

The introduction of technology, ushered in by industrial entrepreneurs, involves corresponding changes in the distribution and control of resources which may loosen the hold of traditional élites. Hagen (1962) suggests that the disdain for modern technology which is common among traditional élites in developing societies is related to questions of status. Such élites attempt to rationalize their status by shunning manual labour—the domain of the lower classes—with which technology is associated. By suggesting that technology and manual labour are somehow degrading or of lowly status, the traditional élite uses its cultural leverage to impede industrial entrepreneurship. Another common by-product of this tension is that industrial entrepreneurs tend to be culturally isolated while prospering economically—as long as they share the profits with the ruling élite. This is, broadly speaking, the situation in Nepal.[3]

This dynamic resolves itself differently in each society and defines the environment in which economic development occurs. When the objectives of rulers and business elements are diametrically opposed, economic stagnation or political unrest are predictable (Marx, 1958b). Some common ground must be found. In more 'mature' economies, political and commercial élites will come to terms with one another out of mutual dependency, and more 'rationalized' systems of control over power and resources will evolve (Durkheim, 1964).

In sum, the attitudes and behaviour of the ruling élite are important in determining the cultural, political and economic milieu in which entrepreneurship takes shape.

Beyond social marginality. In traditional settings, economic change often emerges from a dialectical struggle between 'outsider' groups who

---

[3] See Chapter III.

innovate in an attempt to regain or assert power, status, or riches, and 'insider' groups concerned with maintaining the status quo. This process does not occur without cost to the society. Typically it happens relatively slowly, diverting economic and human resources in the struggle for compromise and change. By contrast, in a situation where traders and industrialists are welcomed and easily incorporated into the mainstream, the pace of economic development is markedly accelerated. One example was the United States in the process of industrial development, in which

> As far as the general public was concerned the business executive was playing to an appreciative audience. Trade or manufacturing, even on a small scale, carried no social stigma. Financial success could immediately raise the executive to the topmost level of American society. This pull of unrestricted opportunity was absent in the more rigid societies which characterized the rest of the civilized world. (Cochran, 1971, p. 100)

This example is perhaps the most extreme foil to the traditional society. It does, however, keep in perspective the variety of incentives and constraints to economic innovation that exist in different socio-cultural circumstances.

SOCIAL ORGANIZATION

Some of the social and cultural institutions and practices which characterize, delimit and determine change in transitional societies—particularly those of South Asia—are discussed in this section. The list includes codes of reciprocity, religion, caste, the joint family, child-rearing, and the role of women. The extent to which community, culture and family inhibit or encourage behaviour conducive to entrepreneurship will be a major thread throughout this discussion.

Traditional agrarian societies have been characterized as hierarchical, custom-bound and ascriptive (Hagen, 1962). These are not chance factors but rational responses to the actual circumstances in which subsistence farming societies live. Arbitrary factors which condition the weather, birth, disease, death or misfortune must be reconciled and fitted into an acceptable world-view. The individual, with a limited understanding of how these forces operate, is unable to recognize his ability to alter events. Thus he attributes good fortune and calamities alike to forces greater than himself—the gods, fate or, in the Hindu context, *karma* (Hagen, 1962; Sadie, 1964). Economic and social relationships also contribute to the individual's sense of powerlessness. Individual identity, productive and consumptive relationships, status and wealth are ascriptively defined in a relational 'enveloping' view of the self in society and the universe: what Durkheim (1964) calls the 'conscience collective'.

This situation is by no means static, however. New political, economic, and institutional forces inevitably trigger change and adaptation in behaviour and belief systems. Education is an important mechanism for expanding the perceptions (and options) of rural individuals. Improved transportation and communication networks have likewise extended the horizons of isolated communities. Urbanization is perhaps the most powerful vehicle for change. Not only does the city embrace a greater plurality of cultural and behavioural patterns, it also offers a rich diversity of economic opportunities. The generalizations put forward in this section assume that while the traditional agrarian sector remains an important social and economic backdrop for developing societies (for the great majority of Third World inhabitants are still rural-based) the locus of change—both cultural and economic—is the city.

Reciprocity and equalization of wealth. Several prominent anthropologists have suggested that reciprocity—the pattern of necessary prestations and exchange of gifts, goods and services—is fundamental to the organization of all societies (Mauss, 1954; Levi Strauss, 1969). For farmers living at the margin, or for even more primitive hunting and gathering communities, the community is the individual's insurance against destitution. While gift-giving and individual exchange is the fundamental form of reciprocity, other more complex forms are also common. Economic reciprocity may take the form of rotating labour or credit systems; religious ceremonies which redistribute wealth to the poor; systems of hospitality exchange; or even landlord-tenant relationships which involve mutual dependencies. Codes of reciprocity insure that what resources are available are shared evenly in the community. This maintains a resource balance, and protects the individual and the family from loss which could in turn render them dependent upon the community.

Reciprocity in traditional societies is based on a view of society and the universe as an organic whole in which all the parts require equal attention and support. Individual identity is fixed in relation to social structures, whether the family, the tribe, the caste, the clan or others.

The determinants of occupation and the relationship between producer and consumer is consistent with this organic conception. Reciprocity relationships are kept intact through normative social controls and institutions such as caste.

When such hierarchical and ascriptive belief systems prevail, innovative behaviour—or the introduction of new modes of exchange which disrupt the equalizing force of reciprocal structures—is typically perceived as a challenge and threat to the status quo. The agent of such change is considered deviant. The village money-lender, for instance, is a direct challenge to equalizing forces at the village level because he accumulates wealth at the expense of other community members (Fricke, 1984). Thus, social sanctions against individuals who venture into new money-making activities are strong. Hunter (1969) aptly sums it up:

> If patience, endurance and the highest sense of family and social obligation are among the great virtues of traditional village life, suspicion, faction and fear are on the reverse of the coin. Village societies are levelling societies, in which attempts by equals to gain individual advantage are constantly suspected and bitterly resented. No doubt this springs from fear that the fundamental security of the village will slowly be lost if one individual after another can reach a platform of prosperity from which he might not need the help of the community and could therefore excuse himself from helping them. (p. 40)

The literature suggests that entrepreneurship emerges at the point at which reciprocity begins to weaken in favour of individual initiative and profit accumulation (Levi Strauss, 1969; Mauss, 1954; Marx 1958b). However, as we shall see in Chapter IV, reciprocity and entrepreneurship can co-exist, and even reinforce each other, in traditional settings. In particular, when reciprocal structures are such that large portions of the community have access to entrepreneurial opportunities simultaneously, such institutions even serve to *promote* entrepreneurship, at least in the short run, by equalizing risk.

Religion: Hinduism and Buddhism. Is religion the opiate of the people, as Marx claimed? Does it hold societies back from developing? Is Hinduism as rigid and restrictive as Weber claimed it to be? While there is no way of measuring the precise impact of religion on economic development or entrepreneurship, assumptions can be made about religion-derived behaviour that might predispose a group towards economic or technological innovation and change. However, it is important to keep in mind that there is always a difference between the theory and practice of religion. Religion is not an abstract, separate concept to the South Asian; it is the axis around which all aspects of life rotate. In this sense, it borders on synonymity with culture itself, and as such is vulnerable to constant adaptation and reinterpretation in the face of compelling economic and political forces. History has demonstrated the myriad ways in which human beings have been able to reorganize their belief systems to suit the times.

Nepal is a Hindu kingdom, and the prevailing socio-cultural synthesizing force comes from the Hindu belief system. However, Buddhism, which entered Nepal from India[4] and, later, via immigrant groups from Tibet, co-exists harmoniously with Hinduism in the country. What has been the impact of these two major religions on the development of entrepreneurship in Nepal?

Hinduism, and the caste system which is associated with it, is an extremely complex area of research and debate. The key aspect of the Hindu social order which is fundamental for a discussion of entrepreneurship is the built-in and overarching inequalities inherent in the caste system, and the implications these have for status, occupation and access to resources and power.[5] Kingsley Davis (cited in Kolenda, 1978) echos the view of several other scholars (Weber, 1958a; Berreman, 1972) in his comment that 'The Hindu social order is the most thoroughgoing attempt known in human history to introduce absolute inequality as the guiding principle in social relations.' For Weber (1958a), caste has a negative impact on economic development:

> Estranged castes might stand beside one another with bitter hatred—for the idea that everybody had 'deserved' his own fate did not make the good fortune of the others more enjoyable to the socially underprivileged. *For so long and insofar as the* karma *doctrine remained unshaken, revolutionary ideas or the striving for 'progress' were inconceivable.* [Italics are author's.]

[4] Lumbini, the site of the Buddha's birth and a pilgrimage place for Buddhists, is in Nepal.

[5] In traditional Hinduism there are four major social estates or *varnas*. The ancient texts delimited the duties and dispositions of individuals born into specific *varnas*. Over time, concerns of ritual pollution were incorporated into the *varna* system, which translated into injunctions against intercaste commensality (in particular intermarriage and interdining). Such injunctions became part of the caste hierarchy as it has evolved

Dumont (1970), taking a less negative position, suggests that although castes are unequal in status, the system insures that all are cared for and that the state or community is an internally self-sufficient, organic whole. Certainly something can be said for this pattern of social organization, particularly with reference to agrarian societies of the past. Here, the basic division of labour whereby higher castes were responsible for spiritual and political affairs, leaving production of the material necessities of life to the lower castes, possessed a certain logic.

Other scholars (Singer, 1972; Srinivas, 1962; 1968; Kolenda, 1978) go further, arguing that the caste system is in fact highly flexible and adaptive. As evidence of this they cite, firstly, India's process of modernization. They also emphasize the fact that Hinduism (as distinct from Judaism, Christianity and Islam) incorporates a diversity of belief forms, tolerates dissenting sects, has no formal conversion mechanism, and has no congregational basis.

At an operational level, Kolenda (1978) maintains that caste is essentially a relationship based on exchange. The dominant family in a village (who also owns most of the land), receives labour and gift prestations from lower castes in return for protection and ritual services. This relationship is given form through the *jajmani* system, whereby Brahmin castes perform life-cycle ceremonies and other rituals (providing a valuable link with the gods) while castes within the Kshatriya category offer protective and administrative services. Both categories (typically also the traditional landholders) exchange surplus grain in return for services and products supplied by the lower castes. The lower castes, however, absorb the ritual pollution that results from the (manual) production of those goods and services (Wiser, 1958). The degree of pollution depends on the nature of an individual's occupation. Thus butchers and tanners, who deal with dead animal products, and sweepers, who clear human excrement, are lower down the caste ladder than craftsmen such as jewellers or other metalsmiths (Kolenda, 1978; Marriott, 1976).

Change, then, whether economic or social, was hardly encouraged by the caste system as it arose in an essentially agrarian economy. Systems of exchange and the interdependency of producers and spiritual and economic overlords sustained a hierarchy which, in turn, provided a rationalization for occupational roles and the domination of ruling elites over production and profit (Marx, 1958a). Weber (1958b), in his comparative analysis of the Protestant and Hindu ethics, saw *karma*, anti-materialism and the Hindu's supposed 'salvation anxiety' as creating apathy and fatalism, and placing brakes on the creativity necessary for entrepreneurship. An empirical study from Rajasthan, in India, supports these contentions: 'Though the members of the three upper castes ... strongly criticized each other's caste for its members' failures, shortcomings and pretenses, no one expressed the wish to have been born in another caste than his own. The caste-roles were unquestionably taken for granted. *This ... discouraged ambition and initiative in the individual.*' (Carstairs, 1961, pp. 321–2) [Italics are author's.] Similarly, Banjadi (1985), in a study of small-scale entrepreneurs in Nepal, found that a major obstacle to expansion, and the reason for missed business opportunities, was the fatalism characteristic of small industrialists. Most of the entrepreneurs in his sample attributed both successes and failures to 'luck' or 'fate'. Their culturally-derived outlook on change thus impeded their business initiative.

High-caste Hindus, in Weber's view, will feel a sense of guilt about entrepreneurial endeavour because its acquisitive objectives run counter to the other-worldly asceticism which is the cornerstone of the Brahmin's *dharma*. And since the Brahmin is at the pinnacle of the social structure, asceticism becomes a cultural norm.

While Weber's assertions may find some reflection in empirical reality, recent studies indicate that caste injunctions can and are being reinterpreted—particularly in the urban setting—to allow high-caste Hindus to participate in commercial activity. Singer (1973), in his study of successful entrepreneurs in Bombay, found many high-caste Hindus among them. One method adopted by Brahmins and Kshatriyas seeking to rationalize their entry into business was to 'compartmentalize' the two domains of business and religion. Furthermore, they often invoked, and reformulated, religious principles to justify their occupational choice ' "Without God's will nothing can move, but if you think God is going to give you everything on a platter, you are a fool ... Asceticism," they maintain, "is putting more in than you take out." ' (Singer, 1978, p. 337) Thus, for Singer, Indian culture is far more pragmatic than Weber gives it credit for: 'If a man's present condition is determined by his past actions, and his future will be determined by his present and past actions, then he is the master of his fate, as Weber recognizes. Why then, should he become passive, pessimistic, fatalistic, and an incompetent failure?' (Singer, 1978, pp. 287)

The example of Singer's entrepreneurs suggests that caste lines and *dharmic* dictums are malleable. And, as Singer's entrepreneurs demonstrate, it is at the urbanized, prosperous, 'enlightened' cutting edge of the culture that change is most likely to occur.

In certain circumstances, low caste status can also be a catalyst for commercial endeavour. Nandy's (1973a) description of a low-caste agrarian community in West Bengal which took to industry as part of a bid for 'sanskritization' suggests that in the reformulation of acceptable economic roles, social and spiritual roles are also open for redefinition. Kolenda (1978) suggests that because most industrial jobs are new, they are perceived to be 'ritually neutral'. Nonetheless, certain industrial jobs, in particular those involving cleaning or other forms of manual labour, are shunned by higher castes. Not surprisingly, because most administrative jobs in industry require education, they are generally filled by individuals from higher castes.

The relationship between Hinduism and entrepreneurial activity therefore reveals some contradictory elements. While entrepreneurship is not seen as an activity of high moral purpose, it is tolerated because it is necessary (Lambert, 1964). While Hindu beliefs may retard the development of entrepreneurship in the culture as a whole, economic opportunities have allowed specific communities under specific circumstances to reinterpret the belief structure to suit their material objectives. It is only when entrepreneurs are able to redefine religious doctrine—to themselves and the community at large—in a way that allows them to innovate in the economic sphere, that they gain the social space necessary to engage in business.

A disproportionate number of entrepreneurial communities in Nepal are Mahayana Buddhist. Buddhism, in its evolution as a dissenting sect from Hinduism, sought to reject the caste system (though this was never achieved completely) and Hinduism's emphasis on the ascriptively derived purity of the brahminical order. Like those of Hinduism, the tenets of Buddhism also stress detachment from worldly desire, and incorporate the concept of individual *karma*. But human existence tends to be viewed more pragmatically. There is a strong emphasis on what Buddhists term 'this precious life'—the opportunities opened by incarnation in a human body, which should not go wasted. The acquisition of material wealth through hard work is seen as a legitimate way to realize such potential.[6]

---

[6] In this sense, the relationship between Buddhism and Hinduism has analogies with the relationship between Protestantism and Catholicism: the former deriving from, and, in an important sense, a reaction to the latter. Weber (1958a) in his study of Protestant entrepreneurship, found the work ethic fostered by Protestantism of particular significance. The similar ability of Protestants and Buddhists to reformulate orthodox doctrines in a

Long-established traditions have contributed to this pragmatism. In Tibet, as well as in most Himalayan Buddhist communities in Nepal, it has been the practice for one son in a family to join a monastery, thereby acquiring religious merit for himself and his family. In return, the family and the community are expected to support the monastery and the religious leaders associated with it. The sizable monastic populations of Tibet and northern Nepal have traditionally lived by the bounty of wealthy merchants who donate vast sums to religious institutions. An individual who acquires wealth can gain religious merit and social status through such donations.

Status hierarchies in these communities tend to be far less rigid than those of their Hindu counterparts. The very fact that anyone from among the laity can become a monk or nun illustrates the absence of immobilizing caste restrictions. Furthermore, success in the economic sphere adds to an individual's religious status—provided he takes steps to share his wealth.[7] Buddhist businessmen may make generous donations to monasteries, stage lavish ceremonies or give to the poor in order to acquire religious merit. Such investment, expected to yield both immediate and next-life returns, has the effect of redistributing wealth within the community.

In general, the absence of rigid caste categories within Buddhist communities ensures a much greater degree of upward mobility—social, spiritual and economic—than is characteristic of Hindu society. Under Buddhism, business is an acceptable option for any member of the community who choses to engage in it.

Further comparisons between the two religious systems may be helpful in clarifying attitudinal and behavioural linkages between religion and commercial endeavour. At the outset, it is important to point out that Buddhism arose in large part as a reaction to the increasing concentration of power and wealth within a brahminical élite; it is a tradition based on more egalitarian principles.[8]

---

manner which allowed for material accumulation without abandoning the ascetic and other-worldly considerations of their 'parent' creeds, is notable.

[7] Note the emphasis on reciprocity inherent in this approach to entrepreneurial endeavour. Also the similarities with Protestantism in which, as Weber (1958b) notes: 'To wish to be poor was ... the same as wishing to be unhealthy; it is objectionable as a glorification of works and derogatory to the glory of God.' (p. 163) For the Buddhist, begging is tantamount to a sin; there is no Buddhist equivalent of the Hindu *sadhu*, for whom begging is an indication of his spiritual status.

[8] It is interesting to note that in India a sizable number of Scheduled Caste, or 'untouchable', people have sought to escape their lowly and oppressed status within Hinduism by becoming Buddhists.

The juxtaposition of giver and receiver within the two socio-religious systems sheds light on their respective relations with entrepreneurship. For the Hindu, as we have seen, material prestations flow upward, reinforcing the control of the higher castes over resources and services. Buddhist communities, on the other hand, are by nature more egalitarian: the 'haves', of whatever station, are enjoined to share their wealth, not only with spiritual elements in the community but also with those who 'have less'.

Karma—understood as the continuity between past and future lives—is an important concept in both Hindu and Buddhist theology. In Hinduism, *karma* is a fixed, immutable aspect of the individual's incarnation. An individual's caste *dharma* is seen as virtually impossible to alter in a single incarnation; it is by accepting and fulfilling his *dharma* (and not trying to move beyond it) that the individual gains religious status. For the Buddhist, on the other hand, *karma* is alterable even in this lifetime through actions which increase or decrease the individual's stock of religious merit. The individual is therefore seen to wield far more control over his actions and fate.

Although release from material attachment is an important aspect of both religions, the approach differs substantively. In the Hindu system, only members of the higher or 'twice born' castes are eligible to take on the role of the ascetic with the possibility for spiritual release. Under Buddhism, however, anyone from among the laity has the option of entering monastic life. This effectively equalizes the opportunities for spiritual advancement. And whereas the Hindu emphasis on asceticism translates into brahminical disdain for manual labour, Buddhist asceticism supports an ethic of hard work and the idea that profits should not be squandered self-indulgently but reoriented to the poor or to spiritual elements in the community.

The mode of religious practice also reveals contrasts. The relationship of the Hindu to his gods tends to be subservient: the worshipper typically approaches his deities with an attitude of supplication, awe, or even fear. In the Tibeto-Buddhist tradition, in contrast, the attitude towards religious practice tends to be pragmatic: a Buddhist worshipper expects returns on his investments, be they donations, the sponsorship of ceremonies or the making of pilgrimages.

Further differences between the two religions seem relevant to the question of economic behaviour. Von Fürer-Haimendorf (1975), writing about Himalayan trading groups, has suggested that in the case of Hindu groups, strict taboos which prevent the acceptance of food and water from lower castes and non-Hindus limit social intercourse with other groups and may even curtail geographic mobility. Buddhist traders, on the other hand, enjoy strong traditions of hospitality and friendship with members of other ethnic groups, a factor that seems likely to enhance their business activity. Differences in family organization and structure also appear relevant. Whereas a typical Hindu family is extended and hierarchical, with relationships and sex roles ascriptively defined, its Buddhist counterpart (at least in the Himalayan region) tends to be more fluid and egalitarian, and is generally nuclear. The position of women tends to be far more circumscribed and protected in Hindu families, where concerns with ritual pollution typically limit female mobility. Women within the Tibeto-Burman tradition, on the other hand, can and do enter into commercial activities quite independent of their male kin (Acharya and Bennett, 1981).

Buddhism, in short, offers an aspiring entrepreneur certain clear advantages, especially when contrasted with the rigidities of orthodox Hinduism.

The joint family. The contemporary role of the joint family—which has its roots in traditional, agrarian society—has been the subject of considerable debate. Is the joint family a social anachronism, out of step with processes of modernization and urbanization? Or does it still have something to contribute to societies undergoing change? Empirical studies suggest that the nature and adaptiveness of the family unit varies considerably across cultures and economic circumstances.

The extended family is still a central cultural and economic institution in South Asia. It plays a key role in the maintenance of resource reciprocity, in the allocation of labour, in promoting economic security and in cementing lineage and religious networks. It provides the economies of scale that enable a family to farm a piece of land, buy or build a house, diversify into new areas, consolidate earnings, and support dependents—from children to the aged or infirm. In Hindu culture, even if families live as nuclear units (with separate kitchens), they may still reside under the same roof as a closeknit kinship unit (Kolenda, 1968). For the present discussion, the joint or extended family is understood to embrace 'affiliated' nuclear families, as long as an element of hierarchy persists and family members continue to define their role in relation to an overall family head.

Bauer and Yamey (1957) maintain that the collectivism of the extended family inhibits innovation because the rewards have to be shared. Other sociologists also contend that the breakdown of the extended family is inevitable in the face of the introduction of the cash economy and economic development. As opportunities for wage labour become available, the impetus towards resource reciprocity (including the exchange of labour) becomes weakened. In the urban context, Owens (1971) suggests that unless several members of a family become partners in business, the family will tend to split up when one member boosts his earnings—whether from business or employment.

However, breaking with the extended family involves economic and psychological risks; these the would-be nuclear family, or single individual, must take into account when examining immediate prospects and likely future financial vulnerability. In transitional economies it is not uncommon for a family member who is employed in industry to elect to remain in the joint family because of low wages and the real or perceived instability in the demand for his labour. The joint family offers a bridge between the security of the land and the unfamiliarity —but potentially greater economic opportunities—of the city. A joint family can, what is more, extend its resource base by augmenting its agricultural income with remunerations from urban employment. In the short run, at least, there are sound financial reasons for the survival of the extended family in the context of economic change.

Even in the long run, however, family cohesion and economic interdependence are not necessarily economic liabilities. Extended family 'corporations' dominate large-scale industry in India and are also common among many commercial communities in Nepal (see Chapter III). These domestic corporations owe part of their success to their ability to put trusted family members in key business positions— obviating the need, in some cases, for the screening and selection of outside managers. In such families, marriages are often arranged according to a larger business game plan or strategy. However, the best candidate for a top business job may not always be available from the pool of family members. This is increasingly pertinent in more sophisticated industries which require from managerial personnel a high level of technical expertise. Likewise, an insufficient supply of capable sons or grandsons can spell the demise of a powerful firm unless sons-in-law can be drawn in (Singer, 1973). Family firms in India have partially resolved this constraint through the institution of the managing agency, which both conserves limited entrepreneurial talent within the family and extends the range of its business potential (Nafziger, 1971).

At the village level, the extended family may not work to the same advantage. Many small businesses are established with the explicit purpose of providing work for unemployed or underemployed family members. As a result, family and business objectives are inextricably intertwined, and the business often mirrors the personal relations and hierarchical structures of the family. Rational business practices, innovation and expansion may be sacrificed to family pressures and priorities (Banjadi, 1985; Cochran, 1965). Except in cases where the head of the household manages his family resources with entrepreneurial flair, family-based businesses tend to be limited in size, scope and vision. Often, too, their lifespan mirrors the longevity of the head of household.

The existing literature supports the assessment of Quigley (1985) that economic development makes the breakdown of the extended family 'possible but not inevitable'. Where family bonds of reciprocity and cohesiveness remain strong, enabling everyone to move up in life or at least share equally in the profits of the family undertaking, the joint family can work as an efficient economic unit. But when one individual ventures off to start an independent business, or gets a job with a significantly larger salary than that of other family members, the old unit is unlikely to withstand the pressures towards break-up. This is particularly apparent when the entrepreneurial member physically removes himself from the locus of family control, perhaps migrating from the farm to the city; while he may send money back to the family, ownership of the business can no longer be seen as family-based. In Nepal, this trend presents special problems for rural Hindu families, for whom the extended family is the norm. It is less of an issue for Buddhist communities, wherein the nuclear family is the norm.

Child-rearing practices. That human personality undergoes its most profound shaping in childhood seems now beyond serious dispute. Current theories of child psychology suggest that the foundations of personality, cultural belief and behaviour are established in the first five years of life. It is therefore within the family that the child forms its first views on such matters as creativity, innovation, risk taking and achievement. Whether these characteristics can be altered in later life is a matter of debate (McClelland and Winters, 1969); but, clearly, child-rearing practices establish the foundation for the way a community, or larger population, interacts with its social environment.

Furthermore, the investment which parents and society make in children comes with definite social and economic expectations. In traditional societies children are the most tangible form of economic security, promising parents succour in old age and ensuring the survival of the lineage. Such expectations influence the way parents handle child-rearing; they also shape the child's self-perception.

Hagen (1962) describes child-rearing in the traditional context as early indulgence followed by strict control. The overriding message from parent to child in the first half-decade of the child's life is that he is incapable of decision-making, or retaining information, even on small matters. Respect for his elders is also stressed.

Describing child-rearing practices in Java, Geertz (1969) notes that 'the assumption seems to be that the child is completely without resources of his own with which to face these little everyday problems ... There is no attempt or desire to let the child develop initiative or independence.' (p. 167) McClelland and Winters (1969) see the Indian joint family as encouraging dependency relationships:

> In a typical Indian joint family ... the father directs, supervises, and controls his son's activities so extensively that the child's autonomy is expressly inhibited. Further, the traditional Indian father exerts strict control over his wife's activities outside the home, with the effect that she in turn invests a large proportion of her energy in loving and caring for her sons. As ties of dependency between mother and son increase, it becomes unlikely that the son will take pleasure in autonomous achievement. (p. 281)

Parental domination is often critical rather than constructive. In a study of child-rearing practices in rural India, Minturn and Hitchcock (1963) recorded 499 out of 500 consecutive remarks of an Indian mother to her child as critical of what the child was doing; only one was considered positive. McClelland (1969) suggests that this approach to child-rearing gives rise to a fear of failure in the child which in turn restricts later propensities for risk-taking.

Hagen (1962) proposes that such messages, whether subtle or explicit, create in the child feelings of dependency, fear of failure (hence fear of trying new things), and perhaps suppressed rage against the parents. The latter may often be turned against younger siblings or those of the opposite gender; this may be one route by which the authoritarian family is replicated across generations. Under such circumstances, the individual's need for approval and acceptance is strong. McClelland (1969) describes a role-playing exercise he witnessed in India in which adults acted the roles of parent and child. The individual playing the child found he 'could not concentrate on feedback from his performance if he was constantly involved in trying to act primarily to please his parents.' (p. 169)

Given this reality, the innovative individual or community faces harsh social judgement, perhaps even ostracism. Such a person or group challenges not only the cultural status quo, but tugs at the primordial fears and inhibitions of his community of origin, for whose members change and challenge were threatening as children.

However, child-rearing practices, along with other facets of traditional society, are not immune to change; with socio-economic change come important modifications. Hagen (1962) has made an important contribution in this area. In his study he examines child-rearing in the context of the economic transformation of a formerly non-commercial community. He suggests that a community that has suffered a decline in, or 'withdrawal' of, political, economic, social or religious status will at some later stage seek to reassert that status through commercial endeavour. In such a situation, the anger generated by the suppression of a community's traditional status may be internalized; a wife may turn against her husband for his failure to maintain the standard of living expected of him; her achievement expectations may then be transferred to the son. This translates, over several generations, into a strong tradition of maternal encouragement, combined with paternal pressure on sons to restore family or community fortunes. In combination, these factors may stimulate an entire new generation of innovators and risk-takers intent upon re-establishing community status. Such a family situation produces children who are at once cognizant of the barriers to success in the world and unafraid of meeting them as challenges. This generation, presumably still blocked from traditional sources of status and wealth, is thus compelled to choose non-traditional avenues to achieve those ends. And one such avenue may be business.

Hagen's theory of status withdrawal, then, offers one explanation for the transformation of formerly non-entrepreneurial communities into active commercial entities. But it is also important to look at child-rearing practices within long-established commercial communities in traditional societies. Marginality theory suggests that such communities operate on the basis of internal definitions which not only foster innovation and risk-taking but also lend the individual the self-confidence necessary to withstand wider social criticism. Commenting on the 'marginality' of entrepreneurial communities, Lambert (1964) suggests that 'their isolation is also necessary to them because it enables them to raise their children with a set of norms in direct contrast to those of the rest of society.' (p. 276) Communal cohesiveness, based on rituals or traditions which separate the community from the society at large, allows for child-rearing practices that may be notably different from those of the mainstream culture.

Writing on the Indian family, McClelland and Winters (1969) maintain that families that nurture entrepreneurship—unusual, even anomalous in the Indian context—tend to be headed by 'a mother less indulgent than the average and a father who is physically absent or relatively uninvolved in the upbringing of the son.' (p. 307) In such cases, sons may find themselves relatively free to express their individuality, and may assume decision-making responsibilities while comparatively young.

Fathers do not have to be absent for sons to develop entrepreneurial traits, however. Nor do child-rearing practices in entrepreneurial communities differ fundamentally from the prototypes described above. In the oriental context, children from entrepreneurial communities are by no means raised to be highly individualistic—a trait long considered by Western thinkers a prerequisite for entrepreneurship. The child (typically the son) from such a community will, of course, eat and sleep business from his babyhood. His education (both formal and informal) and marriage will be geared to the furtherance of the family business. This is in contrast to the child of the subsistence farmer, who obviously lacks the means and the role models necessary to take risks, seek out new opportunities, and innovate in new areas of the economy. Nonetheless, like that of the children of farmers, the individual identity of children from entrepreneurial communities is still fixed in the familial hierarchy which provides both context and support for a commercial career. In the long run, even if a junior member of the family manages a business independently, he is still required to defer to his family elders and the dictates of his caste or clan.

The Japanese example presents an alternative to the Western highly competitive and individualistic model of entrepreneurship. In this case, innovation takes place through group co-operation. Status within the group is defined firstly by seniority and only secondly by success.

The individual is careful not to upset the seniority hierarchy, despite any personal advantage which may be gained from doing so. While conformity to a hierarchy and the suppression of individual achievement-orientation may, from a Western perspective, seem to work against entrepreneurial success, we may refer again to the reciprocity paradigm which offers some explanation for successful entrepreneurship in oriental culture. For the oriental, social cohesion is ranked above individualism. Within the entrepreneurial community, or the corporation, an individual's need for both affiliation and achievement is satisfied through structures which define his position in relation to the whole. Whereas in the Western model the individual seeks to assert his uniqueness in relation to the group, in the Eastern context the individual, even when he is an entrepreneur, functions most comfortably as part of a larger organization.

The contrasts between Western and oriental modes of child-rearing can be summed up thus. While the Western parent, and society, provide an environment in which the next generation is expected to assert its right to differ, challenge and change, the Asian child is reared to conform, to respect, emulate and perpetuate the world-view and behavioural systems of his parents and culture. The child of an entrepreneurial community in the East, then, is reared to undertake risks and innovation while at the same time conforming to the basic tenets of his culture. Indeed this sense of group identity is an important factor in his ability to go about his work.

To the extent that individuals in traditional societies make an investment in their future, the most important investment is in their children. Having children, particularly sons, is the most tangible form of security, not only for old age, but also for the continuity and stability of the family line. For most ethnic groups in a patrilineal culture like Nepal, the first duty of the son is to his parents. He is brought up to respect and obey them, and to provide for them in their old age. Daughters in both Hindu and Buddhist communities are of only secondary importance, as they marry out of the natal household, thereby transferring their economic duty to their husband's household.

Such parental investment in the son carries important implications. In the first place, children are probably the only assets which are not at risk of arbitrary removal (except, of course, through illness or death). In agrarian economies, more children means more hands in the fields. In a transitional, monetizing economy, one or more sons can be sent off to earn while other family members (including the sons' wives) work the land. In either case, the incentives for large families are strong. The important point is that the son sees his relationship to the family unit primarily in terms of duty and personal indebtedness. Imbued from childhood with the ethic of service to the parents and household that nurtured him, the son will tend to view the surplus he generates not as his own private affair but as the prerogative of the extended household (Hagen, 1962).

Parents, therefore, tend to view investment in their children's education as primarily an investment in family continuity. Even if education raises the child's earning potential and mobility, parents still hope to garner the economic benefits by tethering the son to familial responsibilities. Cultural norms reinforce the point that the financial benefits education brings must be passed on to the family (Bauer and Yamey, 1957).

Child-rearing practices in traditional societies also suggest several things about the role of women in those societies. If it is true that dependency on the mother stifles creativity and independence in the child, one would expect different child-rearing patterns where women are less homebound and more economically and socially mobile. In the case of Nepal, Acharya and Bennett (1982) contrast the role of women in 'Indo-Aryan' and in Tibeto-Burman communities:

> The role of mother is highly valued in all Nepalese groups. Nevertheless female role expectations differ widely from community to community. While for women of the higher caste Hindu communities there is no respectable alternative role to being a wife and mother, alternative role models do exist for women in the Tibeto-Burman-speaking communities and if a woman decides not to marry and be a wife, she will have other channels of gaining social status. Nevertheless, even for the women of these communities there are no other roles equally coveted or acceptable as that of mother. (p. 96)

The relationship between the status of women and child-rearing practices conducive to the development of entrepreneurship is discussed further in Chapter III.

FACTORS OF PRODUCTION: ATTITUDES AND VALUES

Successful entrepreneurship is determined in large measure by the availability of, access to, and the nature of the factors of production.

Capital accumulation, the efficient organization and mobilization of a work force and new forms of technology are all important ingredients in entrepreneurial activity.

Attitudes to saving in peasant societies. Traditional peasant societies have long been associated with a relatively weak savings capacity. Some commentators have gone as far as to argue that in the agrarian context, savings or investment for the future have little meaning or value (Sadie, 1964). Peasants are seen as having little motivation to accumulate wealth when the surplus capital, labour or grain generated by a household is siphoned off by landlords, local bureaucrats, or money-lenders (Linton, 1964). In addition, the peasant stands surrounded by threats: from the weather, which can destroy an entire crop; or from life-cycle events (a marriage, a funeral) which can absorb all his reserves.

The peasant may react in one of two ways. One response is to spend whatever is available, getting into debt if need be. A 'present tense' orientation in which the future, or 'fate', is left to fend for itself is adopted. However, since the gods are empowered with control over fate, heavy expenditure on ritual and ceremony is the peasant's major investment in the future. This tends to absorb a great proportion of the actual, and anticipated, marginal surplus and is a major contributor to rural indebtedness (Lambert, 1964; Fricke, 1984).

A second response is to limit production to what can be immediately consumed or preserved within the family unit. Here, a peasant works hard when it is time to plant or harvest, feasting and paying obeisance to the gods in agricultural off-seasons (Linton, 1964).

The peasant's inability to save therefore appears linked to his general lack of control over the products of his labour.

The work ethic. Perceptions of work, its value and meaning, appear to vary considerably from society to society. While in the West 'work' is undertaken for its own sake as well as the financial rewards it brings, this is not always the case in agrarian societies. 'Keeping busy' is fundamental to the Western world-view, with its emphasis on individual identity; leisure, in contrast, is the hallmark of success in many developing countries.[9] Analysts have provided several explanations for

---

[9] Similarly, the emphasis on slimness which prevails in Western industrialized nations contrasts sharply with the preference for a more portly physique—indicative of both leisure and wealth—in many developing countries.

the low level of 'achievement orientation' in many developing country contexts. Suwal (1982) for example, has this to say on the work ethic in Nepal:

> It is understood that most Nepalese are happy-go-lucky type people. They simply do not want to do certain types of jobs despite the high economic return potential ... Non-Nepali labourers are seen slowly replacing Nepali labourers in carpentry, wiring, etc., because of their efficiency and time consciousness. The only two jute mills in the country find it hard to get Nepali workers to replace non-Nepali workers working with them. In one study, it has been found that Nepalese society is predominantly affiliation and dependency motivated. The desire to achieve something is very low. (p. 104)

In fact, the work ethic is shaped by hard economic realities. In the agrarian context, work is governed by annual cycles in which bouts of hard labour alternate with periods of 'leisure' or enforced idleness. Despite an increasingly unfavourable land-person ratio, there is a disinclination among rural residents in Nepal to undertake complementary income-generating activities, seek out off-season sources of employment, or adjust to the requirements of industrial work when they do undertake off-farm employment. This is in contrast to India, for instance, where the agricultural workforce actively seeks alternative employment during slack seasons—even if such alternatives are inadequate or sometimes not available. It has been suggested that even when income-generating opportunities come their way, certain peasant farmers prefer their leisure because they are by nature non-acquisitive (Weber, 1958b; Sadie, 1964).

The situation is certainly not as simple as this, and many other factors must be taken into account. First, the availability of industrial employment in Nepal is extremely limited, given the backward nature of the economy. Secondly, in an agrarian setting such as Nepal's, where labour is interchangeable and income the communal property of the family unit, the benefits accruing to the individual for taking an outside job may not be substantial (Bauer and Yamey, 1957); indeed, wages in Nepal's factories are low (Chao, 1975). Thirdly, low levels of savings plus increasing competition from imported goods preclude investment in cottage industry for most rural families. Cultural traits may exacerbate the problem. The idea of working according to an external, arbitrary timetable may be foreign to rural residents; compliance with the year-round demands of industrial employment may meet with behavioural resistance, at least in the early stages of economic development (Mead, 1964). What is more, farming may be seen as superior to other types of productive labour, especially among Hindus. While small peasant farmers may earn less than tailors, butchers, carpenters, masons or other non-agricultural workers, cultural factors may discourage a farmer from seeking training in potentially more lucrative skills (Linton, 1964; Lambert, 1964). A further factor is the very familiarity of agriculture; income generation via other sectors may be perceived as risky, foreign and the domain of others. As a result of all of these factors, many farmers 'choose', usually by default, to live a marginal existence on shrinking plots of land rather than seek out an often non-existent job in a factory, or start a new business with non-existent resources.

In sum, the work ethic demanded by industrialization does not materialize out of thin air, even when circumstances seem conducive for this. There is a time-lag in the responsiveness—or rather, the ability to respond—of the rural labour force to new opportunities for employment, even assuming that such opportunities exist on a meaningful scale.

Attitudes towards technology. The transplantation of technology into traditional societies creates interesting behavioural reactions. In most developing countries, technology which is imported in the name of development carries with it unfamiliar cultural norms that may not fit the new environment. While consumers, labourers, and industrialists may be eager to acquire new technologies, they may not make the behavioural and organizational changes necessary for their proper utilisation. An example here is the wristwatch, a coveted status symbol in rural communities to whom punctuality, schedules and appointments are largely alien. Donor agencies that attempt to introduce new technology to villages—perhaps in the form of a water pump, an irrigation scheme, or a tractor—often return years later to find the new addition broken and unused. Margaret Mead (1964), in the context of Samoa, provides this characterization of the problem:

> All change was now seen as terribly difficult and against the real will of the people, who only thought they wanted tractors because they were symbols of Western superiority but who really hated regular hours, clocks, machines, hospitals, the dictates of nutritionists, sitting in school, and learning to think in realistic Western terms. (p. 137)

Where new technology is a recent and unfamiliar phenomenon, it is small wonder that rural underemployment continues despite a growing demand for factory labour. The benefits of such technology may be recognized at one level; but the technology may also be seen as involving far-reaching changes in human relationships and the structure of society. Land is seen to embody security; technology, an unfamiliar risk. Even technology which could, in theory, raise agricultural productivity is eyed with suspicion by a farmer asked to undertake the dual risk of financial investment and crop failure.

New forms of technology may be equally unfamiliar to the entrepreneur in such environments. Rural or first-generation urban entrepreneurs, unless they were educated abroad, commonly lack sufficient technical training and have no innate feel for technology. In this sense, the would-be innovator must struggle not only against cultural conservatism but also against his own limitations.

NATIONAL POLICY ISSUES

Although this chapter has focused primarily on social and cultural variables, economic, market and policy factors are, of course, centrally important in determining the nature and pace of economic development and entrepreneurship. While economic decisions made at the international level have an obvious and direct bearing on entrepreneurship in developing societies, this study will focus primarily on policy issues at the national level. A brief survey of these issues is essential to balance the cultural orientation of this study: cultural factors should by no means be seen as the *sine qua non* of entrepreneurial development.

David Dunlop (1983), in a study carried out for the U.S. Agency for International Development, identified some of the market and policy factors common to six countries with successful private sector growth in the recent period.[10] The first factor highlighted by Dunlop was a national policy of import substitution, by which governments sought to cut foreign exchange expenditure on imports and stimulate demand for locally manufactured products. Policy here would often take the form of high tariff walls, plus incentives to indigenous industries: tax holidays, tax rebates, access to foreign currency for the importation of

---

[10] The countries covered in this study are Cameroon, Costa Rica, the Dominican Republic, Malawi, Sri Lanka and Thailand.

raw materials and so on. But while protectionism—designed to shield infant industries from foreign competition—may be successful in the short run, its long-term impact on industrial efficiency and competitiveness may not be wholly beneficial. Critics have argued that the artificial environment which protectionism creates can be detrimental to industrial development in the long run (Adam Smith and Bela Balassa, cited in Hageboeck and Allen, 1982). It has also been pointed out that, in the short run at least, foreign exchange may not be saved by such policies—particularly if the new indigenous industries rely heavily on imported raw materials, technology and technical personnel (Griffin and Enos, 1973). Such policies may also have the effect of increasing consumer demand for imported products (Power, 1973); a black market in imported 'protected' items emerges in response; and attempts to control this further sap the resources of the State. If the black market is lucrative enough, entrepreneurial talent that should be flowing into industry may get diverted (Papanek, 1971). Government support for industries which utilize and strengthen indigenous resources and the effective implementation of protectionist policies may, however, more than compensate for such problems.

Dunlop's second factor was governmental export promotion to generate foreign exchange. Policies here might include tax rebates, warehousing concessions and reduced or subsidized freightage rates. For such policies to be effective, entrepreneurs would, however, require consistency and continuity on the part of the government (Hageboeck and Allen, 1982).

Thirdly, Dunlop emphasized the importance of agricultural growth—seen as the source of capital for national industrial take-off and diversification. In the countries included in his study, overall rates of growth in the agricultural sector were higher than those of comparable low- and middle-income countries. Significantly, the proportion of the total labour force engaged in agriculture had, in almost all the six countries surveyed, declined after 1960, indicating an absorption of manpower into industry.

A fourth factor was governmental attention to small-scale industries. In the countries studied by Dunlop, small businesses played an important role throughout the economy. Other analysts have highlighted the responsiveness of this sector, once incentives are made available (Ashe, 1985; Zivetz, 1987).

Policies that promote the more equitable distribution of income constitute the fifth element. Programmes which stimulate a redistribution of income, in the process creating a stronger home market and investment base, normally involve reform of existing land tenure relationships, reinforced by enlightened educational policies that promote universal primary education and a range of vocational training options. While many governments support training programmes of this kind, some studies suggest that on-the-job, apprenticeship training may be a more effective route to the creation of entrepreneurs (Nihan and Jourdain, 1978; Zivetz, 1987).

Subsidized interest rates which improve the attractiveness of funds offered by formal lending systems constitute another key area of government action. This is particularly crucial in transitional economies where money-lenders are often the sole source of credit for smaller entrepreneurs, unfamiliar with the working of official agencies. Loans from the money-lender can carry an interest burden up to ten times higher than loans from formal agencies (Chuta and Liedholm, 1979). Subsidized interest rates will clearly attract entrepreneurs facing such a situation; but a government also needs to streamline and simplify loan procedures if such clients are to make use of the option (Zivetz, 1988).

Increased flows of donor assistance to the private sector in developing societies also appears significant. In all the countries surveyed in Dunlop's study, the private sector received at least 50 per cent of external aid as loans or credits.

The taxation of imports and exports was a further policy area highlighted by Dunlop. Such revenues made up more than 25 per cent of the national revenues generated in four out of six of the countries in Dunlop's study. While this indicates a productive base which is strong and healthy enough to tax, potential entrepreneurs would obviously want their anticipated profits to outweigh their tax burden (Singer, 1972).

Finally, state involvement in one or more sectors of the economy—most commonly in basic infrastructure, utilities, and health and educational services—was characteristic of the countries studied by Dunlop. An extensive and active public sector is, of course, justifiable on a number of counts: the state brings to the economy its greater fiscal and administrative capacities; its intervention can help promote egalitarian policies. Dunlop suggests, however, that the public ownership of a substantial proportion of large-scale plantations and trading companies in the six countries he studied might in the long run prove incompatible with private sector entrepreneurship. In the short run, this may be a pragmatic response to capital and resource constraints in the private sector; public sector ownership of such enterprises can stimulate private sector enterprises through sub-contract and marketing relationships, but must make a conscious effort to do so. This will be explored further in Chapter IV.

This brief overview has examined some of the ways in which policy measures can and do affect the environment in which industrialization and entrepreneurship take shape. But, as we shall see in the case of Nepal, government policy is not a sufficient prerequisite for industrialization. Contextual factors such as the strength of existing market forces and the society's cultural norms may override or at least qualify the impact of such policies on private sector development, as we hope to show in Chapter IV. There is a fine line between too much and too little state intervention; what is appropriate in one context may be counter-productive in another. As Aharoni (1977) aptly concludes:

> It is now recognized that too much tilting against market forces may be inefficient, wasteful and even disastrous ... attitudes, religious beliefs, institutional arrangements, the political and social structure and cultural factors are all significant in assessing economic policies and materially affect both the ability of the government to implement a policy and the impact of this policy on the economy. (p. 116)

CONCLUSIONS

The discussion of entrepreneurship and economic change has touched on a range of issues in an effort to present the major variables which provide a framework for the case study of Nepal that follows. One point to emerge is that the risk involved in economic endeavour has a strong cultural as well as economic dimension. The would-be entrepreneur must contend with a range of cultural obstacles: negative attitudes towards capital accumulation or new technology; the rigidities of the caste system; cultural modalities which reinforce reciprocity and the equalization of wealth within rural families; and child-rearing practices which do not foster individual creativity or risk-taking. The entrepreneur therefore takes on the burden of stimulating alterations—whether consciously or by default—across a range of social and institutional structures. Perhaps the most compelling example of this is the caste system which, historically, has worked to buttress traditional élites. Commercial communities have, in their bid for power and profit, necessarily sought to redefine caste, and the socio-religious injunctions against material betterment and upward mobility implicit in the caste hierarchy.

In transitional societies, the entrepreneur may face a certain degree of social hostility because he is seen to threaten longstanding economic and social interdependencies. An entrepreneurially inclined community therefore requires a strong sense of identity and purpose; this internal definition may be based on social-religious norms; it may derive from the group's immigrant or refugee status, or from its bid to reclaim lost status or wealth. A combination of these factors is also possible.

The extent to which entrepreneurial communities succeed in effecting changes in the larger environment in which economic development takes place is also determined by external factors, both economic and cultural. The responsiveness, appropriateness and viability of state policies are clearly important factors in the emergence of sustainable industrial and mercantile enterpreneurship.

The entrepreneur can therefore be seen to stand at a crossroads of sorts—the point at which economic and cultural processes of change meet. In the context of post-colonial economic development, and the democratic, humanitarian ethic to which foreign aid and Western influence have at least paid lip service, social upheaval has been inevitable. Societies in transition are, of course, never tension-free. More conservative, traditional elements in the society—whether the rulers or the ruled—find themselves challenged by new economic forces. The nature and pace of the economic change entrepreneurial communities are able to effect—as measured by not only their own financial success but also their ability to introduce new technologies and production methods—are important indicators of the nature and pace of economic and cultural change in the wider society. This is not to say that entrepreneurs constitute the only force for change in transitional economies. But in a country where economic change requires a restructuring of traditional control over resources, the entrepreneur, with his nose for innovation and change, may have a key role to play. As entrepreneurs increase their resource base, traditional elites can perhaps be persuaded to yield some of their political power. Similarly, commercial elements may find it advisable to forge alliances with traditional power-holders in order to achieve their ends. The 'power' which the elite gives up is the price to be paid for a broader-based economy and the range of economic gains this brings with it. If the reshuffling of political power takes place under ideal circumstances, some sort of balance between traditional ruler and entrepreneurial challenger may emerge.

These themes will be taken up again in the case-study of Nepal that follows. While we will maintain that the entrepreneur constitutes the vanguard of change, it should also be remembered that the entrepreneur is the product of his own culture, and as such is also vulnerable to change. The tensions involved in political restructuring and cultural redefinition require that the individual entrepreneur and his community also engage in significant internal redefinitions. The process, then, has dialectical aspects: the agent of change is himself required to undergo transformation.

Finally, it is not the purpose of this study to establish whether Nepal is 'typical' of developing societies undergoing far-reaching change. The primary aim is to understand entrepreneurship and economic change in one country, within the theoretical parameters suggested by the existing literature.

Chapter Two

Entrepreneurship in Nepal: An Overview

> *Economic development was not then a national goal. The socio-economic structure was essentially feudalistic, and entrepreneurship among the people was frowned upon. The ruling class was not only afraid of technical innovation, but also feared changes in the values and aspirations of the common man. It recognized that the development of industries would create conditions favorable to the formation of organizations which would lead to a new awareness among workers regarding the sharing of political and economic power. Therefore no efforts were made to start consumer goods industries that could have potentially exploited new monetization of the regional economy and the increased purchasing power of the people.*
>
> – P. C. Lohani, 'Industrial policy: the problem child of history and planning in Nepal', in Rana and Malla (eds), 1973, p. 39.

PORTRAITS FROM NEPAL

One. Prakash, the eldest son of a Brahmin family in Kathmandu, was raised in an orthodox household. He was taught to respect and obey his elders, to observe the religious duties prescribed by his caste *dharma*, to maintain the codes of ritual purity and avoid pollution of his person, his household and his caste. At six, Prakash, was sent to school. His father, a middle-level officer in a bank in Kathmandu, was keen for Prakash to continue his education through college and obtain a government position which would provide him economic security and prestige. At twenty-two, Prakash finished his university degree in economics, and through his maternal uncle, a civil servant, obtained a junior-level position in a government office. The youngest of his four brothers, Manesh, showed less scholastic aptitude; moreover, by the time his turn came to be educated, the family had exhausted its financial resources. As a result Manesh opened a small business. Having secured government positions for the first three sons, the family was content that the last son earn his keep through this decidedly less prestigious occupation.

Two. Ram Bahdur, the second son of a large Newari household in a hill town, learned about business in the bazaar, helping his father in their small store that sold cloth, grain, tea, cigarettes, and other essential commodities. When Ram was twenty-five, his father died. Ram continued to live in the joint family, sharing responsibility for the store and the farm with his brothers. Five years later, Ram had the idea of setting up a small poultry farm. His brothers were opposed to the idea, and he had to borrow from his wife's family to buy the chickens and wire mesh. When he began to make profits from this business, the brothers quarrelled, and Ram split away from the joint family.

Three. Angkaji Sherpa, the youngest of three sons, learned as a child to move with the seasons. In the summer the family would plant potatoes and then trek up to the high pastures to graze their animals. Usually his father went on trading expeditions to Tibet once or twice during this season, taking grain and butter from the hills of Nepal and livestock from Solu-Khumbu, and coming back with factory-made goods from China and tourist items from Tibet. Of Angkaji's two brothers, one joined the monastery and the other used to help his father on these trading expeditions. When Angkaji was eighteen, a friend of his father's asked him if he would like to work for his trekking company. Eager to see new things, he agreed. Because of his skill with the tourists, and aptitude for learning English, Angkaji was quickly promoted from a porter to a cook and then to a tour leader (*sardar*). He worked as a *sardar* for six years, leading treks and a few climbing expeditions and making good money. Then he left the trekking agency of his father's friend and set up his own with the help of a few friends from his native village.

Four. Thupten fled to Nepal from Tibet and the invading Chinese in 1959, along with his mother, aunt, two sisters and a younger brother. He was thirteen when he arrived, and had been educated only up to the fourth grade. His family had been migratory herders and traders in a small town near the Tibet-Nepal border. They came to Nepal with only the few valuables they could carry, and were soon destitute. Six months after their arrival, the family moved into a camp for refugees.

Like all the other inmates, Thupten spent some time each day weaving in the camp carpet factory. When a camp school was established, he began to attend. When he was twenty Thupten became assistant manager for the carpet factory which had begun to successfully export to Europe through the Tibetan society. By saving and working at home, the family accumulated enough money to establish their own business. When he was twenty-six, Thupten and his family moved to Kathmandu where they opened a small carpet factory.

Five. Mohan was born in Northern India into a large Marwari family, originally from Rajasthan. He grew up with business all around him, and had worked alongside his father for as long as he could remember. Almost everyone in the family was in business. When the family got together there was much talk about the price of this and that and what new markets could be tapped. Mohan's father owned a rice mill and an oil mill in Bengal. The family were also traders, and had been for many generations. Sometimes his father would travel to the Terai region of Nepal to negotiate the purchase of rice and oilseeds. When Mohan was eleven he went with his father for the first time. Later, in college, Mohan befriended a Nepali whose family had sent him to study in India. A few years after they graduated, Mohan moved to Nepal, and with the help of his friend as well as some distant relatives living in Kathmandu, he opened a rice mill in the Terai. Later on, he opened a small industry to manufacture confectionery items and also began importing Indian-made commodities. His connections with the Marwari community in Nepal and India helped in getting the finance, technology and goods necessary for these businesses. When he was twenty-two, his parents arranged a marriage with a girl from his own community, who came to live with him in Nepal.

Six. Although Ramesh's family was from Thak Khola in Northern Nepal, he was born in Pokhara, farther south, where his family had migrated in 1960. Ramesh's father, who had traded with Tibet when they still lived in Thak Khola, opened a small hotel in Pokhara. Ramesh was sent to school in India when he was twelve. He studied through university and got a degree in engineering. When he returned, he married and joined a road construction contracting business in Pokhara. He borrowed money from his community's rotating credit scheme to make his initial investments.

All these portraits are fictitious; at the same time, they are based on real individuals. Nepal remains a heterogeneous nation, where geographical isolation works to reinforce linguistic, caste and religious divisions and where the homogenizing impact of urbanization is still weakly expressed (only 6 per cent of the population lives in cities[1]). It therefore becomes possible to 'invent' portraits such as those presented above with some confidence of accuracy, and to generalize about the community-based factors which push a particular individual or family in entrepreneurial directions.

The first point to be highlighted is that the line between ethnicity and caste is somewhat blurred in the case of Nepal. The country is a patchwork of discrete communities—Thakalis, Sherpas, Tibetans, Gurungs and numerous others—each with their own language, homeland and definable culture. For the purposes of this study, Brahmins, Marwaris and Chhetris are also viewed as discrete communities, for in many ways their internal culture and patterns of life justify the use of such a label.

In this chapter, and the one that follows, we will explore different communities in search of the factors—economic and socio-cultural, predominantly—that seem to have predisposed them to (or, in some cases, set them against) entrepreneurship. An attempt will be made to place these factors in historical and geographical perspective. On the basis of this detailed examination, a theory of entrepreneurship in Nepal will then be presented.

AN HISTORICAL OVERVIEW

In order to understand entrepreneurship in Nepal today, a look back at the past is essential. A careful reading of history explains certain features of Nepal's current economic reality: the dominance of the ruling élite over the nature and pace of private sector commercial activity; the systems of patronage that link the public and private sectors; the powerful presence of India; and the role of Indian entrepreneurs in Nepal's industrial sector. The evolution of industrialization in the country has been characterized by a struggle between conservative, feudal or semi-feudal elements and a non-agricultural private sector.

---

[1] According to the Statistical Pocketbook (1986) published by the Central Bureau of Statistics, Kathmandu. This defines 'urban' as concentrations of more than 10,000 people and lists 23 'cities', most of them in the range 20–50,000. Nepal's urban population is likely to have increased significantly since the official data were collected in 1981.

Map 2

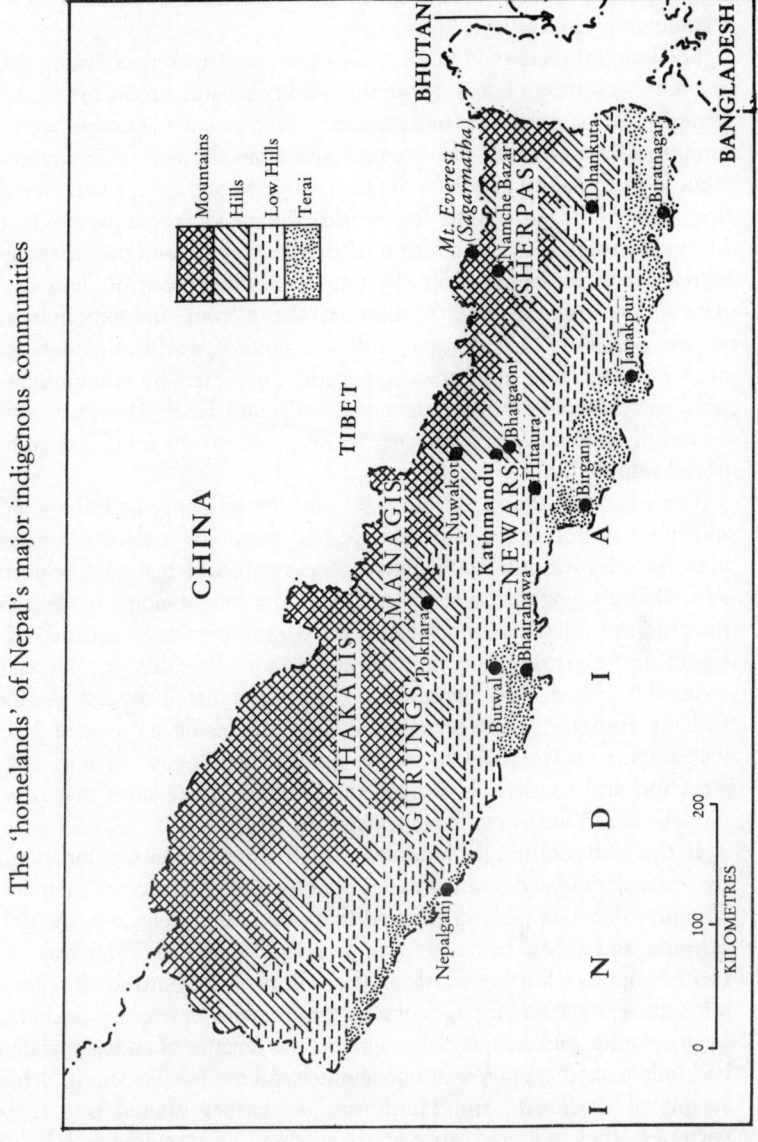

The 'homelands' of Nepal's major indigenous communities

Only recently has the latter, to a limited extent, been able to separate itself from direct state control. Perhaps because of such problems and obstacles, only certain communities have distinguished themselves in commerce and industry.

The last 200 years of Nepal's history can be characterized as, on the one hand, a series of feuds within the ruling élite and, on the other, the struggle for survival of heterogeneous subsistence agrarian communities, isolated from one another and from the centre of government in Kathmandu by virtue of geography. Before 1951, when Nepal first opened her doors to the world, the major preoccupation of successive ruling élites was with territorial expansion and the amassing of resources and land under central, family-based control. This was achieved in large measure through extraction from, and exploitation of, the peasantry. Intercourse with the outside world, and outside market-places, was limited to the trade conducted by communities residing on Nepal's long borders with India and Tibet. There was also a carefully controlled transit trade which profited only a small stratum of the population.

The advent of democracy in 1951 and the influence of foreign aid and increased contact with the Indian economy brought greater opportunities for indigenous entrepreneurship, which should be seen as a relatively new phenomenon in Nepal. But long-standing tendencies towards centralized economic control continue to work against any significant expansion of the private sector. In addition, Nepal's industrial sector has, historically, been dominated by immigrant Indians. Indigenous entrepreneurial communities have focussed their investments on the more lucrative, quick-return areas of trade, construction and tourism. It is only since the early seventies that new, Nepali-owned industries have sprung up.

In the 12th century, the landmass which is now Nepal was inhabited by scattered, isolated and culturally heterogenous farming communities. The prevalence of malaria ensured that population density in the rich farming and forest lands of what is now the Nepali Terai was extremely limited. Further north, in the valleys of the central hill region, self-sufficient subsistence agricultural communities developed. Secluded by geography, separated by language and the practice of endogamy, they had only limited contact with one another and the outside world. While strains of Buddhism and Hinduism had earlier filtered into these societies, they adhered strictly to neither, and maintained belief systems which were (and to some extent remain) quite distinct.

During the 12th and 13th centuries, immigrant Chhetris, perhaps linked with the princely Rajputs of Rajasthan in India, migrated along with their Brahmin priests to the western hills of Nepal. From there they moved slowly eastward, establishing petty states as they went (Adikhari, 1984). The Chhetris introduced new farming techniques which increased agricultural yields. They also superimposed stronger Hindu practices on to indigenous cultures, as evidenced by the adoption of the taboo on cow slaughter and the appearance of the caste system, previously unknown in the hills (Rose, 1971; Gaige, 1975; Adikari, 1989). Another Chhetri innovation was the *jajmani* system of exchange labour. Under this system, an artisan was obliged to supply his patron with services or goods in return for a fixed amount of grain. In this way, the new Chhetri rulers who had acquired large landholdings were also able to acquire the services of tailors, tanners, cobblers, potters and even musicians. An additional source of artisan skills and services was the Newar community of the Kathmandu Valley, whose migration to the new Chhetri states was encouraged. The Newars, skilled in commerce as well as artisanry, early on assumed an important supportive role in the Chhetri administration. A network of Newari merchants served to increase trade links between communities.

Because of Nepal's economically strategic location between the lowlands of India and the high Tibetan plateau, trade has played a role in the economy of the country for at least thirteen centuries. The few trading routes which dissected the country from north to south were Nepal's only important contact point with the outside world. But these tracks seem to have had only a marginal cultural and economic impact on the communities which they traversed, the only exceptions being small élite groupings with outside contacts that developed in Kathmandu and Lhasa.

Border trade has also played a role in the economies of communities residing along the frontiers with India and Tibet. Given the transportation difficulties within the country, economic interaction with nearby market places along both borders was the logical outlet for agricultural surplus and handicraft products. Trade relations were facilitated by the fact that communities on either side of the border often had a common language and culture. The Kathmandu Valley, besides being the largest fertile valley in the country, was also strategically located on the Indo-Tibetan trade route. As such, it was the logical starting-point for the conquest and consolidation of the country. By the mid-18th century, dissension among the Malla rulers of the three states of the Valley was considerable, resulting in a politically unstable situation. Consequently, in 1762, when Prithvi

Narayan Shah, a powerful Chhetri ruler from the hill state of Gorkha, entered the Kathmandu Valley, he was able quickly to overcome the three city-states. The dynasty he established brought together more than fifty warring states, and Nepal became a politically unified entity for the first time in its history (Stiller, 1973).

The close to 100-year-rule of the Shahs therefore served to unify Nepal. Administrative expansion stimulated a demand for goods and services and strengthened links between the capital and remote, far-flung communities, even if in a very preliminary way. But so intense was the exploitation of the peasantry (the basis of Shah rule) and so strict the regime's control over trade that these changes did little to stimulate local economies or any spirit of entrepreneurship.

Much of the energy—and resources—of Prithvi Narayan Shah and his successors was put into military expansion and territorial conquest. This effort generated a demand for labour—to produce the required arms and to provide infrastructural support for armies at the village level. The potential for paid employment and indigenous entrepreneurship inherent in this situation was never realized, however. Typically, the Shahs utilized their control to levy taxes and institute a system of forced labour. Such was the nature of the first important encounter between remote rural communities and the central authority. With little accruing to the labourer for his services, there was very limited stimulus for hard work; with both resources and profit centrally controlled, there was very little incentive for entrepreneurship. As Regmi (1971) comments:

> There seems little doubt that slavery and forced labour systems had a deleterious effect on economic activity. Both these systems impinged on the liberty of the common people and prevented them from attending to their regular occupations ... these systems ensured that the economy remained stagnant even during a period of intensive military activity. Prospects of the expansion of economic activity and the accelerated flow of money incomes which generally accompany such activity were belied by the obligation of the people to work without wages .... [and] aggravated by the general tendency of government officials and other influential persons to utilize [the systems] for their personal requirement. (pp. 111 and 123)

The peasant economy was forced to divert its meagre surplus (whether of supplies or labour) to arbitrary forces, both local and central, from which there was no recognizable return. Not surprisingly, the result was stagnation in both agriculture and handicraft production (Regmi, 1971).

Gorkhali rule lasted until 1832, when palace politics—in essence, a prolonged power struggle between the monarchy and powerful aristocratic families—came to crisis-point. That year, matters reached an impasse, described by one commentator as 'the worst type of political anarchy' (Adikhari, 1984). In 1846, the ancient rivalry between competing factions and the Shah dynasty was resolved in a bloody struggle inside the palace known as the Kot Massacre. Jang Bahadur Rana emerged as absolute leader, with the young Shah king as titular head. This marked the beginning of 104 years of Rana family rule (Adikhari, 1984).

The Rana regime perpetuated the legacy of exploitation and central control at the expense of national economic development. Central control was maintained through a network of monopoly contractors, the backbone of Rana administration in an overwhelming rural nation. Rana rule also continued, and extended, the isolationist policy of the Shah dynasty, taking advantage of the luxuries available in nearby foreign markets while stifling markets inside the country. The development of economic infrastructure and the sponsorship of enterprise were firmly discouraged in an effort to maintain absolute political and economic control. Although the Rana regime did undertake certain legal reforms, the peasantry fared little better than it had done under the Shahs. As before, the role of government under the Ranas was primarily extractive; the nation's human and natural resources were treated as a private Rana domain. One writer estimates that between 25 and 50 per cent of all revenues collected in Nepal under the first Rana prime minister were appropriated by him (Kumar, 1967). The opulent life style of the Ranas is still apparent in extravagant buildings in Kathmandu which survive from that era and today house government offices.

As in most traditional societies, land was the most important economic asset in 19th century Nepal. The Rana family used grants of land to develop an elaborate administrative network; the beneficiaries were loyal civil and military servants who, besides the opportunities for local extraction implied by their position, enjoyed tax-free status and privileges in the areas of trade, manufacturing and mining. In short, the Rana administration functioned on the basis of patronage. Under the *ijara* and *thek* systems, designated tax-collectors were entitled (and expected) to squeeze as much as they could from the local peasantry, their remuneration for services rendered being the difference between what they could collect and the fixed amount due to the State (Regmi, 1987). The system of *jagir khane* (literally, 'to eat land'), whereby land was granted to civil servants as payment, is an expression which remains part of the common idiom today, normally used with reference to government service.

Part of the Rana's strategy for securing control over the underpopulated but agriculturally valuable Terai region was to encourage its settlement. Nepalis from the hills were ill-disposed to do so because of the heat and malaria. Consequently, the settling of the Terai from 1890–1930 was placed in the hands of Indian zamindars who were entrusted with tax collecting administrative authority in return for allegiance to the State. This also included the settlement of indigent peasants to make the land prosper (Gaige, 1975). During this time, it was common for Indian traders to exploit Nepali farmers by working through local tax collectors to force grain sales at a price lower than the going market one. The tax collectors would in turn sell the grain to the Indian merchants, collecting a profit in the transaction (Blaikie et al, 1980).

Trade was also controlled by the State, and to the same end as tax collection and monopoly privileges:

> State intervention made it possible for government to manipulate the terms of trade to the detriment of the producer and the trader. The difference between the price actually paid by the state and the price that the producer and the trader would have been able to get in the market, in the absence of state intervention, was appropriated by the state in the form of profits. (Regmi, 1987)

Thus, at every level state and local institutions served to extend and reinforce the tentacles of Rana administration. The system worked, from an economic point of view, because individuals within the system were in a position to profit, provided they shared their profits with the state. Social organization, too, helped the system along: hierarchical structures of kinship; caste networks; patterns of patronage and reciprocity: all these tended to reinforce the upward flow of resources and power.

The institution of *chakari*, still a common and acceptable way of obtaining favours from government officials, illustrates the power of patronage in exchange relationships in Nepal. *Chakari* describes the behaviour appropriate for someone seeking a favour, a position or some other assistance from an official. The individual performing *chakari* ingratiates himself by doing errands for the official, or presenting him with small gifts; he must flatter and generally make himself useful and agreeable. *Chakari* was not confined to any class of citizenry, but was—and is—employed at every level; it is a culturally acceptable mechanism for making the system work.

Like the Shahs before them, the Ranas kept Nepal as isolated as possible from external influences. Although Prime Minister Jang Bahadur Rana journeyed to England in the 1850s, ostensibly to bring back new ideas in art and science, no new industries or technological advances resulted—save the importation of European luxuries for the enjoyment of the ruling family. Roads connecting India with Kathmandu were purposely ill-maintained to restrict social and economic intercourse, and to prevent smuggling and the escape of political prisoners (Regmi, 1987). However, in the late 19th century, as India's railways moved closer to the Nepali border, trade between the two countries began to increase.

It was only during the Second World War, when imports of commodities were at a low level, that the regime showed a brief interest in domestic industrial development. Between 1939 and 1951, 65 companies were registered, with a combined authorized capital of 7 crore Indian Rupees and 21 lakh Nepali Rupees (Pradhan, 1984).[2] The new crop included rice-mills, oil extraction plants and factories for the manufacture of such basic commodities as matches, soap and paper (World Bank, 1972). The majority closed after the war. Nonetheless, two aspects of this first-time foray into industrialization are of interest here. First, the fact that many of these industries were begun as joint ventures between the ruling élite and Indian industrialists is significant. Such collaboration signalled a new recognition on the part of Nepal's ruling élite that profits were to be made, and indeed a competitive edge to be gained, by inviting Indians to come to Nepal along with their expertise. What is also important however, is the low level of financial risk which the Ranas were willing to take in such ventures. Their financial involvement was merely a drop in the bucket relative to their overall wealth. Always aware of their political vulnerability, the Ranas had historically invested heavily in land and commerce in India, at once stifling indigenous growth and investment and leaving themselves vulnerable to their eventual demise. The Indian industrialists gained access to new markets, new sources of raw materials, labour and protection from Indian excise taxes under the patronage and protection of the Ranas. In exchange, the Ranas benefited from the capital and entrepreneurial talent of the Indian industrialists. Both of these trends are still apparent in industrial alliances between the ruling élite and Indian entrepreneurs today.

Such factors may have contributed to the popular overthrow of the

---

[2] 1 crore — 10,000,000 (ten million); 1 lakh — 100,000 (one hundred thousand). Today, the exchange rate is approximately US $1.00 — N Rs 30.00. At that time, it was probably closer to $1 = N Rs 10.

Rana regime in 1950. With the fall of the Ranas not long after Indian independence, the Shah dynasty reinstated itself, but with a new democratic mandate: King Tribhuvan in 1951 undertook to introduce democracy and political reform. However, such was the gap between people and rulers, and so intense the feuding among élite factions, that a unified government could not be established. The years 1951 to 1959 saw considerable unrest in the country. In 1959 the King ordered elections, and a parliament was installed. But this attempt at democracy proved premature for a government with one foot still in its feudal past; the following year, the King revoked the Constitution, dissolved parliament and banned political parties.

In 1962 a new Constitution was promulgated by the King. This introduced the partyless panchayat system,[3] along with a commitment to egalitarian national development. Major reforms were introduced, including a new legal code, the *Mulki Ain*, a land reform programme, and a 'back to the village' campaign. But if good intentions motivated these programmes, the actual results were disappointing. Growing opposition from Nepal's banned political parties ultimately forced a national referendum in 1980. In this, voters opted—by a slender margin—to retain the panchayat system, which then underwent revision. Indirect nominations at the panchayat level were replaced by direct elections of district representatives to the National Assembly. In addition, the selection of the prime minister (formerly in the hands of the king), was delegated to the National Assembly. However, one third of the membership of the National Assembly is still appointed directly by the king: the palace remains the apex of political power.

The restored monarchy has, since 1951, demonstrated a basic ambivalence towards its stated goals of egalitarian development and democracy. External influences such as Nepal's aid donors and the Indian democratic movement have certainly made an impact on the rhetoric, and may even have stimulated some tangible advances. But some Nepali intellectuals maintain that the country's increasing dependence on foreign aid and growing links with the Indian economy may have actually worked against development objectives (IDS, 1984).

---

[3] The panchayat system, adapted from India, was initially designed as a five-tiered governmental structure (*panch* meaning five). Local representatives were elected to a village assembly, which in turn elected a representative to the village panchayat, and so on through the district, zonal and national assemblies. In Nepal, the zonal tier was subsequently done away with. Today district representatives are elected directly by the people to the National Assembly. An important feature of the panchayat system in Nepal is that it disallows the formation of political parties, so that each representative in theory represents only his constituency and is not beholden to any party organization.

Development efforts continue to be heavily subsidized by donor countries; in 1987, for example, such aid constituted 75 per cent of the development budget. And it could be argued that as long as foreign aid is forthcoming, the ruling élite can afford to maintain the profoundly inegalitarian political and economic status quo.

Since 1951, too, the growth of the government bureaucracy, which was supposed to promote development, has served rather as a sponge for a young, disgruntled, educated élite (Blaikie et al, 1980). New government processes, designed to decentralize authority and promote equality, function in large measure on the traditional basis of patronage and caste.

Foreign aid, which was to infuse the system with investment capital to give Nepal a running start, has been siphoned off by those in power; used thus, it has tended to perpetuate the autocratic power of the monarchy (Gaige, 1975). Industrialization, which was supposed to provide alternative sources of income for farmers and revenues for the government, has served instead to tighten Indian control over the Nepali economy. It has also been used to shroud a complex network of illegal trade behind a facade of constructive development.

At the village level, however, some changes are evident as a result of the modest reforms since 1951. Certainly more people have access to health, education, transportation, communications and legal aid. Consumption patterns have also undergone some change. Even in the most remote bazaar towns (and particularly in towns with access to a metalled road), villagers can now buy machine-made fabrics and ready-made garments, packaged foodstuffs, radios, watches, and other manufactured items which were virtually unheard of even 15 years ago. Most of these items are made in India or China. Once exposed to these goods, villagers want, and expect, more. At the same time it bears emphasis that in the area of agricultural production, there has been little progress. Once a grain-exporting country, Nepal has in recent years been forced to appeal to relief agencies for food aid. A 2.6 per cent population growth rate—one of the highest in the world— has added to the problem.

Today, industrialization increasingly figures in Nepal's development rhetoric. Population pressure and the inability of the country to feed itself make this an obvious panacea for the country's ailing economy. However the control which the ruling élite has historically wielded over the private sector, and its long-standing lack of interest in indigenous entrepreneurship, are still evident. A narrow élite continues to maintain control over national resources, even if this control is becoming less and less direct. At the same time the complexity and size of the commercial sector is growing. The élite perpetuates its position not only by joint-venture partnerships with the business sector but also through bureaucratic procedures that entangle private investors and render them dependent on officialdom. Procedures such as registration, licensing, and applications for foreign exchange operate as implements of state control; this approach to administration has recognizable precedents in the *ijara* and *jagir* systems inherited from the Ranas. As a result the Nepali entrepreneur cannot afford to be simply a skilful innovator, manager, technician and financier; first and foremost, he must know how to capitalize on 'source and force'[4] in the state bureaucracy; how to work the system.

Government programmes to stimulate cottage industries in rural areas further demonstrate the lack of any true commitment to private sector development. Such efforts commonly take the form of training courses in skills for which there is often no tangible market. Handloom weaving, knitting, cane-working and other handicrafts are usually high on the list. The products of such activity typically face stiff and growing competition from imported machine-made items sold at prices the fledgling producer is unlikely to be able to match. Indeed in many cases the only market is the government-subsidized Cottage Industry Emporium, which tends to be weak on both quality control and marketing. Cognizant of these facts, the canny villager, who may attend such courses for the stipends offered, opts ultimately for the security of agriculture.

Nepal's small rural bourgeoisie likewise continues to view land as the most risk-free asset, rarely investing in other productive activities. Money-lenders, petty traders and retailers normally take the traditional path and invest in larger tracts of land, cultivated in the traditional style. In more recent times, buildings have also become a desirable form of investment, particularly in urban areas. All this does little to stimulate new forms of production at the village level.

It is only fair to point out that such conservatism is also true of Nepal's ruling élite, few of whose members have evidenced an interest in technologically-related investment. While foreign imported products have historically enjoyed a high status in élite circles, the actual introduction of foreign technology for domestic production has been done mainly by foreign donors and foreign investors. Within the indigenous élite, investment is still governed by the historical preference for land and commerce.

Indigenous entrepreneurs in medium- and large-scale industries have

---

[4] 'Source and force' is a commonly used expression in Nepal. It refers to the ability of an individual to garner influence either through monetary incentives (source) or kinship or friendship (force).

strong ties with government officials—ties usually based on kinship or patronage—which give them the all-important 'source and force' to run industries. Because frequent policy changes render industrial investment highly vulnerable, access to 'source and force' provides entrepreneurs with a measure of security. Individuals without resources or connections therefore have little scope to carve new, economically viable investment openings. Overall, then, the relationship between entrepreneur and the state appears to have undergone little change in the past two centuries.

As for trade, the experience of Nepal appears notably different from that of India. Despite the existence of barter trade along Nepal's northern and southern borders, trading activity has never played an important role in stimulating the indigenous manufacture of goods. This reality is even more glaring today. The items of greatest profit to Nepali traders are not bought, sold, or even produced within the country. Primarily luxury goods purchased in Southeast Asian countries, such items are often contraband bound for the black markets of Nepal and India. And the profits from such trade are generally not banked in the country, either.

Despite the downfall of the Ranas in 1951, strong vestiges of the patronage and exploitation which characterized the old system survived. The more brazen methods of extraction which typified the Rana regime were no longer possible in a new context in which world opinion, the views of donor countries, and the nearby example of democratic India were making their impact. Nonetheless, more subtly expressed cultural forms of patronage were to be incorporated into the workings of the government bureaucracy.

Economic development in Nepal over the last 35 years therefore presents a mixed picture. While resources, commodities and services have been made available to a larger segment of the population than before, their distribution, production and price are still subject to strong centralized control. Economic change and technological innovation confront a situation still dominated by patronage relationships; to be a successful entrepreneur involves considerable skill in working the system. In this situation, immigrant Indian entrepreneurs with access to capital, technologies, and wider markets have been able to move into gaps in the private sector and make the most of their advantages over their Nepali counterparts.

THE GROWTH OF MODERN INDUSTRY AND
ENTREPRENEURSHIP : INDIA AND NEPAL COMPARED

A look at industrialization in India provides a useful point of comparison with Nepal. It is also the logical starting-point for an exploration of the extent to which entrepreneurs in Nepal have become dependent on Indian markets, capital, technology and expertise.

India's long coastline and history of successive invasions have contributed to a long experience of international trade. The seeds of the country's present-day industrial and commercial activity, however, were probably planted in the 18th century, the era of triangular trade between China, India and Britain. British colonization of India, completed by the mid-19th century, spurred demand for raw materials, labour, new markets for manufactured items, and locally based entrepreneurs. It also financed the expansion of the country's infrastructure, notably its seaports, railways and roads.

The rise of industrial entrepreneurship in India was therefore largely the result of contact with a colonial power. Moreover, this came at a time of deep-going change in the West: the era of the industrial revolution, the growth of capitalism and expanding international trade. Foreign firms, dependent to some extent on indigenous trade, credit, and distribution networks for the purchase of raw materials and the sale of finished goods, exposed these networks to new contacts and markets, and brought in a certain amount of capital (Timberg, 1978). The fact that the British were obliged to work closely with indigenous managers and entrepreneurs appears to have stimulated the development of an entrepreneurial class, led largely by those from the ranks of traditional trading communities. The British relied particularly heavily on the services of the Indian *banian*.[5] He became a key intermediary for procuring raw materials and organizing labour, internal markets and the export of goods (Timberg, 1978). In this way, British firms served as the training ground for many future Indian entrepreneurs.

By the 1930s, if not earlier, some Indian entrepreneurs began breaking away from their British partners and establishing their own industries. The emerging industrial entrepreneurs often came from major banking and trade concerns, particularly those owned by, or associated with, foreign industry or commerce. A larger, more educated and technically oriented cadre of 'imitative' entrepreneurs came on the heels of these pioneers. Many had had their 'apprenticeship' training in larger companies, and broke away to form similar industries of their own.

Industrialization in India was, therefore, a complex process, the

---

[5] Timberg (1978) defines the *banian* as 'a person by whom all purchases and sales of goods, merchandize, and produce are made and through whom all shipments are made on account and on behalf of the merchant or mercantile firm in whose establishment he is *banian*.'

result of many interweaving factors. One was the development, by the colonial power, of the infrastructure essential for colonial exploitation: this helped transport raw materials and finished goods to a wider market. A second factor was the introduction of the factory system by a colonial regime eager to capitalize on India's cheap labour and abundant raw materials; this resulted in migration from rural areas to urban factories by a quite substantial labour force, who eventually adapted to new types of economic organization. Also important were the expanding markets for trade before World War I, which provided the prerequisite capital and expertise for launching industries during and after the war. Lastly, there was an emerging class of imitative entrepreneurs upon whom the expansion of the indigenous industrial sector rested.

While industrialization was transforming the Indian economy, Nepal, never colonized, land-locked, and protected from interaction with economic and political forces beyond her borders, remained virtually isolated from the outside world. It is not surprising that when the process of industrialization in India did at last began to spill over into Nepal, it was the Indian entrepreneur who introduced it. Nor is surprising that it is the Indian entrepreneur who still maintains control of this sector.

When the Indian railway system reached Nepal's southern border, Indian merchants were swift to capitalize on this new source of labour and raw materials. Not only was Nepal virgin territory as far as raw materials were concerned, it also represented a new market-place for Indian manufactured goods and an attractive site for industrial development. By establishing industries in Nepal, Indian industrialists could, in addition, circumvent exise duties in their own country.

It can be argued that the lack of a colonial past has proved a handicap to Nepal's industrial development. Whatever its negative impact, colonialism in India provided markets and infrastructure as well as an unintended training-ground for industrial entrepreneurs. The entrepreneurial class which emerged during and after British rule continues to play an important political and economic role in post-colonial India. Nepal, in effect entering the world market in 1950, came with none of these advantages. The significance of this time-lag should not be underestimated. When India entered the market-place, there was a demand for her raw materials, labour, and financier and commercial talent. Nepal, with far less human and natural resource potential to begin with, with limited infrastructure, with virtually no experience in industry and only limited, geographically confined experience in trade, was in a disadvantaged position. This was particularly so with respect to her giant neighbours, India and China, both of which were already decades ahead in terms of industrial development.

A further impediment to Nepal's industrial development has been her political relationship with India. While the potential exists for Nepal to apprentice herself, economically speaking, to India, a strong sense of nationalism within Nepal has stymied such possibilities. National pride, stoked by the strong cultural and economic influence India already exerts over the country, has hindered Nepal from taking full advantage of the opportunities offered by Indian entrepreneurship at her doorstep. The garment industry, discussed in Chapter IV, is a case in point.

The concentration of Nepal's industrial development in the hands of traditional 'public sector' forces—a roundabout way of noting the continuing clout of Nepal's royal family and those close to it—has proved another handicap. Such industry as there is has taken shape largely outside the domestic private sector, overseen by the bureaucracy and funded mainly by foreign aid and Indian investors.

Nor has industrialization been helped by a distrust of outsiders—and outside influences—which is still evident in ruling circles today. Indeed, Indian entrepreneurs in the industrial sector have met with suspicion and criticism, notwithstanding the fact that their activity is an important source of revenue for governmental coffers—and individual civil servants. At a more general level, this attitude translates into mistrust of foreign technology and modern production methods, providing further disincentives for domestic entrepreneurs to venture into industry.

In sum, many of the factors which inhibited the development of entrepreneurship in the country persist today. But despite this rather pessimistic picture, several indigenous communities have, by accepting the constraints of the system and skilfully operating within them, been able to make their mark in the private sector. These communities, to be explored in the next chapter, would appear crucial to Nepal's economic future; in a sense, their fortunes will be an important barometer of the kingdom's development progress.

THE ETHNIC DISTRIBUTION OF ENTREPRENEURSHIP IN NEPAL

The figures presented in this section provide data on the representation of various communities in Nepal's industrial sector. The statistics—even those from reputable institutions and official reports—are provided with certain caveats, however. As is the case in many developing countries, the collection of reliable statistics in Nepal has been given insufficient attention. Very little hard information on industries, in particular the owners of industries, is available. Furthermore, given the geographical constraints on census surveys in Nepal, the results of existing data collection efforts must be interpreted with a measure of scepticism.

The interpretation of the data is further hindered by policies which may skew census returns in favour of 'small' industrialists.[6] Until very recently, attractive import incentives and tax exempt status were available to promote small industries. Many firms which are in fact medium-scale (or have grown to that size) have been registered as 'small' to take advantage of these facilities. Inefficient monitoring by the government and bribes to appropriate officials allow entrepreneurs to retain their status as small industrialists even when they have well outgrown that category. Recent policy changes which have eliminated these incentives may change the pattern of registration, but the effectiveness of such policies remains unclear.

In Nepal, foreigners are barred by law from owning small industries and are entitled only to 49 per cent ownership of medium-scale industries. It is therefore common practice for foreigners wishing to invest in industries of these categories to recruit a 'sleeping' Nepali partner whose name appears on the registration form.[7] The presence of an influential Nepali partner in medium- or large-scale industries may also strengthen the access of an expatriate entrepreneur to the all-important 'source and force' necessary to run a business successfully in Nepal. For Tibetan refugees and first-generation Marwari entrepreneurs (neither of whom enjoy Nepali citizenship), such considerations are particularly important. Given this reality, Tibetans and Marwaris may be underrepresented, and Brahmins, Chhetris and Newars—the communities from which Nepal's sleeping partners tend to be drawn—overrepresented in the data set out below.

The first set of data, Figure 2.1, shows the representation of different ethnic communities in the ownership of Nepal's manufacturing industry, analyzed in terms of its medium- to large-scale, small-scale, and micro-scale sectors. Ninety-one small- and medium-scale

[6] This is done by underestimating the projected total fixed assets in the registration application.
[7] **Foreigners** may own **large-scale** industries outright.

FIGURE 2.1

Ethnicity of Nepali Entrepreneurs by Number and Size of Industry

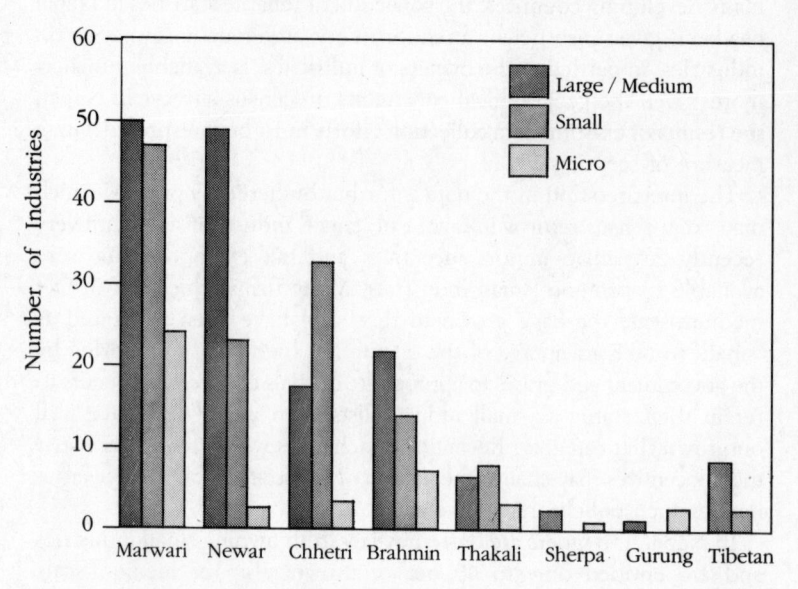

SOURCE: Department of Industries, Kathmandu.

NOTE: Small industries are here defined as those with fixed assets below Nepali Rupees 5,00,000 (approximately US $23,000); medium under two million Nepali Rupees (approximately US $95,000) and large above ten million Nepali Rupees (approximately US $470,000). Cottage industries are only required to register if they need government facilities such as import licenses or temporary tax exempt status. As there are an estimated 200,000 such industries and small commercial ventures (and many more in the informal sector), no attempt to classify them has been made.

milling enterprises have been included here: they account for nearly a quarter of the total industries in the country and reflect the strong bonds between the industrial and agricultural sectors. This figure was compiled by extracting the names of industrial proprietors from registration information on file at Nepal's Department of Industries. Ethnic background was then deduced from the names.

Figures 2.2 provides an approximate distribution of the same ethnic communities in the total population; with the exception of Brahmins and Chhetris, all the groups appear to be overrepresented in industry relative to their proportion of total population.

FIGURE 2.2

Population and Industrial Ownership
Distribution According to Ethnicity

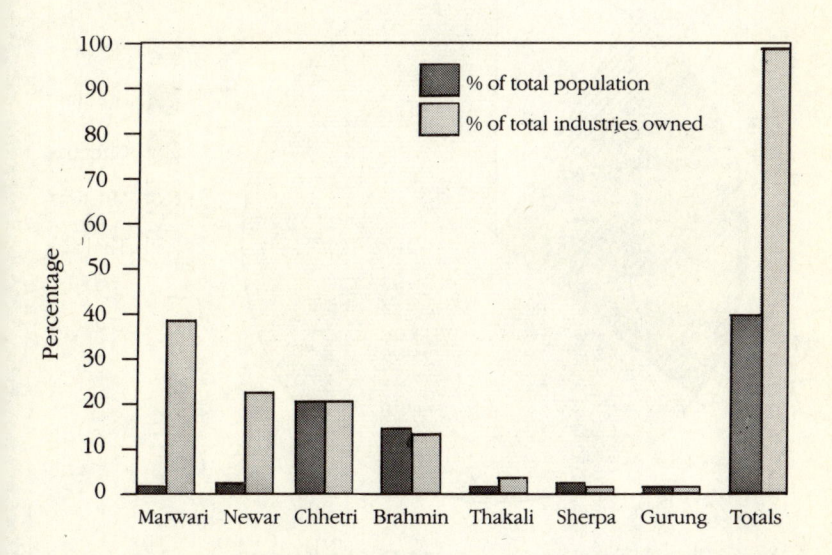

Figure: Bar chart showing % of total population and % of total industries owned across Marwari, Newar, Chhetri, Brahmin, Thakali, Sherpa, Gurung, and Totals.

Source: Department of Industries, Kathmandu.

Figure 2.3, while not based specifically on the manufacturing sector, provides additional insight into the ethnic distribution of business holdings in Nepal.

Because of the largely small-scale and agriculturally-based nature of business in this region, it is not surprising to find that Newars and high-caste Hindus predominate. As described above, Newars pioneered cottage industry and trade in this part of Nepal, while Thakalis carved out a niche in construction, retailing and tourist-related concerns.

Newars also dominate rice- and oil-milling concerns, as Figure 2.4 shows. The data reveal Brahmins and Chhetris to be primarily involved in retailing, generally considered a relatively low-risk activity. Given the agricultural roots of much of the business in this region, it is not surprising to find a small number of Marwari enterprises relative to overall national figures, nor to discover that most such businesses are

FIGURE 2.3

Owners of Business by Ethnic Group in West-Central Nepal

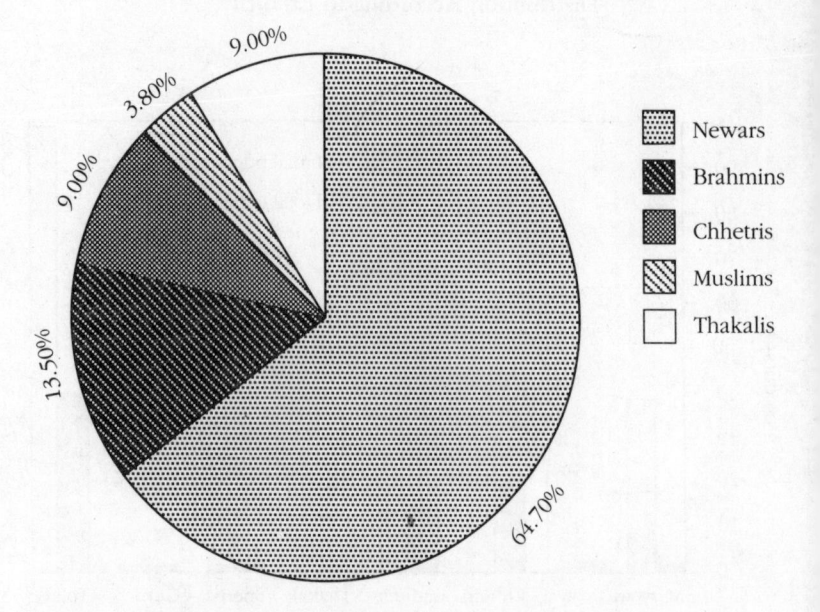

- Newars: 64.70%
- Brahmins: 13.50%
- Chhetris: 9.00%
- Muslims: 3.80%
- Thakalis: 9.00%

Source: Piers Blaikie, John Cameron and David Seddon, *Nepal in Crisis*, Oxford University Press, Delhi, 1980.

in the cloth retailing sector. Outside the major urban centres, Marwaris tend to capitalize on their links with external suppliers of imported goods—which are in constant demand in rural Nepal.

The breakdown of the membership of the Pokhara Chamber of Commerce provided in Figure 2.5 highlights sharply the dominant role of the Newars in the private sector activity of the region. Relative to their population size, Thakalis are well represented in this forum as well. The absence of Marwaris from this figure is notable. As a rule Newars and high-caste Hindus tend to dominate Chambers of Commerce throughout Nepal, although in Terai towns, where ethnic distinctions are more blurred, this is less the case.

A similar trend is shown in Figure 2.6, which depicts the participation of various ethnic groups in one of the major trading associations in the country. The Nepal Trans-Himalayan Traders Association (described in more detail in a later section on the carpet industry)

FIGURE 2.4
Ethnic Distribution in Different Businesses in West-Central Nepal

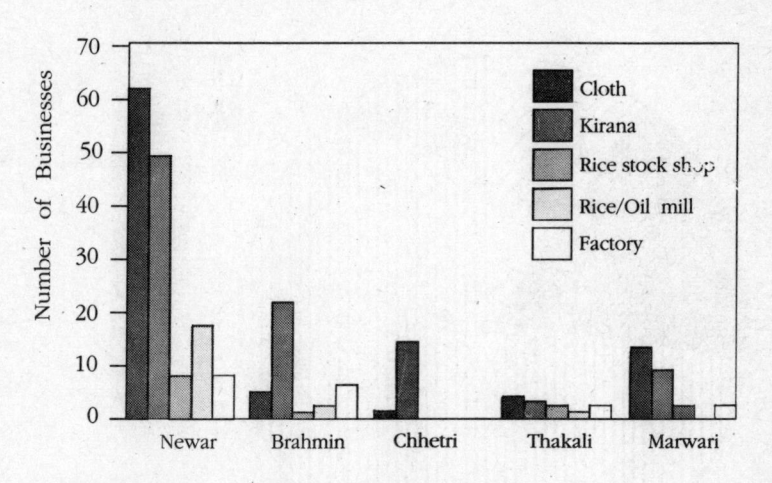

Source: Blaikie, Cameron and Seddon, 1980, pp. 160–1.

FIGURE 2.5
Members of Pokhara Chamber of Commerce by Ethnic Group

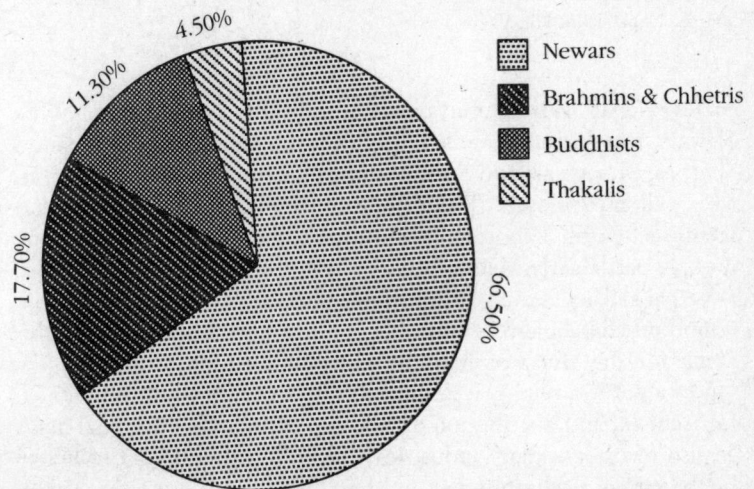

- Newars: 66.50%
- Brahmins & Chhetris: 17.70%
- Buddhists: 11.30%
- Thakalis: 4.50%

Source: Pokhara Chamber of Commerce.

FIGURE 2.6

Members of Nepal Trans-Himalayan Traders
Association by Ethnic Group

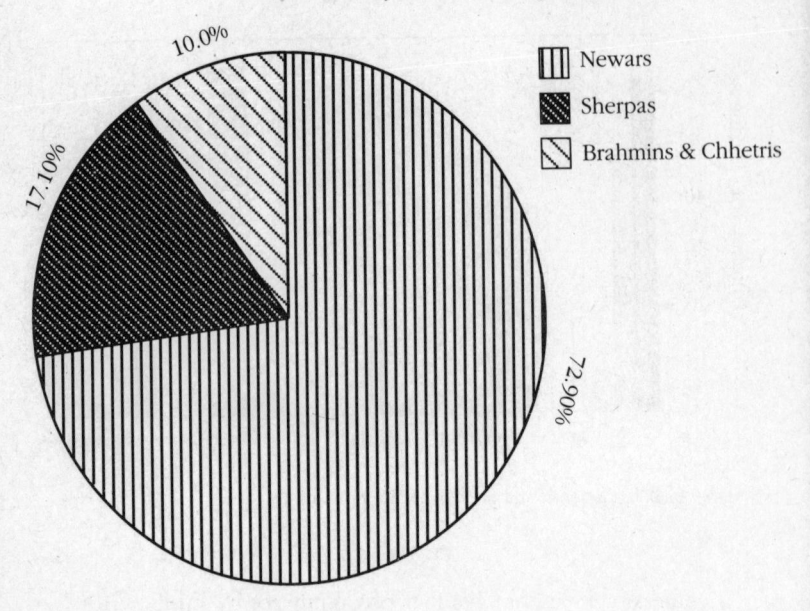

- Newars
- Sherpas
- Brahmins & Chhetris

10.0%
17.10%
72.90%

Source: Nepal Trans-Himalayan Traders Association.

trades Nepali agricultural products for wool with Tibet. While Newars, with historical trade links to Tibet, dominate this association, Sherpas, who are also involved because of their proximity to Tibet, are also well represented. This figure is illustrative of only one segment—albeit an important one—of the trade sector. Other ethnic groups, particularly Marwaris, are major players in trade with India.

Nepal's Salt Trading Corporation, one of the largest and most important shareholding companies in the kingdom, provides another arena for the study of minority community business activity. The corporation is a semi-private limited firm with government contracts for trade in, and distribution of, salt, sugar, and other essential items. It also owns subsidiary industries. Figure 2.7 provides a breakdown of the ethnic background of its shareholders.

FIGURE 2.7

Distribution of Shares in Nepal's Salt Trading Corporation by Ethnic Group

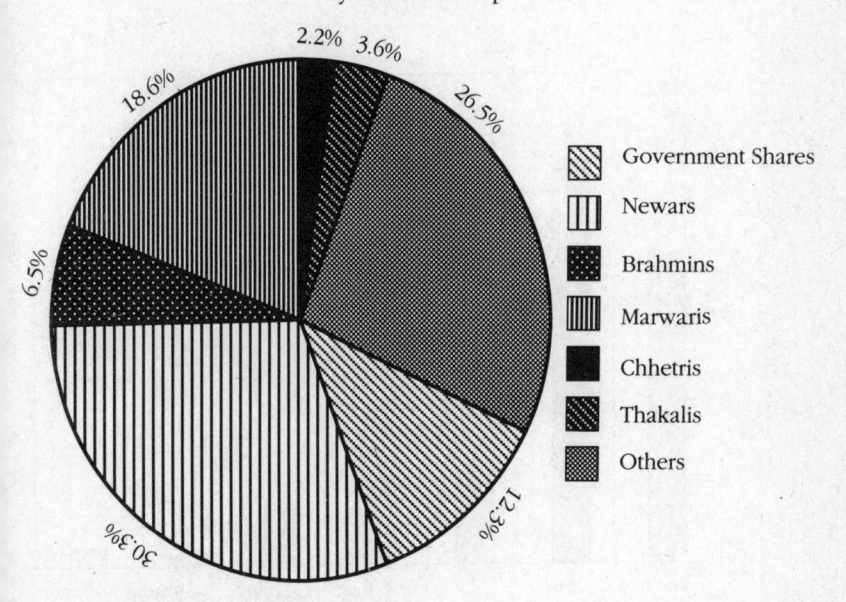

- Government Shares
- Newars
- Brahmins
- Marwaris
- Chhetris
- Thakalis
- Others

2.2%, 3.6%, 26.5%, 12.3%, 30.3%, 6.5%, 18.6%

Source: Salt Trading Corporation, Nepal.

Figure 2.8 shows the ethnic distribution of owners of tourist and trekking agencies, important contributors to the Nepali economy. Many of the agencies are small-scale enterprises owned by two or more individuals, as often as not from different ethnic groups. Together, such operators make a significant contribution to national economic life; tourism, an important source of employment as well as foreign exchange, has grown significantly over the past decade.

The picture that emerges from the data is that Marwaris dominate Nepal's large-scale industrial and trade sectors, while the Newars are the major small-scale traders and cottage industrialists. Relative to their size in the total population, the Sherpas are well represented in the tourist industry and the Thakalis in industry and contracting. With the exception of Brahmins and Chhetris, who make up a sizeable percentage of the population (though exact statistics on this are not available), all these groups are extremely small relative to the national

FIGURE 2.8

Ethnic Distribution of Owners of
Tourist and Trekking Agencies

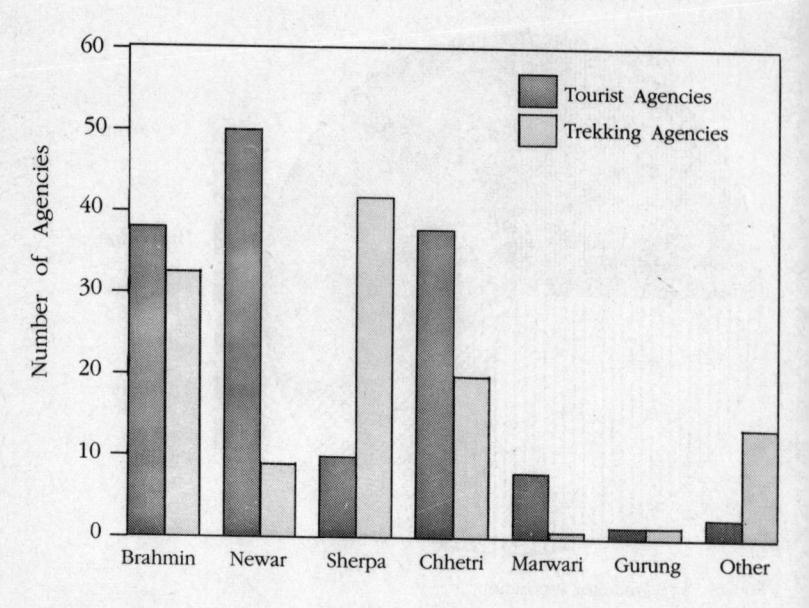

Source: Ministry of Tourism, Kathmandu.

population. In the chapter that follows, each of these communities—that have, in the face of Nepal's difficult history and sundry disadvantages, scored some entrepreneurial success—will be placed under closer scrutiny.

Chapter Three

Entrepreneurial Communities in Nepal: Some Case-studies

In this chapter, seven cultural communities in Nepal which have demonstrated varying degrees of entrepreneurship are considered in some depth. The discussion will attempt to highlight the specific interface between socio-cultural forms, economic organizing principles and historical circumstance which has promoted entrepreneurship in each of these communities. These case-studies are not intended to be comprehensive ethnographies, although ethnographic sources, where available, inform the discussion. The broad brush with which each culture has been painted in this attempt to extract and examine the factors most relevant to entrepreneurship necessitates brevity; while this may offend the sensibilities of the specialist historian or anthropologist, the aim here is to extract the major threads from each case-study and establish similarities and contrasts in order to weave a general picture of entrepreneurship in Nepal.

THE NEWARS

The Newars are one of the oldest and largest communities in Nepal to engage in business activities. While nowadays they are sprinkled all over Nepal, their origins are in the Kathmandu Valley, where they developed a culture rich in ritual, ceremony, and craftsmanship. The fertility of the Valley is largely responsible for the occupational diversity of the Newars. Handicraft production, trade, and commerce were further stimulated by Kathmandu's location on the major India-Tibet trade route, while the Gorkhali conquest of 1769 escalated the demand for Newari goods and services. During the two centuries of Nepali history following unification, the Newars established themselves as the leading mercantile community in the kingdom. Their domination of business in the country was enhanced by the lack of competition from other communities and the reliance of successive ruling élites upon the Newars for their business skills. Over the last three decades, however, the Newars have been facing competition from other communities which have outpaced them in the private sector.

There are conflicting theories about the origins of the Newars.[1] It is generally agreed, however, that they were the original inhabitants of the Kathmandu Valley. Recent research—based primarily on legends—maintains that Newari society was consolidated in the twelfth century under the three great Malla kingdoms of the Kathmandu Valley. While the culture had already been influenced by Hinduism in important ways, in the 14th century, King Jayastiti Malla, with the assistance of Hindu advisors from north India, organized the Newars into sixty-four occupational castes, mirroring the Indian caste system.

There are also Newari Buddhists who follow the Tantric form of Buddhism, with strong influences from Tibetan Buddhism.

Among the Newars, the most important castes are the *Jyapoos*, or farmers; various craft-specific castes; and merchant and administrator or *Shrestha* castes. While in theory the caste system serves to structure only the Hindu segment of Newar society, the compelling influence of Hindu culture has forced Buddhist Newars to conform to a similar hierarchy (although strict pollution restrictions may not be relevant to them). Buddhist priests, or *Vajracharayas*, rank above the *Shakya* (artisans) and *Uray* (business strata) (Gellner, 1986). Hinduism and Buddhism co-exist harmoniously within the Newar culture, with considerable mingling of the two faiths.

Before the invasion of Prithvi Narayan Shah in the latter half of the 18th century, the Newars (primarily the Uray Newars) were engaged in trade with Tibet. The Tibetans, wary of the East India Company and the British presence in India, gave the Newars preference over Indian merchants.[2] Such preferential treatment was reinforced by later Nepali rulers. Additionally, the heat of the malarial lowlands of Nepal was as distasteful to the Newari traders as were the rough Himalayan passes to the plains Indians. Thus the division of the trade route was conditioned by both politics and geography.

[1] While G.S. Nepali (1965) contends that the Newars came originally from southwestern India, Levi (1905) suggests that this is highly unlikely.
[2] However, there were Kashmiris in Lhasa in the 19th and 20th centuries, according to researcher Todd Lewis (in conversation with the author, 1986).

The Gorkhali conquest of the Kathmandu Valley, perhaps facilitated by Newari 'meekness', signalled a major turning point for the Newars.[3] For the first time they faced political domination by an outside regime. After the Gorkhali invasion, some Newars left the Valley, fleeing taxation and interference from the new government. Others followed Gorkhali inducements to undertake commercial and administrative activities in outlying districts. The Gorkhalis, preoccupied with territorial expansion, relied on the Newars for the necessary commercial back-up. Many Newars were given *ijara* monopoly privileges to tax and trade in important sectors such as mining, paper-making, and agriculture (Regmi, 1986). The Newars established important commercial centres at Pokhara, Tansen, Butwal and Baglung in central Nepal. Those not involved in administration engaged in petty trade, retailing, and cottage industries (Regmi, 1971).

The *ijara* monopoly contracting system, and similar taxation agreements, persisted well into the Rana regime. The Newars also controlled a large percentage of trade, particularly in the hills (Regmi, 1986). Through these and other mechanisms, the community assumed new positions in the administration. These gave them expanded access to power, prestige and, more specifically, to land through *jagir* land grants—the form of payment for administrative services rendered.

Concerned with projecting their own caste superiority, the Chhetri Ranas raised the status of Hindu Newars while subjugating the Buddhists, in particular the Uray traders. They went so far as to promulgate a policy whereby traders returning from abroad were required to perform purification ceremonies to cleanse themselves of the pollution acquired through contact with non-Hindus. Buddhism does not concern itself with such ritual pollution, and this dictum was a sore point with the Urays, who largely circumvented it (Rosser, 1966). As one Uray entrepreneur recalls,

> My father was a businessman. He used to import silk from China and Japan for the Ranas. During the Rana time, once you went to a foreign country you lost your caste. You had to get permission to get it back. During the Rana time people were not allowed to go to schools. I got my business sense by getting around.

[3] Critics of this position maintain that it is a stereotype propogated by Gorkhali/Nepali culture in response to recent Newari 'nationalism' (see footnote 7). But the fact that three strategic city-states were so easily overcome by outside invaders points to a certain absence of warring spirit. Later events tend to support the view that the Newars have been easily manipulated by stronger political forces.

The Ranas were also anxious to maintain caste distinctions between occupations, and attempted to restrict Brahmin and Chhetri entrance into business (Doherty, 1975). The Newars therefore faced little competition from other communities in the commercial arena. Nonetheless, the Newars never exhibited a strong inclination to invest in larger concerns or more diverse types of industry or trade. This conservative tendency was reinforced by political circumstances which limited their ability to diversify and at the same time offered them alternative, administrative avenues to power. In addition (although little hard historical evidence for this is available), current investment propensities among the Newars indicate a longstanding preference to invest profits in religious and social ceremonies, rather than in retailing, trade or industry.

While the Newars have secured a stronghold in government, their domination of the commercial sector has waned since 1950 when Nepal opened its doors to the world. Newari entrepreneurs have been unable to compete with indigenous and immigrant business elements who have pioneered new opportunities in tourism, factory-based manufacturing, building and road construction, and international trade. Trade with Tibet was curtailed after the Chinese invasion of Tibet in 1959; only a small minority of the Uray population has been able to create new avenues of international trade since then (Lewis, 1986). A few Newars, principally those with strong governmental connections, have become industrial entrepreneurs. Today, most Newars are to be found running basic commodity (*kirana*) shops, grain or oil milling concerns, or cottage industries based on inherited occupations such as tailoring, metal-working, carpentry and cobbling. Handicraft and other traditional forms of production have, however, suffered with the increased flow of manufactured items into the country. Although the Newars continue to dominate the cottage industry and petty retailing sectors, particularly in hill bazaar towns, even these economic strongholds are being threatened by manufactured items from India and China—all of them imported and marketed by other groups.

Considering the former commercial prowess of the Newars, and their headstart in the non-agricultural private sector, why is it that enterprising, innovative individuals from this community have become the exception rather than the rule? The reasons for this are complex. In part they are historical, as we have already seen. However, it can also be argued that the rigidity and conservatism of Newari social organization has retarded the community's diversification into modern commercial pursuits.

Social structures and entrepreneurship: the Newar experience. Newari society is a complex organization of kinship and social sub-groups linked by compelling, cohesifying norms which delimit and define individual identity as well as occupation. An individual's identity and behaviour is ascribed according to his place in the family, the community, specific lineages and caste-defined organizations. Communal cohesion is maintained through an abundance of ceremonies and festivals, and strong restrictions on aberrant behaviour. Nepali (1965) describes Newari culture in these terms:

> The sum total of Newar culture-traits goes to make such an institutional complex that there is complete integration of the individual with the society. The rigidity is too orthodox, while the ceremonials are elaborate and rich. Aberrant individuals find themselves completely rooted out of the rich life offered by the society. (p. 421)

The strong sense of community which typifies Newari culture contrasts oddly with an equally compelling avoidance of economic co-operation. This is demonstrated most clearly by exploring several Newari social organizing structures.

The primary form of Newari ceremonial, economic and political organization is the *guthi*, a social grouping formed to carry out specific tasks. There are several types of *guthi*, the most important being the *sana guthi*, which performs the necessary rituals upon the death of a *guthi* member. There are also collective worship, ceremonial, and lineage *guthis*, which are structured around the worship of a specific deity, the organization of a ritual or festival or the preservation of lineage concerns respectively. *Guthis* typically cross family lines but are caste-bound; they are organic institutions to which an individual normally belongs for his entire life.

Interestingly, however, no specifically modern economic *guthi* has yet emerged within Newari society. In former times artisans of the same caste were known to participate in *desla guthis* which maintained a credit fund and loaned sums of money at low interest to *guthi* members. Evidence indicates that this practice had died out because of the blurring of caste-based occupations and transformations in traditional modes of production as modern manufactured goods have entered the market-place (Toffin, 1977). No new Newari credit systems have replaced the *desla guthis*. The closest approximation to organized co-operation in the productive sphere exists among farming communities, who sometimes organize work-groups at planting and harvesting times—although even these are breaking down today. Such groups tend to be temporary, ad hoc and based on kinship ties (Toffin, 1977). In more recent times it has become a matter of prestige and preference to hire outside labourers rather than engage in the exchange of labour common among most other farming communities in Nepal (Ishii, 1980). In the Newari trading community of Dulikhel, 'an arrangement such as *gwali* [labour given by kinsmen with no exact reciprocity expected] would be almost inconceivable ... where relations between affines tend to be characterized by extreme formality verging on avoidance.' (Quigley, 1985, p. 37; explanation, author's)

As we have already noted, Newars of both Hindu and Buddhist background follow a caste system (or, more accurately, parallel hierarchical structures), with each caste or sub-caste adhering to its own occupation, deity and ritual. Upward mobility has become possible in recent years under the impact of modernization, urbanization, and growing external contacts. In general, such mobility has been contingent upon economic advancement, acceptance into higher caste *guthis*, intermarriage with higher caste individuals (usually a man marrying a higher caste woman who is economically not so well-off), or repudiation of caste. New *guthis* formed of individuals who have changed caste by these methods have also become common.

As a group, the Newars have demonstrated a subtle but consistent upward mobility, involving gradual integration into the administrative and landed élite. Their domination by the Gorkhalis (and, later, by the Ranas) effected internal redefinitions as they assumed important administrative and commercial positions under successive ruling élites. This advance into positions which are valued by the mainstream culture has to some degree been achieved at the expense of the Newars' previous success in business.[4]

Among the Newars, hierarchical forms of relationship predominate,

---

[4] Gellner (1986) cites a personal conversation with K.P. Malla in which the latter estimated that in 1981 Newars constituted 30 per cent of university teachers, 32 per cent of authors writing in Nepali, 24 per cent of journalists writing in Nepali and English, 30 per cent of civil servants, and 8 per cent of those elected to the National Assembly. These proportions have undoubtedly increased since then. In addition, many of the king's closest advisors have traditionally been Newars.

both within and outside the family. The most senior male member of the household is the ultimate authority in all spheres. While the son must show deference to his father, and must perform his death rituals, the male head of the household (who may be a senior uncle or a grandfather), is the ultimate disciplinarian and prime mover. Below him status is determined by age and gender. A son has *de facto* access to property while the father is alive, but it is generally considered improper for him to claim his inheritance during the father's lifetime.

Joint families—consisting of several generations living under one roof, with common ownership of property—are a feature of Newari life, and persist even among urbanized, educated families (Quigley, 1985). However, in recent times there have been cases where the death of a father triggers the break-up of the old unit. This has been attributed to several factors, among them conflicts between the mother-in-law and her sons' wives (Nepali, 1965), and the economic advancement of one or more of the sons. It may also result from tensions inherent in the deferential father-son relationship—a relationship which is mirrored in that between the senior son (upon whom the deceased father's responsibilities and status devolve) and his younger brothers.

The organization of individual Newari businesses tends to reflect the hierarchical structure of the family. In general, one individual rules the roost, running the business or businesses as a family corporation. Although the patriarch may not be involved directly in all the family businesses, he is the controlling authority and decision-maker (Quigley, 1985). In addition, since most Newari businesses are single-product or single-outlet enterprises, there is little scope for sons to branch out on their own. As one Newari entrepreneur reports, 'My father was not happy when I started my own business. Of course, I was in the same family [i.e. he lived in the joint family]. I borrowed money from friends to start my business.'

Of the twenty-five Newari entrepreneurs I interviewed, almost half had begun their businesses only after their father's death. And twenty-two of them had begun a different type of business from that of their father.

The family is, clearly, the most important economic unit within Newar society, and operates autonomously, sometimes even competitively, in relation to other Newari families (Quigley, 1985). While families engaged in both agriculture and business typically hire outside labour to perform the menial farm work, the use of hired labour in non-agricultural activity is viewed with suspicion and caution (Quigley, 1985). The typical Newari shop in a Nepali bazaar town is not only owned but also run by family members. Of the sample of Newari entrepreneurs interviewed, only three had partners who were not family members.[5] An outsider might be hired to run errands but never to handle money.

Furthermore, Newars—in common with other small entrepreneurs—complain that after they bring in outside labourers and train them, the employees invariably run off to start their own businesses. It seems safer to rely on family members. This, however, tends to restrict the possibility of expansion, especially in a situation where only male family members are considered fit to be involved. It is not uncommon for a business to fold when the owner dies, although his son may start another soon thereafter.

Economic co-operation among Newaris therefore appears highly problematic. Research among the Newars of Patan, in the Kathmandu Valley, indicates that a 'a high degree of social and religious co-operation and economic anarchy seems to be normal. There would be economic rewards for co-operation, as they dominate the curio business, but they seem to be incapable of it.' (Quigley, 1985, citing a personal conversation with David Gellner)

This author has had a similar experience. In one case I came across, a metal craftsman was unable to fill a large order because he was suspicious of sub-contracting part of the work to other craftsmen in the bazaar where he lived—despite the fact that they were well known to him. The communal bonds and social interdependencies which are so important to Newar individual indentity are, however, protected by such practices. As one small manufacturer told me, 'I have a hard time getting labourers because I can't hire people from my own locality. If they don't work hard, or if they cheat me, what can I do to them? Some of my neighbours are angry that I don't involve them in my business, but it's easier that way.'

We see here a strong avoidance of co-operation, whether between members of the same community or families, along with the promotion of business structures which mirror family relationships. While these approaches to enterprise—which may preserve social harmony at the

---

[5] All three owned large- or medium-scale enterprises, and one of the three had a foreign partner who provided partial funding and technology.

expense of economic advancement—perhaps suited the Newars' traditional way of life, their appropriateness for new forms of production and an ever-widening market-place appears debatable. Nevertheless, if we look closer at the many Newari castes engaged in business, we find that senior sons are still encouraged to follow a business career. Of the twenty-five Newari entrepreneurs I interviewed, eleven were first sons and seven second sons in their respective families. More than three-quarters of this small sample reported other family members in business. It is not uncommon, however, for at least one son in a family to be educated to a fairly advanced level in an effort to get him a job in the civil service. Aside from the prestige of a government position, this also ensures assistance for the business wing of the family.

The position of women in Newari culture differs little from that of their Brahmin and Chhetri counterparts. The wife must subordinate herself to her husband in ritual and social activity, and her mobility is limited (Nepali, 1965). There are strong mother- and goddess-worship cults among the Newars, and mothers are expected to reflect the nurturing, subservient feminine principle invoked by such deities. Nepali portrays the ideal of Newari womanhood thus:

> She is kind and partial to her own children. She receives obedience due to her kindness and love, whereas a father commands obedience from his children through awe ... the mother has comparatively little social and ritual leadership in the domestic ceremonies connected with her own child, unless her position happens to coincide with the status as the chief lady of the house or the consanguineal group. (p. 271)

It is uncommon for a Newari woman to run a business independent of her male kinsfolk. But women make significant contributions to family-based businesses, particularly in rural or semi-urban areas; here they assist in shops and small manufacturing units. Women perform primary domestic and agricultural functions as well (Acharya and Bennett, 1981).

The Newari business ethic. By separating business from social relations, the Newars have settled on a system which wards off conflict in the economic sphere, and preserves the social amicability so central to their culture. Because the cultural emphasis on communal cohesion tends to exclude economic reciprocity, expenditure on ceremony and ritual (in terms of both capital and time) takes precedence over investment in business. The show of wealth is seen as more important than its accumulation (Quigley, 1986).[6]

Newari merchants also demonstrate conservatism in their approach to diversification and investment in business. As Quigley, writing on merchants in a Kathmandu Valley bazaar town, comments, 'Dulikhel merchants, though geographically mobile, are extremely unadventurous when it comes to investing their capital in enterprises. Rarely do they stray outside of traditional commodities which are in high, everyday demand. They are assuredly not innovators.' (Quigley, 1985, p. 39) The merchants in Quigley's study chose to move out of their community rather than diversify into new businesses.

An additional reason for such entrepreneurial conservatism is lack of ready capital. There are no lending systems, formal or informal, within Newari communities. The desire to avoid economic dependency on non-family elements also limits borrowing for commercial purposes. Roughly three-quarters of the Newari entrepreneurs interviewed started their businesses with their own or family capital.

Lack of capital has, in fact, been a critical handicap in Newari attempts to compete with foreign entrepreneurs who have brought in significant capital (some of it in hard currency) and have been aggressive in taking advantage of banking facilities. Relatively poor access to capital also limits the degree to which the Newari entrepreneur can 'buy' government favours. Nor does his ethnic affiliation always work to his advantage. As one Newari businessman commented to me, '[Foreign entrepreneurs] are not shy about bribing because they don't have to worry about the social implications. For us, the official may be a distant relative, so offering an "incentive" may be embarrassing for us both.'

Once again, social sensibilities would seem to impede entrepreneurial advancement.

It also bears emphasis that Newari entrepreneurship has functioned within a strictly controlled patronage network for the past two hundred years. During this time, entrepreneurs never functioned in a market-place which was expandable and free of stringent external controls. Today, they manifest a business ethic which is conservative

---

[6] Social etiquette requires that individuals attend numerous *guthi*, family, caste, deity, life-cycle, community and other festivals and rituals. Most Newari businesspeople willingly comply, despite the fact that time and money may be lost in the process.

and narrow-visioned, typically focussing on one specific area. This ethic features hierarchical and conservative modes of business organization, including attitudes towards risk-taking, investment and diversification. It also bears the imprint of externally-imposed systems of patronage, a long history of bowing to ruling élites. If the Newars today reveal a lack of business initiative it is because they have learned their conservatism over a long period.

Several factors appear, then, to have hindered entrepreneurship among the Newars. One is the community's rigid hierarchical structure, including dictums which discourage individual initiative while encouraging heavy spending on ceremonial events. A second is the lack of community co-operation in business; this increases the risk for individual and family businesses and tends to work against diversification. Thirdly, the Newars appear the victims of a history which has given them little exposure to outside market-places and contacts. Another factor—not restricted to the Newars—has been the longstanding control by the State over private sector endeavour. Finally, the Newars have been undermined by their own success: able to utilize non-business avenues to prestige and power, they have lost out, as entrepreneurs, to vigorous new competitors. No longer can the Newars be described as Nepal's leading commercial community.[7]

THE MARWARIS

> The Marwari who died went to the god who told people whether they'd been good or bad in their lives and sent them to heaven or hell. The god said to the Marwari: 'Well, you've done some good and some bad things, so you have to spend time in both heaven and hell. Where would you like to go first?' The Marwari answered: 'Wherever I can make a few pisca (cents).'
>
> A Marwari boy was walking along the road with a clay container of curd on his head. He had paid four rupees for the curd. He saw a five rupee note lying on the ground. He let the curd drop, breaking the vessel, and picked up the five rupee note. When he got home, he told his father what had happened; his father praised him.

---

[7] Among Newars in the Kathmandu Valley, there is currently a resurgence of ethnic identity and cultural pride. There is a renewed interest in the Newari language (several Newari language newspapers have a wide distribution in the Valley) and festivals. Newars represent an important political lobby, tolerated under the partyless panchayat system, and assist one another in specific ways to achieve more prominent positions in government and the professions.

As these two stories from Nepal indicate, the Marwaris have changed the character of commerce and industry in the Himalayan kingdom—while not always attracting popular esteem. The Marwaris, of course, represent only one strand in that not insubstantial section of Nepali society that traces its origins back to India. But by virtue of their domination of Nepal's large-scale and medium-scale industrial sectors, the Marwaris merit detailed analysis.

The Marwaris' role in Nepal's development is perhaps best understood in the context of their emergence as an entrepreneurial force in India. Unfortunately, there is little literature on the Marwaris of India, and no scholarly literature at all on the Marwaris of Nepal.[8] However, a preliminary attempt will be made here to explore Marwari social and economic institutions, the role of the Marwaris in Nepal's industrial evolution and the community's political relationships with the ruling élite.

The appellation 'Marwari' is often generically applied to all business people who trace their roots to Rajasthan. The Marwaris were relative latecomers to the industrial scene in India, but their ascendency was swift and lasting. Marwari expertise and interest in trade has often been attributed to Rajasthan's harsh, arid physical reality, which necessitated non-agricultural forms of income generation, as well as to its strategic location at the head of the Ganga and Malwa trade routes (Timberg, 1978). But the Marwaris were to add, to historical and geographic circumstance, certain strong cultural traits—traits that were to help propel them to the pinnacle of private sector success, both in India and in Nepal.

Long before the British in India eliminated their European rivals and established their pre-eminence, the Marwaris were developing their skills as traders and financiers in the service of the princely courts of India. British conquest stimulated a gradual shift in the Marwari base of operations. Between 1860 and 1900 many Marwaris moved from Rajasthan to Calcutta, Bombay and the other centres of colonial rule. Here they established themselves as export-import dealers, stockbrokers, speculators and money-lenders. By the beginning of the First World War, their achievement was impressive: in Calcutta for example, they had acquired a commercial edge over indigenous Bengali traders. This success was bound up with the ability to play several supportive roles for the British. British firms depended upon

[8] Timberg (1978) has written the most comprehensive book on the Marwaris of India. What little has been published on the Marwaris of Nepal tends to be opinionated, even slanderous in nature (see, for instance, Shrestha, 1985).

the *banian*, or Indian middleman, for the procurement of raw materials and labour, and for the distribution and marketing of finished goods. By working in British trading and industrial houses, the Marwaris not only enhanced their business skills but also expanded their financial base and sphere of commercial influence.

As increasing numbers of Marwari firms acquired the role of *banian*, the community followed suit, triggering what Timberg has described as the 'Marwari diaspora' (Timberg, 1978). Big Marwari firms in the major metropolitan centres encouraged the immigration of other members of the community by establishing communal kitchens *(basas)*, shelters *(ashrams)*, caste associations, loan funds and charities, all of which eased the transition to a new environment. These institutions also served to cement Marwari solidarity in the new settlements. Intracommunity credit assistance—what Timberg (1978) calls the 'resource group'—similarly strengthened the network. Large firms helped smaller ones to get started; small firms, in turn, became agents or retailers in outlying areas for the larger firms. By the early twentieth century, Marwari credit and trading links fanned out from the port cities to a wide network of up-country dealers:

> The great Marwari firms were rich in capital. They operated on their own capital, and provided accommodation to a large number of smaller firms. Though these smaller firms belonged to all trades and communities, the familiarity born of a common homeland made 'great firms' key members of the 'resource group' upon which smaller migrant Marwari firms depended. (Timberg, 1978)

The Marwaris were the first indigenous group to invest their own capital in large-scale trade and ship-building in India. After the First World War, some Marwaris began investing in other industries as well (Medhora, 1965). By the time the British left India, the Marwaris had established themselves in the business community as a force—albeit sometimes an unpopular one—to be reckoned with.[9]

---

[9] In 1918 and 1926 there were anti-Marwari riots in Calcutta which were in part due to the Muslim-Hindu tensions in the city at the time (Timberg, 1978). An excerpt from the *Bombay Gazetteers* (Vol. XXII, *Thana*, pp. 113–16) reflects local attitudes towards the Marwaris in Bombay in the late 19th and early 20th centuries: 'They usually came with scanty stock and growing speedily rich carried their gains to their own country ... of late by their great vigour and power of work and by their greater unscrupulousness, Marwaris have, to an increasing extent, been ousting local traders from the money-lending business.'

In 1964, the report of the Monopolies Inquiry Commission set up by the Indian Government estimated that the Marwaris owned a larger share of the major firms in the country than any other single community.[10] The movement of the Marwaris into Nepal can therefore be seen as a natural extension of their expanding commercial base in India.

The 'resource group' had in fact spilled over into Nepal in the late nineteenth century. With the extension of the Indian railway network to the Nepali frontier, Indian businessmen—some of them Marwari— began moving across the border in significant numbers to purchase agricultural products such as foodgrain, oil seeds, jute and sugar-cane. These were then taken back to India for processing. The railway link stimulated the importation into Nepal of a growing volume and variety of Indian manufactured items; it also played a role in the establishment of manufacturing and processing industries in Nepal itself.

Utilizing the capital, business acumen and contacts they brought with them to Nepal, the Marwaris quickly established themselves, making it a point to cement some crucial political alliances. One scholar has asserted that the Marwari partnership with the Nepalese ruling élite dates back to the era of Jang Bahadur (1846–77), the first Rana prime minister, who may have collaborated with the Marwaris in the opium trade with China (Shrestha, 1985). What seems beyond doubt is that the first modern industry in Nepal—a jute mill—was established in Bhairahawa in 1936 by Radha Kissen Chamaria, a Calcutta Marwari. This was a joint venture with the prime minister of the day, Juddha Samsher Rana. Rice, cotton and sugar mills, and a *bidi* (rolled tobacco leaf) cigarette factory followed in quick succession (Gaige, 1975). These industries were established in order to evade Indian excise taxes; they also tapped new sources of raw materials.

The nine Marwari entrepreneurs I interviewed in Nepal all said their fathers were involved in trade with Nepal from India before settling in Nepal.[11] Four traced trade with Nepal to their grandfather's time. The fathers of three of these respondents had traded in cloth

---

[10] According to this report, 10 out of 37 major firms belonged to Marwaris, representing nearly 40 per cent of the combined assets of these firms.

[11] Although most of the early Marwari entrepreneurs came from northern India, and many had already longstanding trading relationships in Nepal, some were refugees from Burma after foreigners were expelled by President Ne Win. Some observers maintain that the Marwaris of Burma were the first to be ousted because of their corrupt business practices, which, according to these commentators, they brought with them to Nepal.

before they established cloth stores in urban areas in Nepal. The fathers of three of the five who were born in Nepal had established industries in the country. Whether first or second generation residents, all the traders had maintained their social and economic linkages with the Marwari community in India.

In the new politico-economic reality triggered by the events of 1950 (growing inflows of foreign aid, improvements in internal communications, expanded links with international markets, the rapid growth of the civil service, not to mention the new rhetoric of equality, democracy and development), Marwari influence on investment, production and marketing practices appears to have been marked. The Marwari presence set new standards for private business and catalyzed significant changes in the relationship between the public and private sectors, both of which were undergoing transformations.

Essentially, the Marwaris established their power bases in the private sector by allying themselves with the Nepal's non-entrepreneurial élite, which served to protect and promote their business interests. The nature of this alliance and its ramifications for business practices is related to the complex cultural and market changes Nepal has undergone since it opened its doors in the fifties.

When they entered Nepal, the Marwaris found a virtual vacuum in terms of 'modern' industrial entrepreneurship. Few indigenous traders, merchants or manufacturers enjoyed the commercial networks or the access to technology, information and capital which had won the Marwaris such success in their own country. Nepal was virgin territory, a point underlined by the absence of any clear notion, within Nepal's traditional élite, of the direction of private sector development. Indeed, the language of the government's early industrial policies was decidedly vague, as we shall see in the next chapter. While the ruling élite understood the necessity for industrialization, it was unwilling to invest in industrial enterprises. Moreover, the new administration was unschooled in modern business practices, the Marwari's forte. While it is true, therefore, that the Marwaris effected major changes in the system, it is also true that the system was uniquely ripe for a Marwari business offensive.

An important aspect of the Marwari's commercial success in Nepal has been their ability to draw members of the ruling élite into joint ventures in industry and trade. To these ventures the Marwaris contribute their entrepreneurship, management, capital and marketing skills; the Nepali partner, for his part, adds money and political protection. On the basis of such ventures (and on less formal links between individual Marwari entrepreneurs and senior civil servants and political leaders) the Marwaris have secured access to influence and services barred to other smaller or less well-connected communities.

In particular, the Marwaris have taken advantage of the special access to import facilities which their links with government have afforded them. Marwari control over both industrial raw materials and imported consumer items has made retailers from other communities increasingly dependent on Marwari business networks. Nepal's thriving black market has been another arena of opportunity; Marwaris, controlling the flow of commodities and raw materials in high demand in both Nepal and in India have, not unexpectedly, fared well here too. In this and other aspects of trade, the Marwaris continue to dominate the flow of commodities between India and Nepal and, to a large degree, between Nepal and other countires. The long open border between Nepal and India offers exceptionally rich possibilities: one scholar has called the Terai 'a smugglers' paradise', or as another puts it, 'any item that is less expensive on one side of the border is likely to turn up for sale on the other side without having followed established customs channels.' (Gaige, 1975, p. 50) Such black marketeering has been aided by ineffectual government policies, a proliferation of legal loopholes and the difficulty of policing the long border.[12] While indigenous groups have also taken advantage of these opportunities, the Marwaris, with their finger on both Indian and Nepali market pulses and their ready access to capital, technology and political protection, have been especially active in such ventures.[13]

[12] In 1951 the USSR, China and some Eastern European countries began sending aid to Nepal in the form of cement, sugar and cloth. Much of this found its way across the border where, naturally, it was sold at a higher price. When in 1966 the Nepali government gave hard currency incentives for jute exporters, India's protectionist policies encouraged the smuggling of jute across the border and its re-export, in the guise of Nepali jute, to third countries. In more recent times, gold and luxury items imported from the Far East through Nepal have found a lucrative market in India. In addition, Indian manufactured goods find their way, unprotected, across the border, to the detriment of Nepali industrialists.

[13] It is, of course, impossible to measure exactly the qualitative impact of any individual or ethnic community in Nepal on complex processes of change. The Marwari role is a very sensitive issue at the moment in Nepal. The statements in this section are not true of all members of the Marwari community. Nor are they unsupported allegations: they are based on extensive interviews with a variety of informed individuals, and in many ways reflect what might be termed the common wisdom.

It should be remembered that Nepal's industrial and trade sectors are still in an embryonic phase, still struggling for a place in the sun in a socio-economic and political environment ruled by tradition. The Marwaris, as talented outsiders, have been able to maximize the opportunities inherent in this situation. By doing so, and because they have maintained a certain social aloofness, they have become the objects of criticism, suspicion and envy, particularly among indigenous commercial groups (Shrestha, 1985). Whether they have in fact inflicted corruption and the evils of capitalism on an otherwise pure and innocent society (as some critics have asserted) seems debatable. We would prefer to argue that immigrants to a sovereign nation—no matter what the relationship of the host country to the immigrants' country of origin—can only exploit opportunities if those in power are predisposed to let them do so.

Nepal's entrenched systems of patronage and favouritism have, as we have seen, persisted into the workings of government today. To these, the Marwaris may have added other forms of inducement. If so, their timing was right, for they were to be quickly absorbed into leadership of the private sector. As large-scale traders and industrialists, the Marwaris were to set the pace for the use of bribery as a tool of business, their access to capital reinforcing other, pre-existing advantages. Forms of patronage long functioning in the system positively beckoned these 'outsider' entrepreneurs in need of certain facilities from the government. But the price of that patronage was to prove high as the system grew in complexity and acquired many more players. Whereas in the past influence had to be established only with the ruling family, now the entrepreneur had to cultivate a bewildering range of individuals as the bureaucracy proliferated.

But ensuring that the Marwaris did well in their chosen avocation was vital to an administration faced with the economic imperatives of national development. The new regime was badly in need of alternative sources of revenue, as well as new productive activities to enliven a stagnating economy. It also wished to maintain control over the pace and direction of the benefits resulting from economic development. The Marwaris appeared an ideal conduit for the achievement of both objectives. Their outsider status was seen as an asset; it meant they were unlikely to challenge the domination of existing élites, dependent as they were upon those élites to allow them to do business in Nepal. A bank manager, asked for his views on lending to Marwaris, reflected a widely held perception of the 'business focus' of the Marwari community:

> That's a good question. Sometimes even the policemen ask us why we lend so much to Marwaris. There are so many Marwaris, there is no room to discriminate against them. One thing we have to accept is that they are the ones in business. They understand the norms of business. They will not join the government service. They will not become teachers. They will not be a volunteer. Marwaris always become traders and industrialists. We don't want to waste our money by lending to someone who does not know how to handle it, so eventually the project becomes a failure. With the Marwaris, their whole life is dedicated to business, and they take the matters very seriously so that their projects are usually successful.

In short, the relationship between the business-minded Marwaris and Nepal's ruling elite displays a strong element of reciprocal benefit.

Social organization and internal definition. The ability of the Marwari community to take advantage of the opportunities implicit in the situation in Nepal is partly attributable to socio-cultural factors which promote a business ethic and have allowed the Marwaris to pursue profit in the face of the social stigma attached to this activity. Despite its outward flexibility, the Marwari community is characterized by social conservatism and traditionalism. Indeed, these very qualities bind the community together and allow it to pursue profit in a context where this is hardly an ethical norm (Timberg, 1978). As one Marwari I interviewed explained, 'Marwaris always think to stay together in one place. The belief is we are one big family. We expect our business to expand all over the world. But when we come back we always want to stay together.'

The Marwari business ethic is based on the concept of the resource group, a network of intra-community entrepreneurs who share capital and contacts. In Nepal, when a Marwari comes to town, he has immediate access to a Marwari-run guest-house *(dharmsala)*. Secure in this base, he may meet distant relatives or friends who will assist him in making business contacts. As a result he may be able to acquire funding, organize subcontracts, establish retailing opportunities, or even gain employment in a Marwari business. If the newcomer is short of capital, several established Marwaris are likely to club together to help him out, arranging loans to be repaid within a stipulated period. As one Marwari businessman told me, 'Usually whenever a loan is extended, the terms—such as the interest rate or repayment period—are softer than current practices because these loans are given more as a gesture of goodwill.'

If the initial loan is repaid on time, subsequent requests from the borrower will certainly be well-received. But it is also incumbent upon the borrower to keep his word. For the Marwari, keeping one's word appears a point of honour, at least where other members of the community are concerned. Recounting the reasons for their success, most of the Marwari entrepreneurs I interviewed cited this code, along with the ability to move quickly when opportunities presented themselves.

Marwari skills in risk-taking and speculation are an obvious factor behind the commercial success of the community (Timberg, 1978). Disdaining Nepal's conventional economic wisdom, with its emphasis on quick-money trading and 'safe' investment in the land, the Marwaris have shouldered the longer term risk of investing in industry. This readiness appears linked with an internal definition—a set of values, rituals and objectives—that has allowed the Marwaris to pursue profit even at the expense of social acceptance and popularity.

Within the Hindu caste system, Marwaris by convention form part of the broad *vaisya* or merchant caste grouping.[14] The Marwaris describe themselves variously as Hindus, Jains, followers of the Sanathan sect of Hinduism, and Vaishnavas. What sets them apart from other Hindus is that they are universally, and strictly, vegetarian. The practice of vegetarianism provides clues as to how the Marwaris have been able to reconcile the materialistic nature of their endeavour with their self-denying religious faith. As one Marwari explained it to me,

> We are vegetarians according to our culture. It is not written anywhere that we shouldn't eat meat, but my great grandfather decided that meat is not essential. You can survive with or without meat. But Marwaris are God-fearing people and since they are closer to God, they don't eat meat, just as the Gods don't eat meat. It's a kind of sacrifice, not eating meat. When you die you don't take anything along: your business, money, friends, family.

[14] Although Marwaris assume the role of the *vaisya* caste category in the communities in which they settle, they adhere to an internal caste system in which there are Brahmins, Kshatriyas (with the surname Oswal), Vaisyas (surname, Agarwal), and Maheswaris (analogous to the Sudhras, although not definitively low caste in the Marwari system. The most prominent businessman in India, Birla, is a Maheswori). All are involved in business, but in general do not intermarry. As a rule Oswals are followers of Jainism, while the others worship Hindu gods. Most of the Marwaris in Nepal are Agarwals, but a few of the most prominent business houses are also owned by Oswal Jains.

Vegetarianism thus becomes, for the Marwari, a type of renunciation. By giving up meat, the Marwaris make a deliberate sacrifice which provides both a religious and a social counterbalance to their wealth. Because the gods do not eat meat, this choice brings them closer to the gods—and perhaps farther from the judgment of their fellow men. It certainly allows them a measure of social prestige in the Hindu context, which values vegetarianism as a form of asceticism.[15]

The ethic of non-violence is carried several steps further by the Oswal Jains, who cover their mouths with a cloth to prevent accidental killing, even of invisible living things. The strict prohibition against the taking of life necessarily inhibits both travel and farming, since motorized vehicles and implements that turn the soil can inadvertently kill small insects. As a result, this sect has, historically, attracted those in sedentary occupations: money-lending, banking, and industry (Weber, 1958).[16] In practice, however, it was impossible for the majority of Marwari traders, for whom mobility was crucial, to adhere to the more rigid codes of Jainism.

While most of the Marwaris in Nepal, with the exception of a few large business houses, are not Jain by faith, they express the ethic of non-violence through their vegetarianism. Indeed, this appears a common thread in the internal definition of the community as a whole. Vegetarianism is defined in the Hindu context as pure (*satuywick*) and conducive to clear concentration. This is in contrast to the *tamasik* diet, embracing meat, alcohol, garlic, onions and other 'stimulating' foods, which is felt to cloud thought and is therefore suitable for groups involved in hard manual labour. Clarity of thought is an obvious necessity for those in business; and the Marwaris may partly rationalize their vegetarianism with this objective in mind. But since the *satuywick* diet is also part of the high-caste *dharmic* code, adherence to vegetarianism brings the community dividends in terms of social prestige.

The practice of vegetarianism tends to set the Marwaris apart from other groups in Nepal, and to restrict commensality.[17] In general, the

---

[15] Indeed, the renunciate—closest to God in the Brahmanical order—has always given up meat.

[16] It is virtually unheard of for Jains to engage in industries which involve the taking of life. Tanneries, meat processing plants and the like are usually in the hands of Muslims or other non-Hindus.

[17] One Marwari told me proudly that in the palace in Kathmandu there is a special table which is reserved for Marwaris because it is vegetarian and 'pure'.

use of meat, alcohol and other foods considered impure by the Marwaris is commonplace among both Hindus and Buddhists in Nepal, where climatic and agricultural conditions deter strict vegetarianism. The strict avoidance of meat would therefore seem to strengthen the Marwari sense of indentity and of a special place within society.

Marwari family structure is another factor that has contributed to the community's success in the world of business. With the senior male at its head, the family functions as a quasi-corporation in which management responsibilities are clearly defined and allocated. Profits are shared equally among all participating male members of the household. While diversification may require individual families to live in different locations, the family typically operates as an economic conglomerate. Although sons may claim their inheritance at any time, business ventures are so intertwined with the structure of the family that it is unusual for sons to move out and embark on an enterprise which is divorced from the extended family. When the third generation is old enough to assume overall responsibility, the second generation typically splits off, taking with it several independent businesses.

While the family corporation is certainly hierarchical in nature, there is also a certain built-in pragmatism that allows individuality to express itself. As one scholar defines it, 'these families have developed techniques for dividing authority and cushioning conflict, which serve them in good stead at some stages of their evolution.' (Cohen, cited in Timberg, 1978, p. 2) The patriarch in a Marwari family neither wields the absolute control nor demands the strict deference required by his Newar counterpart. He is consulted on all major issues, not only on account of his seniority but also to ensure consistency in decision-making. However, adult sons commonly operate their own firms with a relatively free hand. Several instances of sons who wished to embark on new types of enterprise were described by the Marwaris I interviewed. In such cases, rather than sever family ties, the father commonly finds a way of accommodating (and even financially supporting) his son's investment interests under the umbrella of the family corporation. As one Marwari entrepreneur told me:

> If my son wanted to start a new business, I would do everything to help him so that he would stay in the family. After my death they might think of something else. If I am fifty years old and my sons are twenty-five, I will have another ten years to live. I would never want to be dependent on my children, but if I couldn't work in that ten years, then I will be obliged to ask my children to help me.

Eight of the nine Marwari entrepreneurs in my survey were the first or second sons in the family. All the respondents had started independent businesses within the family corporate structure.

The organization of the extended family encourages the Marwaris to diversify as far as the number of adult males will permit. It also serves to minimize risk by allowing the operation of many businesses simultaneously. Consolidation of capital within the family unit further strengthens the commercial position of the Marwari family.

Children are, by Marwari tradition, schooled in business practices from an early age. Eight of the Nepali entrepreneurs interviewed said they had learned their skills in business either directly from their fathers or in another firm where, presumably, their families had encouraged them to work to gain experience. But despite his key role in shaping the next generation, the Marwari father appears somewhat removed from the authoritarian, judgmental father-figure of the Hindu stereotype. This may be linked to the fact that in the early Marwari trading communities, families were often left behind in Rajasthan while the men went off to trade. The prolonged absence of the father perhaps contributed to more liberal child-rearing practices, including the encouragement of independence and free-thinking (Timberg, 1978; Burton and Whiting, 1969).

In more recent times, some wealthy Marwaris began the practice of sending their children away to boarding school (a tradition introduced by the British). Boarding schools continue to provide an opportunity for cementing lifelong affiliations. But while children thereby escape direct parental and community control, they are sent away on the assumption that they will return to take up the family business.

Despite the access to élite schools by a section of the Marwari community, however, Marwaris were until recently less educated and more socially conservative than other entrepreneurial groups in India. The recent past has seen them provide more education for their sons, particularly in business administration and technical skills. In the context of Nepal, first-generation Marwari immigrants are usually more educated than their Nepali counterparts. Six of the nine Marwari entrepreneurs interviewed had achieved the equivalent of a bachelor's degree.

A further feature of the community that should be highlighted is its tradition of philanthropy. The Marwaris of Nepal give generously to a variety of needy causes, cutting across communal lines. Most of the charities that gain Marwari support are socially oriented, with religious overtones. Marwari philanthropy tends to be directed at causes which either benefit individuals spiritually or further Marwari economic objectives, however indirectly. For instance, the Marwari Sewa Samiti, an active philanthropic arm of the community, maintains an *ashram*, or guest house, in central Kathmandu where visitors are charged a nominal fee. This *ashram* is not unlike the *basas* in which the Indian Marwaris used to shelter newcomers to commercial centres. Vegetarianism is strictly observed in the *ashram*. The Samiti also supports a shelter for dying cows near the great Hindu temple of Pashupathinath just outside Kathmandu. Protecting the cow, an animal sacred to Hindus, would appear to ensure a good measure of religious merit. The Samiti also runs a fund which provides assistance to poor families who cannot afford to perform expensive death rituals for their relatives. Once again, religious merit seems guaranteed, given the importance of the death ritual to orthodox Hindus. Indeed, Marwari respondents were candid on this point, noting that gift-giving was done in the spirit of acquiring religious merit. Nonetheless, the social dimension of Marwari philanthropy should not be minimized; as one senior member of the community summed up the position:

> Our community has made great contributions in the fields of health, religion, social and educational services in the Kingdom of Nepal. Almost all of the institutions rendering services in the Kingdom have been set up with this community's financial support ... community members also participate in the administration of these institutions. The community does not restrict itself to industry and commerce.

It should be noted that Marwari largesse has also extended to the political sphere, with certain candidates benefiting from community donations. Such gifts are clearly expected to yield commercial dividends, and underline the element of pragmatism evident in Marwari beneficence.

With their historical trade links and the expertise and capital they acquired under the British, the Marwaris were able to fill a vacuum in Nepal's economy, building an industrial sector in a situation where little indigenous expertise or capital existed. Their position was cemented by their ability to form strong ties with non-entrepreneurial élites. But their success was also linked to certain internal socio-economic characteristics: a robust, cohesive, extended family system; well-defined but not rigid child-rearing practices; informal systems of lending based on intra-community trust; values that encouraged risk-taking and the manipulation of capital; and strong socio-religious beliefs which promoted an ethic of hard work as well as separateness from other communities. Medhora (1961) sums up the reasons for the Marwari success as 'tenacity, perseverance, keen business insight, and most important of all, group solidarity.'

The position of the Marwaris in contemporary Nepal is not without its uncomfortable aspects. The 'Indian' identity of the community occasionally stirs nationalistic sensibilities; a strong internal structure can, on occasion, set the Marwaris apart from the mainstream culture; and their very commercial success has been a source of suspicion and envy. Yet the Marwaris are as close to the seat of power as any community in Nepal. Insiders, yet also outsiders: this would seem to sum up the paradoxical identity of Nepal's Marwari community. To many Nepalis the Marwaris represent the intrusion of capitalism into a simpler, more equitable environment. But, intriguingly, it is this 'outsider' status (added to the community's internal strength) that has enabled the Marwaris to pursue profit in Nepal with such demonstrable success.

THE THAKALIS

Although constituting only 0.6 per cent of the population of Nepal, the Thakalis are considered by some to be the country's most successful indigenous entrepreneurial community. Geographical factors; a rich tradition of trade which allowed Thakalis to amass substantial wealth; the social cohesiveness of the community; and an internal lending system providing access to capital are some of the factors that underlie the Thakali achievement.

While Thakalis themselves are ambiguous on the subject, several scholars believe that the Thakalis came to Nepal in the twelfth century, fleeing religious persecution in Tibet.[18] The community, which is now divided into three sub-groups, the Tamang Thakalis, the Mawataan Thakalis (or Marphalis), and the Summi Thakalis (Jackson, 1976), originally settled in the area around the village of Kobang in the Kali Gandaki River Valley (known to those who inhabit it as Thak

---

[18] The Thakalis were persecuted by adherents of the Bon religion—the precursor of Buddhism in Tibet. There are still adherents of Bon in Tibet today.

Khola). Today, the economy of the Valley remains based on agriculture, pastoralism, and trade, all of which were interlinked in former times. Animals were raised for portering purposes and as a barter commodity. Because agriculture was sufficient to meet subsistence needs, profits from trade were available for investment in further trade.

The Kali Gandaki Valley allows relatively easy access for pack animals travelling through the Himalayan passes to Tibet and southward to Pokhara and the Terai. The Tamang-Thakalis, in particular, were active in this trade, establishing a commercial centre in Tukche Bazaar, south of Kobang, at the end of the nineteenth century. Grain and other goods were brought to Thak Khola at the end of the autumn harvest, stored there through the winter, and transported to Tibet in the spring and early summer when the pass was clear.

The Thakalis acted as both middlemen and transhippers, moving easily between the Terai, the hills and Tibet. This was possible not only because the Thakali homeland provided a strong base for trade but also because of a certain cultural fluidity which allowed the Thakalis to move comfortably between the hill communities (with whom they shared certain belief systems) and the Tibetan border settlements (with whom they had common origins). The Thakali ability to maintain mercantile relationships with both environments was facilitated by adaptive types of 'impression management' (von Fürer-Haimendorf, 1975). The analogy used by the same scholar in the following passage sheds light on this particular Thakali trait:

> It is perhaps this non-committal attitude to ideological matters and their chameleon-like ability to present two different facades to their trading partners in contrasting cultural orbits which fitted them so well for the role of middlemen and helped them to achieve outstanding commercial success. (von Fürer-Haimendorf, 1975, p. 303)

The Thakalis of Thak Khola developed various strategies to maintain social cohesion among a highly mobile community of roughly seven thousand people. Decision-making hierarchies took shape, village assemblies were instituted, and attendance of community festivals and rituals was strictly enforced. The village assembly undertook projects of community importance, such as the upkeep of irrigation systems and the provision of extra help for agricultural operations, for example in bad weather. Each household was represented by its head in the village assembly, and was obliged to delegate one member to work-teams organized under this body. Wealthier families might hire someone to fulfil this obligation, while others might send their most able-bodied member (von der Heide, 1987).

The village assemblies operated under the guidance of the village *mukiya* or headman, who, in turn, represented the village in the Thakali council. The central community council of *mukiyas* was the administrative body for settling internal disputes, establishing new cultural norms and watching over the economic prosperity of the community as a whole. Its decisions were considered binding on the entire Thakali community.

The rise of the Thakali community to its current economic success had its beginnings in the Rana period. The years 1854–56 saw a war between Nepal and Tibet over trading rights through the Kali Gandaki. After the war, border disputes still erupted periodically despite a treaty between the two countries. The Ranas, who distrusted other Bhotia[19] groups, established an alliance with the Thakalis in order to maintain economic and political control of the region. Bal Bir Serchan, a prominent Tamang-Thakali who had acted as official translator in the Nepal-Tibet war, was appointed as *subba*, 'with jurisdiction over trade, customs, and local administration' (Messerschmidt and Gurung, 1974) and magisterial duties in the Thak Khola region. The most important aspect of the *subba* appointment was the monopoly rights it extended on the importation of salt. In return for this, the Ranas levied a flat fee of Rs 12,500 a year (von Fürer-Haimendorf, 1975). Tibetan salt was then an important import commodity and the monopoly increased the economic prosperity and political prominence of the *subba* families and of the Tamang-Thakali community as a whole. While in theory the role of *subba* was to be granted to the highest bidder, in practice it became the hereditary property of the Serchan family for the next 70 years (Manzardo and Sharma, 1975). Economically dominant, the Serchan family also assumed the social leadership of the Thakali community, heading the central council of *mukiyas*.

The salt trade, as well as the active role that the Thakalis played in India-Tibet trade, provided not only wealth but also fiscal and administrative experience. The Thakalis soon began to reach beyond trade, developing entrepreneurial expertise and access to political influence. The latter was gained by applying the adaptability and

---

[19] Bhotia is a Nepali term loosely used to refer to Buddhist groups of Tibeto-Burman origin. Its use is sometimes pejorative.

'impression management' that had proved so successful in the trading arena.

The political alliance implicit in the Rana delegation of powers to the *subba* brought the Thakalis closer to the seat of power in Kathmandu and increased their interaction with the rulers. The Thakalis soon discovered that their eating and drinking habits were unpalatable, even offensive, to their Rana patrons. Traditionally Buddhist, the Thakalis were eaters of meat, particularly yak; for the high-caste Hindu Rana family, yak was classified as beef and hence taboo. The Thakalis also consumed alcohol, which was off-limits for high caste Hindus. The *subba* family therefore instituted moves to give up alcohol and promote mutton in place of yak. The Thakalis also adopted dress more acceptable to the Rana's sensibilities. Most importantly—in the context of a traditional society in which caste and lineage were the basic yardsticks of social status—the Thakalis began claiming they were descendants of the Thakuri of Jumla, a high-caste Hindu community situated in the Thak Khola. In more recent times, Thakalis in urban areas were to take this a stage further, calling upon the services of Hindu priests and celebrating Hindu ceremonies to demonstrate their affinity to the mainstream culture.

In 1928, the Ranas, alarmed at the political power that the *subbas* were achieving, abolished the position of *subba*, and instituted a flat tax on salt imports. This allowed more Thakalis access to the lucrative salt trade. Some traders were by this stage already moving southwards out of Thak Khola in search of new business opportunities (Manzardo and Sharma, 1975).

A sequence of events in the 1950s brought further changes. Following the Chinese invasion of Tibet, trade between Nepal and Tibet was sharply reduced. At the same time, the availability of Indian salt—brought by rail to the Nepali border—diminished the demand for Tibetan salt. Beyond the cessation of such traditional commercial opportunities, the Thakalis also felt the impact of the new situation that followed the overthrow of the Ranas. For one thing, the Thakalis took advantage of the hasty flight of the Ranas to India in 1951 to buy up some of their lands (von der Heide, 1976). For another, increasing numbers of the community moved away from their traditional base of operations. Moving southwards, the Thakalis established themselves in urban centres in the middle hills and the Terai, where they took up road-contracting and established hotels, restaurants and agro-industries. Some even expanded their trading networks into India.

The flexibility of Thakali culture was demonstrated again in the course of these recent changes and upheavals. In the urban centres in which they settled, Thakalis founded special organizations, *Thakali Samaj Sudhar Sangh* (TSRO),[20] to ease the transition to a new environment. The first TSRO was established in 1954 in Pokhara; others were later established in Bhairahawa and Kathmandu. Every Thakali resident of the town and its rural hinterland is a member of the organization, which is run by an executive committee elected by the heads of households plus the hereditary *mukiyas*. The decisions of the committee are considered binding, on penalty of ostracism—although this, apparently, has never been necessary (Manzardo and Sharma, 1975). The TSRO has an important fund-raising role, collecting from businesses and community festivals; such collections are used for the uplift of the Thakali community. There is also a strain of social reform in its activity: for example, the attempt to cut down to size elaborate life-cycle ceremonies. Recognizing the drain that lavish ceremonies were imposing on Thakali purses, the TSRO established limits on the number of guests to be invited to marriage and death ceremonies. It also set limits on spending for other festivals. In this way, the TSRO 'provided Thakalis with a way to eliminate dysfunctional social traits in an orderly way, both cutting costs of ritual events and external litigations, and maintaining at the same time some sense of jurisdiction of the organization.' (Manzardo and Sharma, 1975, p. 38)

Such activity has not been without its critics, however. Some believe that urbanization and the pruning of culturally important events has resulted in the speeded-up assimilation of Thakali culture into that of the mainstream; indeed, there is evidence to support this assertion (von Fürer-Haimendorf, 1975). Von der Heide (1986) has even gone as far as to argue that the economic success of the Thakalis has been retarded by their obligatory involvement in TSRO social welfare activities.[21] Attention and resources, it is alleged, have been divided between economic and social activities. What cannot be disputed is that the TSRO has provided a useful bridging mechanism for Thakalis in transition.

---

[20] A *samaj* is broadly comparable to the *guthi*—a social organization designed to carry out welfare activities.

[21] Von der Heide expressed this view to the author on the basis of extensive interviews with small-scale Thakali businesspeople from many parts of Nepal.

Family structure, the role of women and child-rearing. The Thakali family structure, like that of most Himalayan groups, is predominantly nuclear. When the son marries he is given his inheritance and is then expected to establish his own household and make his own way in the world. The youngest son commonly remains in the family home until the death of both parents, when he is entitled to the remaining portion of the family inheritance, including the house.

An interesting feature of many Thakali communities is a 'retirement' scheme under which the senior member, reaching the age of sixty-one, is no longer eligible to represent the family in the village assembly. In return, he signs an agreement with his sons by which they agree to provide their parents a specified amount of grain and other commodities until their death (Vindig, 1979). Interestingly, it is the son-in-law, and not the son, who is required to perform the death rituals. This is in contrast to the practice of other communities, both Hindu and Buddhist, in Nepal and indeed across South Asia.

The non-extended nature of the typical Thakali family unit might be expected to result in labour shortages at key points in the agricultural year. Several strategies have been developed to tackle the problem. Families with larger landholdings began early on to hire in wage labour. This practice was in contrast to that of other farming communities in Nepal, to whom the hiring in of labour has been exceptional and even distasteful (Vindig, 1979). The strategy also released family members to pursue potentially lucrative trading endeavours and enabled the community to acquire valuable skills in the field of labour management.

The position of women within the Thakali family structure offers another point of contrast with certain other Nepali communities. Women in Thakali society are, in general, more active in commercial enterprises than their Hindu counterparts; moreover, within the nuclear family, female labour makes an important contribution to the household economy. Historically, Thakali daughters and wives engaged in petty trade. Today, women in bazaar towns typically manage small hotels and tea stalls while their male kinfolk are off trading or running separate enterprises. This degree of economic mobility has important implications for child-rearing. The economically active Thakali mother figure offers her children a strong, enterprising role model. Moreover, since their migration from Thak Khola, the Thakalis have emphasized education as a mode of upward mobility. Much of their business success has in fact been due to the parental foresight which encouraged children to enter engineering and other technical disciplines. This has given second- and third-generation urban Thakalis access to business opportunities unavailable to other, less educated communities.

Economic organization. The Thakali internal economy is based on a set of mutually supporting credit systems or *dhikuri*. Under the *dhikuri* system, an individual needing capital can organize a pool to which each participant contributes an equal sum of money. When the initial stipulated time period is over, another member of the group is entitled to this loan, in addition to the interest paid by the first borrower. In this way, capital circulates within the group until each member has had access to the capital, the first borrower paying the most accumulated interest for the privilege of having first access, the last receiving the greatest amount in repayment for the use of his capital (Messerschmidt, 1978). This loan system offers new investors ready access to capital as well as commercial assistance from other *dhikuri* members who now have a vested interest in the success of a co-member's venture. For a trader, the *dhikuri* could provide the kind of instant capital that would allow him to buy on the spot. And the system seems to work: few examples of default have been recorded in the Thakali community of Thak Khola.

The *dhikuri* system demonstrates how the reciprocity and equalizing tendencies that result from group liability in this type of lending system can benefit entrepreneurship and commercial expansion within a traditional cultural system. Although this system encourages individual entrepreneurship, it also binds the individual to the group and ensures that, in theory at least, all members of the community have roughly equal access to capital. In this way the system minimizes individual risk as well as individual profit. The obligation of richer Thakalis to finance less wealthy members of the community through the *dhikuri* could tie up capital which could have been more profitably deployed elsewhere; this seems to indicate an ethical choice of some kind, a commitment to the view that the economic advancement of the community as a whole should take precedence over the amassing of individual fortunes.

Another equalizing force, historically, within Thakali culture, was the custom of making generous donations: to religious institutions; towards the construction of monasteries and temples; and to a variety of life-cycle festivities, often involving lavish hospitality. Such gifts may have served to redistribute (and direct away from commercial investment) the wealth of the community. Today, however, the tradition of largesse is undergoing significant modification, especially in urban centres.

Urbanization and dispersion. The transition of the Thakalis from Thak Khola to urban environments was facilitated by the establishment and maintenance of social and economic institutions which preserved a strong element of internal cohesiveness. Gradually, however, the inherent adaptability of Thakali culture has resulted in a process of assimilation. While the old community service organizations, the TSROs, still operate, and all members of the Thakali community in theory participate in them, they have lost much of their significance for the present generation of Thakalis, especially those settled in Kathmandu. In the heterogenous business environment of the capital, most Thakalis have opted for the path of least resistance and have assimilated with the mainstream culture.

The *dhikuri* system is in a similar process of decline. In Kathmandu, Thakalis are talking about ending the system altogether. Certainly, new problems have surfaced. While smaller *dhikuris* have crumbled, larger ones have been used to finance major business enterprises and have sometimes widened to include partners from other ethnic groups. And in the new urban environment, where the social stigma attached to non-payment is more dilute than it was in the old rural strongholds, default has become more common (von der Heide, 1986). Also suggestive of the fact that traditional governing systems are breaking down in the urban context is the growing involvement of Thakalis in public court cases against one another. Such disputes would, in the past, have been settled internally.

The Thakalis have, historically, demonstrated considerable adaptability, adjusting to a diversity of business locations without sacrificing their communal integrity. This appears related to the fact that Thakali culture provided the individual with the cultural and economic support he needed if he were to take advantage of new economic opportunities. But the very cultural adaptability that served the Thakalis so well through their recent history now, ironically, appears to be contributing to a process of cultural dilution, an assimilation road on which the more positive features of Thakali society may be lost for ever.

THE SHERPAS

> Business is necessary for life but it is not life. People who do business are clever but not wise. Clever people know that a butterlamp is made of wick,

oil and flame. Wise people know that there will be no butterlamp unless each are of good quality individually, *and* that there are harmonious relations among the parts. Life is a good butterlamp. Business is only part of life.

—Kyerok Lama, Khumbu

Rich is the man who has no debt to pay.

—Sherpa saying

In the past, before the mountains were climbed, we were able to grow three crops. But now the summit has been reached and we can only grow potatoes and so we are no longer Sherpa. Soon even the potatoes will be gone.

—A Sherpa elder

The Sherpas of Solu-Khumbu in north-eastern Nepal were, until the 1960s, relatively minor actors in Nepal's commercial sector. This was in part bound up with the remoteness and inaccessibility of their homeland in the foothills of Mount Everest. Their culture, more in tune with Buddhist Tibet than with Hindu Nepal, also seemed to set them apart. However, positioned between the agrarian communities inhabiting the lower and more fertile Himalayan slopes to the south and the pastoral communities across the mountains in Tibet, the Sherpas certainly figured as important economic players in their own region. Although primarily agro-pastoralists, many Sherpas grasped the advantages of geography and pursued lucrative trading activities. Nor were they slow to spot new openings; in recent years, mountaineering and tourism have replaced trade as the major commercial activity of the Sherpas.

The early history of the Sherpas and their date of settlement in Solu-Khumbu remain unclear. On the basis of oral traditions and of texts discovered in Solu, some scholars (Oppitz, 1974; von Fürer-Haimendorf, 1975, 1984) have concluded that Sherpa settlement was motivated primarily by political and religious considerations. They maintain that the Sherpas came to Nepal in the 16th century from Kham in Eastern Tibet, fleeing political persecution by the intruding Mongols. From the lavish parties they reputedly staged en route to Nepal, it appears that the refugees were wealthy. What is less clear is whether the Sherpas braved the northern barrenness of the Khumbu from the outset (the conventional wisdom on the subject) or whether they settled first in the warmer, more fertile valleys of Solu to the south. The fact that more recently evolved clans predominate in the Khumbu suggests that settlement of the Khumbu came later (Draper, 1988). Perhaps a northward migration from Solu to the Khumbu was prompted by trading considerations, for certainly the Khumbu was closer to Tibet. Or perhaps it was shortage of agricultural land in Solu that drove the Sherpas north. For the present, the reality can only be a matter of conjecture.

The introduction of the potato from eastern Nepal in the mid-nineteenth century was to significantly alter the economy of the region. The potato, both a subsistence and a cash crop, considerably improved the livelihood of the Sherpas of both Solu and Khumbu. At about the same time, the region experienced a rise in celibate monastic Buddhism as a result of the widening political influence of the Gelugpa sect in central Tibet. The introduction of the potato; growing trading activity; the patronage of certain Sherpa families by the Rana administration; remittances from a Darjeeling-based community of Sherpas engaged in contracting and other activities: all this resulted in a significant rise of income within the Sherpa community. The major outlet for the new prosperity was monastery construction, since such investment brought the donor social status and religious merit.

The first monastery was constructed in Solu in the late nineteenth century by a trader who had become wealthy by virtue of his role as a tax collector for the Ranas. Several years later, his brother (then residing in Darjeeling) heard about the prestige and power the trader had gained by building the monastery. He returned to Solu, wrested the tax collector position from his brother, and built a second monastery. This story illustrates the point that the penetration of the Nepali state into Solu-Khumbu had the effect of concentrating political and economic power in the hands of single individuals (the tax collectors). Moreover, this coincided with a time when the monastic tradition was vesting greater spiritual power in the hands of the high lamas. For the first time, hierarchies based on wealth and spiritual standing (the two being related in important ways) became apparent in what had, hitherto, been a highly egalitarian culture.

Traditionally, responsibility for social, cultural and economic affairs was rotated within the Sherpa community and was never allowed to be monopolized by one individual or family. The overt exercise of power was generally discouraged; the community followed strong norms of social reciprocity. With the increasing influence of the monasteries, however, the abbot (a reincarnate lama), his wealthy patrons and, indirectly, the Nepalese state became increasingly powerful within the Sherpa community.

The rise of celibate monasticism also encouraged the accumulation of wealth. Traditional Sherpa culture allowed for some redistribution of wealth (an important survival mechanism in the harsh environment of Solu-Khumbu) through the formalized practice of hospitality and gift exchange. With the growth of monasticism, however, contributions to the new religious institutions and sponsorship of individual monks became more important, because such acts were seen as a means of acquiring religious merit. This was accompanied by a greater emphasis on individualism and entrepreneurship. Desire for the acquisition of religious merit in fact reinforced the accumulation of wealth, since worldly success would allow a donor to increase the size of his gifts and hence his spiritual standing. The mutually reinforcing relationship between the accumulation of religious merit and material wealth suggests an important characteristic of Sherpa society: the coexistence of pragmatism and spiritualism.

Although essentially an agro-pastoralist community, the Sherpas had a long tradition of barter trade relations with the Tibetans (Draper, 1988). Animals, hides, dried potatoes (from the Khumbu) and food-grains (from Solu) were traded for salt, wool, dried meat, religious artifacts and gold—the last an important standard of wealth in Sherpa society (von Fürer-Haimendorf, 1975; Draper, 1988). Some of these items would then be bartered in the south for rice, millet, maize and other commodities. But it is important to remember that such commodity exchange was somewhat peripheral to the community's other economic activities and was certainly less important than the practice of gift exchange (Draper, 1988).

Namche Bazaar, now the hub of trekking activity in the Khumbu, was once the centre of the old trade with Tibet, and in fact owes its origins to that activity. It is an entrepot not unlike Tuckhe to the west.

Although the Chinese takeover of Tibet disrupted the old trading relationship for a while, the Sherpas have continued to trade with communities across the border, albeit on a much diminished scale. The nature of the goods has changed somewhat, with manufactured items from India and China being bartered alongside animals from Nepal and wool from Tibet.[22] Cash replaced barter as the main

---

[22] After the Chinese invasion of Tibet in 1959, the population of Solu and Khumbu is estimated to have quadrupled, with Tibetan refugees outnumbering Sherpas 3:1. Many of the new immigrants were traders and some who remained in Khumbu continued to trade with communities across the border (Hagen, 1971).

medium of trade, and gradually it became more common for Tibetan traders to travel to Namche Bazaar rather than for Sherpas to make the difficult journey through the Himalayan passes to Tibet. But the quantum of trade declined and it was fortunate for the Sherpas that new, lucrative opportunities in mountaineering and tourism revealed themselves at precisely this moment.

The growth of interest in mountaineering in the 1950s, followed by the development of Nepal's tourist sector from the sixties, stimulated a whole range of new occupations. There was a call for porters, for expedition leaders or *sardars*, for hotel accommodation and restaurants; and the Sherpas responded industriously. In particular, it was the less advantaged Sherpa small-holder who made the most of the new openings, being in a position to leave the Khumbu for extended periods (Ortner, 1978; von Fürer-Haimendorf, 1984). Later, wealthier Sherpas were to set up travel agency businesses, but the quick response of poorer sections of the community to these changes did allow a significant redistribution of wealth and a widening of employment opportunities.

Much of the initial seed money—and, indeed, the primary entrepreneurial impetus—for the tourist industry came from expatriate investors who recognized the commercial potential of the Khumbu, an exotic, almost legendary frontier zone. The first foreign investors relied heavily on the Sherpas for labour and for detailed knowledge of the locality; and, increasingly, the Sherpas acted as local partners who played a key role in easing business formalities. In turn, the Sherpas relied on their expatriate partners for investment capital and marketing, having—naturally—very limited access to the European and American tourist markets themselves. Most of the original trekking companies evolved in the context of expatriate-Sherpa partnerships of one form or another. The Sherpas were quick to create a variety of opportunities for themselves, and many who began as *sardars*, or even porters, went on to establish their own trekking companies, hotels and restaurants in the Khumbu and Kathmandu. Initially, they faced little competition, since it was only from the late 1970s that entrepreneurs from other communities began to involve themselves in the trekking sector on a significant scale.[23]

To give an idea of the importance of tourism to the Sherpa economy, it

---

[23] Tamangs, Rais, Limbus and other communities from the region below Khumbu have responded to the growing demand for porters, so that Sherpas now represent only a portion of the total. Chhetris, Newars, Brahmins and even Thakalis are also moving into the lucrative trekking industry.

is relevant to highlight that while the Sherpa population of the Khumbu region is roughly 3,000, Mount Everest and its neighbouring peaks attract roughly 10,000 trekkers a year—twenty-five per cent of the tourists who come to Nepal for trekking or mountaineering. Earnings from this inflow may, however, be modified by the fact that many trekkers come on pre-paid 'package' treks, while others may be eager to live as cheaply as possible (Bjonnes, 1983). Aware of the dangers involved in becoming over-dependent on the trekking business, many Sherpas are now looking for other opportunities, both in Solu-Khumbu and in Kathmandu.

Sherpa religious and cultural practice. Sherpa religion is based on the tantric Nyingma sect of Tibetan Buddhism. This emphasizes the realization of the unity of opposites through pragmatic pursuits as well as spiritual ones. As we have already noted, the generation of wealth and the accumulation of merit are reciprocally stimulating factors in Sherpa culture. Conversely, poverty is believed to reflect bad *karma* (Ortner, 1978); the individual is encouraged to work hard, and honestly, to raise him or herself above this state.

While the Sherpa socio-religious belief system encourages entrepreneurship and a work ethic based on the accumulation of surplus on the one hand, it also shapes some rather distinctive spending patterns. Sherpas feel almost compelled to divert a portion of their surplus to monasteries, the sponsoring of festivals and individual monks, complex, reciprocal gift exchanges, and lavish hospitality. If this were not done, the Sherpa would feel excluded from the all-important network of social relations—and this would certainly strike at his business prospects.[24] Interestingly, Sherpas rarely go into business with each other. This is not because of any absence of trust; the intention seems rather to avoid any threat to existing trust and good relations within the community. Even money-lending—a common phenomenon in Sherpa society—is organized in such a way as to minimize the danger of long-term indebtedness, exploitation or abuse of trust. In short, while Sherpa cultural-religious practice serves to encourage individual entrepreneurship, it does so in

---

[24] For the Sherpas, reciprocity is not limited to human relationships. Their relations with their gods (and even with inanimate objects) demonstrate the same concept of the interconnectedness of all forces. When the Sherpa communes with the supernatural, he offers food and hospitality, expecting returns in terms of healing, wealth or the resolution of problems (Draper, 1988).

complex ways in which the maximization of profit may not be the main objective.

Other Sherpa cultural traits demonstrate the flexibility which has helped the community both in its trading pursuits and in its ready adaptation to the new tourist sector. While the Sherpas do follow codes of ritual purity and inter-dining, these are notably more flexible than those of other communities, especially Hindu ones. The Sherpas themselves claim a readiness to eat any kind of food with any kind of person; this allows them to participate in a wide variety of social networks, essential for both trading and tourism.

Outside their community, Sherpas have developed an elaborate network of personal contacts and friendships, often on the basis of 'fictive' kinship. The clearest example of this is the ritual friendship relationship known as *thouwu*. In this relationship, which is also practised by other groups in Nepal, the two participants treat each other as virtual siblings (von Fürer-Haimendorf, 1975). For the Sherpas, *thouwu* relationships outside the community bring several benefits: a place to stay in the fictive sibling's town or village; guaranteed assistance; and, perhaps most important of all, a reliable source of business information. The *thouwu*, however, is rarely a trading partner; once again, Sherpas seem anxious to avoid situations which might threaten their social relationships.

The Sherpas of Solu-Khumbu often form *thouwu* relationships with Rais, Limbus, and others in the farming communities to the south; they do not, however, form them with Tibetans. Relations with Tibetan traders remain close, however, and many Sherpas have distant kin across the frontier. Such close relations with Hindu communities are less common, possibly because the inter-dining restrictions upon the latter makes shared hospitality difficult.

Perhaps more than any other indigenous community in Nepal, the Sherpas have managed to 'get along' with Western visitors, whether tourists or business partners. This reality is indicated by the number of Sherpas who have been sponsored to study and work abroad, and the many business alliances forged between Sherpas and European and American agencies in the tourist industry. The ability of Sherpa entrepreneurs to sustain ties with non-Sherpa partners is perhaps linked with their skills at impression management. This ability has been fundamental to the success of trading communities throughout the Himalayas, as already noted in our discussion of the Thakalis. The Sherpas, in particular, have been able to capitalize on such skills by responding to Western contacts, economic opportunities and modes of business activity. Far from compromising their culture, this may have actually consolidated their cultural identity, especially in comparison to communities that have failed to develop such external contacts.[25]

Sherpa economic organization. When one compares the Sherpas with other high Himalayan entrepreneurs, the former do not seem to have gone all out to grasp the economic opportunities before them. There appears to be a delicate, on-going balance in Sherpa society between economic activity and the desire to sustain relationships. Several factors would seem to underlie this. Firstly, Sherpa society has, historically, been influenced by egalitarian principles which allowed communities living in a harsh environment to protect their less wealthy or fortunate members by offering them access to resources and social support. Social status, in this context, was based not only on wealth and individual integrity but also on the ability to forge strong reciprocal relationships with neighbours and friends.[26] Being part of the network of relations was fundamental to all aspects of life—ritual and social as well as economic. Being outside spelt disaster. Draper cites the example of an elderly nun who, prior to taking this avocation, had alienated her family by unilaterally disposing of her deceased husband's property to outsiders. She was ostracized to the extent that when she became ill, no healer would treat her and she was left entirely isolated, her subsequent death hastened by starvation (Draper, 1988).

A second factor is the absence of economic institutions geared specifically to the needs of entrepreneurs. Although these exist for agriculture (in the shape of reciprocal labour groups known as *ngalok*), no equivalent mechanisms provide credit or other forms of business support. Money-lending is carried on outside the parameters of kinship and community: indeed, interest rates can be as high as 33

[25] Although von Fürer-Haimendorf (1984) suggests that tourism has served to dilute Sherpa culture in the Khumbu, Draper (1987), in a more recent study, contends that the nature of the Western presence in the Khumbu has rather encouraged a consolidation of Sherpa culture. One of the factors that draws tourists to the Khumbu, contends Draper, is the 'exotic' culture they encounter there. An increase in investment in religious ceremony and institutions by the Sherpas appears to bear this out.

[26] It is revealing that the Sherpas refer to the past era—*samen lemu*—as the good era, a time of greater interconnectedness between people. The present era—*samen kokpu*—is, in contrast, the bad era when social relations are breaking down in the face of economic individualism (Draper, 1988).

per cent. Like the Newars, the Sherpas appear to shun the whole notion of reciprocity in the sphere of business.

In the past, the *thouwu* ritual friendship relationship may have compensated for the absence of such economic mechanisms, at least in the context of trade. In more recent times, expatriate partners would seem to have taken up this extra-community partnership role. Certainly it is significant that the Sherpas have been most successful in trade and tourism, both modes of activity reaching outside the community and embracing the 'outsider'.

The family and the role of women. The Sherpa family is essentially nuclear. When the son marries he establishes his own household and has immediate access to his inheritance. As with the Thakalis, the youngest son traditionally remains in the family house, looking after his parents and inheriting the house upon their death. Once a son leaves the family, he is free to engage in trade, even if his father was a farmer, or tourism, if his father was a trader. But in this new venture he is on his own: 'The risks he takes are entirely his own, for no kinsman is under an obligation to come to his rescue or liable to pay his debts should a venture fail.' (von Fürer-Haimendorf, 1975, p. 287) To an extent, then, the absence of a joint-family structure and the economic support it involves may handicap a fledgling Sherpa entrepreneur.

As with the Thakalis, Sherpa women are relatively free to engage in entrepreneurial activity. Such activity raises the income-generating potential of the nuclear family, and provides entrepreneurial role models for children. In Namche Bazaar and other tourist centres in the Khumbu, women are often to be found running shops, hotels and restaurants while their husbands are away, often for the entire trekking season. Moreover, in the absence of their menfolk women assume responsibility for family property and general economic matters.

Nepal's Sherpa community has undergone far-reaching change in the recent past. From a society based on agro-pastoralism and trade, it has re-oriented itself towards a new service industry, tourism—to the extent that the economy of the Solu-Kumbhu region is now reliant on this sector. Several cultural and religious factors appear to have eased the transition. Sherpa Buddhism may have sanctioned the pursuit of profit, at least in some measure; Sherpa family relationships, revolving round a nuclear structure, would seem to have fostered economic individualism; practices such as the forging of ritual friendships with outsiders seem to have enhanced Sherpa skills in the art of 'impression management' and of functioning outside the community.

Nevertheless, the process of change has been marked by impediments. Sherpa notions of social reciprocity and sometimes overgenerous hospitality may work against entrepreneurial success. The absence of formal credit arrangements within the community appears another handicap. The nuclear family, too, seems a far from unmixed blessing for aspiring entrepreneurs, a point underlined by the far greater economic success of the joint-family-based Marwaris.

Today, the Sherpas find themselves a 'marginal' community within Nepal, confined largely to one geographical location and unable to make much of a national impact beyond the sphere of tourism. Yet this is a community able to draw upon considerable latent talent and with an instinctive feel for economic opportunity. Whether the Sherpas will be able to grasp such openings and diversify into other areas of Nepal's economy has yet to be seen.

THE TIBETANS

In 1959, after the Chinese invasion of Tibet, many Tibetans fled southward to avoid religious persecution and political domination. While roughly eight thousand Tibetans have made their homes in Kathmandu and Pokhara, perhaps six thousand still reside in refugee camps in various parts of the country (Office of the Dalai Lama, 1986). A small community, the Tibetans of Nepal nevertheless provide a useful case study of successful entrepreneurial endeavour. The rapid adjustment of the Tibetans to their new environments, in India as well as in Nepal, is, in fact, remarkable testimony to what one scholar has dubbed 'adaptive strategies' (Gumbo, 1985). These strategies have, on the one hand, enabled the rebuilding of social and religious institutions in exile and, on the other, allowed younger Tibetans a good measure of flexibility in integrating into their host societies.

The process of adaptation is all the more remarkable given the baseline on which the Tibetans had to build their new life. Most fled their homeland in a haphazard manner, arriving in Nepal without any resources. The majority were nomadic herders from Central Tibet who sold what precious possessions they could carry to sustain themselves during the hard mountainous trek to Nepal. Destitute Tibetans were, by the early sixties, a familiar sight throughout Nepal.

International aid, however, was not slow in arriving. Several aid agencies, notably the office of the United Nations High Commissioner for Refugees, and the Swiss Association for Technical Assistance (SATA), were instrumental in establishing refugee camps (there were four by 1961). Initially, all such aid was channelled through the Nepal Red Cross, a non-governmental organization. Following a fresh influx of refugees fleeing the Cultural Revolution in China and in the wake of the dismantling of the Kampa guerrilla camps on the Tibetan border by the Nepali government, another four camps were opened during the 1970s. Aid was also forthcoming from the governments of India and Nepal. Both made available tracts of land for camps and colonies of settlers, often helping to establish schools and other institutions. Because of the need to preserve a working relationship with China, neither government gave formal recognition to the Tibetan Government in Exile (TGE) that was established in Dharmsala, in northern India. However, Tibetans were extended most of the privileges available to citizens of the two countries.

In addition to such international support, the Tibetan refugees arrived with the advantage of a leadership that remained more or less intact. The Dalai Lama, the religio-political leader of the Tibetan people, quickly re-established a governmental infrastructure in his Dharmsala refuge. The TGE was to become the co-ordinating agency for the welfare of Tibetans across South Asia, helping to generate aid and acting as a mouthpiece for the community in exile.[27] Its task was eased by the faith the Tibetans placed in their leader and by a sense of optimism within the dispersed and largely destitute community that was of vital importance as the refugees battled the hardships of the early years.

Beyond these factors, certain socio-cultural traits of the Tibetans appear to have come to their aid in the challenge of adjusting to a new society and a new way of life. Ugen Gumbo, basing himself on the experience of Tibetan refugees in the Kathmandu Valley, has listed five principal factors: the ability of the Tibetans to maintain their traditional family structure; the resurgence, in exile, of traditional mutual aid organizations (based on regional affiliations which such organizations helped to preserve); the persistence of a conservative

---

[27] There is no consensus among Tibetans as to the role or structure of the TGE, nor do all refugees agree on the position Tibetans in exile should take towards China. All agree, however, on these three points: the supremacy of the Dalai Lama; adherence to the Buddhist faith; and the goal of 'liberating' Tibet.

belief system; the reinstitution of monasticism in exile; and continued general adherence to Buddhism (Gumbo, 1985). Such factors appear to hold the key not only to the success of Tibetan 'adaptive strategies' but also to the blossoming of Tibetan entrepreneurship in the adopted home of Nepal.

Family structure. Traditional Tibet was notable for the existence of polyandry and polygamy alongside monogamous marriage patterns. Such forms may have enabled agricultural families living in a harsh physical environment to keep their resources undivided from generation to generation. Ugen Gumbo's research among Kathmandu-based refugees suggests that polyandry survives to this day; eight per cent of the families he studied practised bifraternal polyandry. It seems probable that economic factors lie behind this survival, but further research is in order.

Within its monogamous units, the Tibetan family is not dissimilar to that of the Sherpas or the Thakalis. While sons are permitted to stay with the parents after marriage, it is more usual for them to establish their own household—finances permitting— and for one child, either male or female, to remain with the parents as caretaker. If the family has no son, they may elect to arrange a marriage for their daughter with a man prepared to live in the family household. The son-in-law then takes his father-in-law's title, and is entitled to his inheritance. He is also expected to take over the family business.

Whatever its structure, the Tibetan family is the nucleus of the community's business activity. In the carpet industry, to take one example, the mother assumes the responsibility of minding the spinning unit along with the grandchildren. The father or the eldest son will typically provide overall management of the business, including marketing and the procurement of raw materials. A younger brother may look after the accounts, while wives and sisters may supervise factory production or manage a retail outlet. While Tibetan family organization remains hierarchical in the sense that the patriarch controls all major decisions—whether social or financial—it is not uncommon for parents, when they reach a certain age, to vacate the business in favour of their sons. This indicates a basic pragmatism that allows the Tibetan family to adapt itself to new economic activities.

Socio-economic organization. Mutual aid associations known as *skyid-sdug* (literally, 'happiness-sadness') were commonplace in old Tibet, as were reciprocal exchange systems (*dga-nye*). The former were organized to assist families in times of marriage, death and sickness— the 'happy-sad' periods of the name. This assistance was not simply financial but could embrace logistical and emotional support as well.

In exile, the institution of the *skyid-sdug* re-emerged first in the form of pan-Tibetan organizations.[28] When these were unable to respond to the demands of the large and dispersed population of Tibetans in exile, new organizations formed around regional and sub-regional affiliations. While initially concerned with political activities, the new *skyid-sdug* gradually acquired a socio-economic focus, offering help to their members in times of need, sponsoring social events (some of which were designed to generate income for the organization), and establishing small businesses towards a similar end. Gumbo (1985) suggests that the re-emergence of the *skyid-sdug* in exile has led to a resurgence of regional identification, which was important in traditional Tibet.

Dga'-nye, another traditional form which lives on today, is a system of reciprocal exchange between kin as well as non-kin. It applies to a variety of situations: agricultural operations, hospitality and moments of crisis. While strict accounting to ensure a balanced two-way exchange is not maintained, gifts and favours are expected to even themselves out and, in exile, *dga'-nye* is more common among wealthier Tibetans who are in a position to reciprocate.

There are no formal lending institutions among the Tibetans in exile. Indeed, there appears to be a preference for re-investing savings, even if this requires the accumulation of capital over long periods of time, rather than for borrowing large sums of business capital. Co-operative societies formed within the refugee camps were designed, in theory, as sources of credit; in practice, however, the role they played here proved negligible.

Old Tibet had its professional money-lenders; not unexpectedly money-lending survives in exile. Unless the person is a relation or a trusted friend, such loans usually carry the burden of heavy interest.

---

[28] The 1960s saw two organizations, the United Tibetan Association and the Tibetan Women's Association, established along the lines of *skiyd-sdug* to provide a social and political voice for Tibetans, perform welfare activities and settle community disputes. These organizations were short-lived because their ambitions outweighed their economic resources (Gumbo, 1985).

Because most Tibetans lack both formal citizenship[29] and collateral in the shape of land or buildings, bank loans are usually out of the question. Given these constraints, it is not surprising to find that as much as ninety per cent of the Tibetan carpet industry in Nepal functions solely on the basis of internal family resources.

Cultural practices and religious beliefs. While traditional Tibetan beliefs and practices survive in exile, especially among the older members of the community, change is apparent among the youth. Predictably, those born and raised in Nepal have adopted many of the attitudes and social practices of the host country. While this has been achieved without sacrificing their basic Tibetan identity (including their adherence to Buddhism and the goal of a 'free Tibet'), such change has allowed younger members of the community growing flexibility and mobility in economic and social activity (Gumbo, 1985).

Tibetan skill in preserving old ways while adapting to new circumstances would seem the result of several factors. The absence of serious social hostility in either India or Nepal, indeed the sympathetic attitude of host populations, certainly eased the process of transition (Goldstein, 1978; Miller, 1978). Miller attributes this friendly welcome in part to the fact that both India and Nepal are pluralistic societies into which newcomers are absorbed with relative ease. In addition, the Tibetans learned to be circumspect about social habits such as meat-eating and alcohol consumption which might offend Hindu sensibilities.

In the case of Nepal, the Tibetans had the additional advantage of proximity to indigenous groups with Tibetan Buddhist roots—Sherpas, Tamangs, Rais and other Himalayan and hill communities—whose cultural practices were already familiar. There were other similarities, too: Nepal, like Tibet, is ruled by a leader whose powers are believed to be divinely inspired. Finally, never having been colonized or conquered themselves, the Nepalis have been sympathetic to the plight of the exiled people of Tibet, particularly as their flight was linked with religious persecution.

The survival of Tibetan Buddhism in exile was aided by the escape

---

[29] Although Gumbo (1985) maintains that citizenship is open to Tibetans in Nepal, many refugees do not acknowledge this. The TGE, reflecting the sentiment of many refugees, contends that taking up citizenship of another country is equivalent to giving up the struggle to return to their homeland. Those few entrepreneurs who have taken Nepali citizenship for business purposes have done so quietly and not without the disapproval of the community.

of some eight thousand monks along with the Dalai Lama. This represented a very high proportion of the total monastic population of the country prior to the Chinese invasion. The re-establishment of the monastic tradition has been crucial for preserving the cultural integrity of the exiled community. It has been sustained by the growing economic success of the Tibetan community in exile. In the Kathmandu Valley alone, there are now nine separate monasteries, supported largely by the Nepali Tibetan community (although generous donations by Buddhist communities in other parts of Asia and by Western well-wishers have also helped). Families still place children in monasteries as fledgling monks and nuns, often for socio-economic rather than religious reasons. Indeed, poorer families who would not have been able to send their children to the monastery in Tibet represent the most important source of novice monks and nuns in the Valley (Gumbo, 1985).

A positive attitude to life and its challenges appears characteristic of Nepal's Tibetan refugee population. Despite the hardships of exile, many Tibetans exhibit a quality of life superior to that of their Nepali neighbours. As a Kathmandu-based lama once observed,

> By the blessings of the three jewels ... Tibetans are very different. If you observe a Tibetan who gets Rs 300 as a teacher and a Nepalese who gets Rs 600 as a teacher and look at their homes, you would find that the Tibetan has more to eat and is doing better by far. It has to be the 'fruit' of the divine grace ... of the Buddha Dharma. (Gumbo, 1985, p. 247)

In interviews with Tibetan refugees in India, Miller (1978) came upon a similar pulse of optimism: 'respondents who recounted how all their possessions were left behind, in order to save their lives, repeatedly stressed that those material objects could be replaced through dint of determination and application.' (p. 386) While the Tibetans recognize themselves as refugees, the belief, strong even among the younger generation, that they will return to Tibet one day acts a powerful *raison d'être*.

Entrepreneurship in exile: the carpet industry. The task of creating a new economic base for the Tibetan population in exile proved the community's most difficult—and ultimately most successful—challenge. Few of the Tibetans who came to Nepal had any experience in industry, and those with some commercial expertise were versed only in the old, small-scale border trade between Tibet and high-altitude communities of Nepal. Initially, in both India and Nepal, most of the new refugees were employed in road construction, farming, or in infant camp-based handicraft industries.

Much of the impetus behind the creation of the Tibetan carpet industry in Nepal came from SATA. Carpet weaving, a traditional cottage industry in Tibet and a marketable skill in the context of Nepal's expanding tourist sector, became the focus of refugee training and economic organization. By the mid sixties, the carpet industry was well established within the framework of the camps, but marketing remained underdeveloped: carpets were only trickling their way to consumers. With the help of SATA, the Carpet Trading Corporation (CTC) was established to help camps co-ordinate the inflow of raw materials and the export of finished carpets. It also managed a showroom in the Kathmandu-based Jawalakhel camp to sell carpets to tourists.[30] In addition, SATA subsidized a European importer in order to expose the carpets to the European market.

The evolution of the carpet industry is exemplified by the experience of two co-operative firms established in the late sixties. The camps had been unable to absorb all the refugees, and there were at that time substantial colonies of unemployed Tibetans living near the Buddhist *stupas* (shrines) of Swayambu and Bodha. The Dalai Lama sent assistance from his headquarters in Dharmsala to investigate the possibility of setting up additional carpet industries, following which co-operative carpet industries were established in both locations. The initial capital was supplied by wealthier Tibetans in Nepal and by Dharmsala; no outside aid was involved.

The centres went into production in 1968 with just twelve weavers. For four years, they incurred heavy losses; without access to outside markets, they had to depend on the local tourist trade, then much smaller than it is today. But the Tibetans made active efforts to establish an export connection, and, in 1972, a German buyer agreed to import fifty metres of carpet on a trial basis. This was the breakthrough the Tibetans had been waiting for. The buyer established a market in Germany and agreed to import as many carpets as the industries could supply. Several years later, the centres established an exclusive reciprocal agreement with OCM of London, a major carpet importer. Today, the co-operatives' export body, the Himalayan Carpet Export Company, services several refugee camps, seven

---

[30] The CTC currently manages about six per cent of carpet exports from Nepal.

co-operative production centres and half a dozen or so small-scale producers who do not have their own export outlet. The original co-operatives have spawned numerous progeny.

The carpet industry in Nepal has become the economic mainstay of the Tibetan population, employing more than two-thirds of the refugee work-force. It also provides work for a large number of unskilled Nepali labourers. The success of this venture has exceeded all expectations: Tibetan carpet exports today represent Nepal's major source of foreign exchange (Trade Promotion Centre, Kathmandu, 1985).

The Tibetan carpet industry in Nepal falls into three broad categories. Firstly, there are semi-corporate or corporately owned factories within the camps. Secondly, there are the private co-operatives such as those initiated with support from the Dalai Lama in Swayambu and Bodha. The third category is that of independent concerns based on household ownership; in many cases, these developed out of the first two types, and are particularly relevant to our discussion of entrepreneurship.

The refugee camps and the co-operatives-based carpet factories have provided an important training ground for would-be entrepreneurs. With the imperative of economic survival, the backing of the community, and an ever-expanding market-place, the smartest and most enterprising Tibetans have broken away to establish independent factories on the strength of their own savings and what they could borrow from within the community. In addition, camp-based families have been able to save money by weaving at night on their own looms.[31] Even if they faced limitations on capital, the early independent producers were assured a percentage of the export market through the Himalayan Carpet Export Company. Such exports were complimented by a growing local tourist market. In more recent times, individual entrepreneurs have pioneered new markets and established links of their own with a much wider network of overseas buyers.

The Tibetan carpet industry today manifests an element of healthy competition between its various components. But it remains a fact—given the nature of the industry—that when one suffers, all tend to suffer in the long run. When there is not enough wool, the industries which have the capital and connections are naturally in a position to

---

[31] Industries established within the refugee camps encouraged this practice by allowing families to weave up to two carpets per month at home. These were then marketed through the showroom established in Jawalakhel. In addition, dividends from camp factories were distributed among members.

stockpile and gain an advantage. But fluctuations in raw material supply have never been of sufficient duration to drive significant numbers of producers out of business—although the availability of wool is currently a serious constraint. The most important variable remains the market, and as long as a producer can maintain a standard of product comparable to that of others, he is assured of a buyer. The Nepal Carpet Association operates as a platform for sharing ideas and information which the independent carpet producers—whether large or small—see as beneficial to all.

The success of Nepal's carpet industry is due in large measure to the fortuitous 'fit' between the skills of a refugee population and the requirements of the tourist and export sectors. In addition, the present generation of Tibetan entrepreneurs has had the advantage of fluency in the local language as well as in English and of familiarity with Nepali social practices and business culture. The adaptability of younger Tibetans, which we have examined in some detail, seems linked to the priority the community ascribes to education and self-improvement.

It should also be noted that although the transition from nomadism, agriculture and petty trade to the manufacture of carpets has demanded new types of labour organization, the psychological and social strains involved have perhaps not been unduly harsh. Indeed, Gumbo (1985) provides this alluring, perhaps over-romanticized picture of life in a Tibetan carpet factory:

> Unlike most mechanized factories where workers sit at machines all day and may have to put up with deafening noise, these handicraft factories offer a wide range of human diversions ... An outside observer cannot fail to notice the lively atmosphere: two or more younger workers might be listening to a third, who has seen a Hindi movie and is summarizing its plots; several older workers might be singing a prayer in unison; an older man with a nomadic background might suddenly burst into a solo rendition of a nomadic song from a corner, while from another section one or two younger workers might be singing aloud a 'hit' Hindi movie song .... Meanwhile, children run around freely, crying, laughing, playing and shouting. All the while, everyone's hands are busy at work ... (p.145)

The emergence of Nepal's Tibetan refugee population as a successful entrepreneurial community in its own right is unique and revealing. Community cohesiveness; the sheer will to survive economically;

cultural patterns which adapted easily to new surroundings; the identification of a product—the handmade carpet—subject to growing demand at home and abroad: such factors provide part of the explanation. But the ability of this resilient community to pick up the pieces and get on with life in exile seems bound up in important ways with a strong sense of identity, a tenacious adherence to Buddhism, boundless faith in the Dalai Lama's leadership and an eventual return home. A combination of optimism, adaptability and viable economic options has helped make the Tibetans successful entrepreneurs in their adopted home.

THE GURUNGS AND THE MANAGIS

Two other minor actors in Nepal's commercial sector deserve mention in our discussion of entrepreneurial communities. The Gurung community, with a long history of service in the Indian and British armies, has in recent years increasingly channelled repatriated earnings and pensions into business endeavours. The Managis from northeastern Nepal are an old-established trading community with a reputation for dealing in contraband. They are of special interest to us because of their well-organized trade networks.

The Gurungs. The Gurung community is based in the central hill region of Nepal. Military service has long been an important source of supplementary income to this community's primarily agrarian way of life. The organizational skills learned in military service and the exposure to other societies appear to have contributed to the emergence of successful entrepreneurs in the Gurung community in recent years.

A strong strain of egalitarianism and reciprocity is evident in Gurung social and economic organization (Doherty, 1975; Messerschmidt, 1978). For example, in the Pokhara area, the Gurungs have pooled their savings from military service to start transport businesses. These have a definite military flavour, organized as they are on the basis of age and experience 'within a group participation framework' (Doherty, 1975). Interestingly, top management posts are rotated.

The relative social and economic mobility of Gurung women gives the family additional opportunities for income generation. Women often run restaurants, small tea-houses and hotels.[32] Thus, for many families, income is derived from agriculture, military service and business simultaneously.

Co-operation and reciprocity appear the cornerstones of Gurung entrepreneurship, allowing the community to move out from its traditional agrarian base and pool manpower and economic resources in the pursuit of profit.

The Managis. The Nyishang community from Nepal's Manang District (popularly known as the Managis) is today actively involved in trade with Southeast Asia. The Managis have affinities with the Sherpas and Thakalis in that they hearken from the Himalayan border region, are Buddhist by religion and culture, and spring from a traditional economic base of agriculture, pastoralism and trade. In fact, the Managis have an impressive history of long-distance trade; initially involving Burma and India, this later reached into Southeast Asia, aided by special concessions granted by the monarchy as early as 1789. This ancient trade was in exotic items: live dogs, goat and sheep skins, yak tails, leopard skins, herbs and musk from the Managi homeland were traded for manufactured items from India and Burma (Gurung, 1976). The colourful character of the activity continued well into modern times; the 1950s saw Managi traders importing such items as tiger-claws, jewellery and gemstones from Rangoon, Penang and Singapore via Calcutta for sale in India as well as in Nepal. Official support for such activity, too, remained very much alive. When the government placed restrictions on the import of certain goods in 1967, traders able to identify Nyishang as their homeland were granted specific concessions. One provision allowed the Managis to import goods to a value of Rs 30,000 as personal baggage. Luxury items, mostly bound for the Indian black market, were brought in under this dispensation, while under-invoicing on a significant scale added to the inflow of goods.

The 1960s saw the scope and scale of Managi trade rise, especially after the introduction of a direct air service to Bangkok and improved links with Hong Kong. By the 1970s the Managis were to be found in Singapore, hawking synthetic leather products from Bangkok and religious curios from Nepal. From this it was logical to develop

---

[32] In Doherty's (1975) Pokhara sample, 58 per cent of the businesses were operated by women whose husbands were serving abroad in the army.

dealings with the lucrative Indian black market, with the focus on the import of gold.

While Managi trading on the edge of the law has not gone unchallenged by competitors, the following comment appears to sum up the picture of step-by-step expansion in an indulgent environment:

> For the Managis there has been a rapid but continuous development from a background in which concealment of petty goods and cash was practised as a routine matter, through more profitable involvement with animal products and organs ... to a hugely profitable contraband in gold.(Cooke, 1982, p. 90)

The secret of Managi business success appears linked with the clandestine, co-operative organization known as the *tshong roo*. This entity is made up of Managi traders and—in the more developed groups—wealthy businessmen from other communities. The *tshong roo* makes loans to individual traders, and has on hand the international contacts and information essential for successful trafficking in contraband. Loans, given on an interest-free basis for members of the Managi community, carry an interest rate of 10 to 15 per cent for non-Managis and require the deposit of collateral. Only when a new member is able to pay back his loan is he admitted to full membership—an initiation procedure that tests his trustworthiness and business skill (Cooke, 1982).

The *tshong roo* also operates to establish relationships with customs officials; some receive a lump sum for each shipment they wink at, while others are kept on a retainer basis. This organization therefore appears to act as a forum for the sharing of risk, capital and contacts. While offering wealthier merchants a measure of protection against the risks involved in the type of trade in which the Managis have historically engaged, it also provides access to capital for novice Managi traders.

Given their history of long-distance trade, not to mention the profits to be derived from operating at the very edge of the law, it is not surprising to discover that Managi investment in other spheres of economic endeavour (for example, industrial production) is decidedly limited.

CONCLUSIONS

What generalizations are possible on the basis of our case-studies of entrepreneurial communities in Nepal?

The first point is that although there exists no single formula for success in business—in Nepal as elsewhere—the communities explored in this chapter do reveal certain common practices and characteristics. Most of them exhibit a pronounced sense of community identity, derived from an impressive degree of internal cohesiveness. They come equipped with a background in trade. Many have evolved internal lending systems that work to promote enterprise within the community. Most of these communities have inbuilt sanctions on the accumulation of wealth. However, in many cases, they also place importance on relatively egalitarian social organization and a measure of reciprocity within the community. In the main, too, these communities have placed no obvious barriers in the path of female entrepreneurship.

It is also clear that history did not arrange for these communities to have equal access to market opportunities, capital, business networks or even government connections when they lined up at the starting point. Indeed, such a situation is unlikely outside of the laboratory; were it possible to control the external factors of history, geography, policy and politics it would of course be far easier to measure the precise impact of various socio-cultural institutions on entrepreneurship. We have assumed, however, that the past thirty-five years of economic development in Nepal have somewhat equalized entrepreneurial opportunities (not to mention obstacles). From the vantage point of the present it has been possible to hazard assumptions about the relative importance of social, cultural, political, historical and market forces in the development of entrepreneurship in each community and to re-examine the determinants of entrepreneurship as set out in Chapter I.

Social marginality. The case-studies suggest that not only are Nepal's entrepreneurial communities socially marginal, but also that entrepreneurial activity, at least in Nepal, is inherently marginalizing. All the entrepreneurial communities considered (and here we put aside the Brahmins, Chhetris and Newars, whom we shall consider in a moment) fall outside the political and cultural mainstream. This reality is reinforced by the fact that in Nepal control over resources has traditionally been exerted by a 'public sector' elite dominated by Chhetris, Newars and Brahmins.

Historically, the Newars represented the bridge between political and commercial concerns, and as a result of this unique position were able to gain access to positions of political power. This historical experience appears to have made entrepreneurship less of an economic imperative for the Newar community. As a result of this, and of inhibiting socio-cultural structures, the Newars have not demonstrated an ability to take up new market opportunities. For such 'mainsteam' groups, business endeavour has been facilitated by lineage and caste links with those in power—perhaps the most important aspect of their commercial success, such as it is. The basis for entrepreneurship within these mainstream communities is, therefore, notably different from that of the other communities considered in this chapter.

Taking the argument one step further, our examination of marginality theory has assumed that the central government controls resources and power and that access to these is to a large extent determined by caste and community affiliation. Private enterprise may offer 'outsider' communities an entry point to privilege—but only when a significant shift takes place in the power structure. Until such a change is effected, such groups will remain, by definition, on the socio-political margins.

But in the culturally heterogenous context of Nepal, the fact that a community lacks control over resources, power and prestige is insufficient to explain the relationship between social marginality and entrepreneurship. Indeed, the large majority of Nepal's rural inhabitants who belong to minority ethnic communities have not turned to entrepreneurial pursuits. Several other factors must be considered.

Geographical factors. Geography has played a major role in shaping entrepreneurship in Nepal. It has been those communities whose agricultural economies could not easily be sustained in the harsh Himalayan environment that turned to trade. In addition, all the communities examined here (with the exception of the Newars) have their homeland in regions which were politically and culturally remote from Chhetri political control. Such isolation appears to have strengthened local communalism, while trading activity perhaps predisposed these groups towards entrepreneurial pursuits. Beyond these factors, certain internal organizing principles and structures would seem to have influenced certain communities in the direction of enterprise.

Social organization. Entrepreneurship in Nepal's minority communities is accompanied by a strong internal definition which provides the communal cohesion necessary to withstand criticism from the mainstream culture. Is it possible to make generalizations about an 'optimal' internal definition for entrepreneurship? And does this cohesion necessarily subsume individually under the interests or dictates of the group?

In the Nepali context, adherence to communal norms appears the key to entrepreneurial success. Typically, the individual internalizes the support of the community as a way of embarking on innovative activities in a conservative environment: without this support, he or she would be lost. Thus individuality is expressed in the context of the group—whether the family or the community—and is sanctioned by group norms.

Such communal cohesiveness, when viewed in the context of a prevailing culture not very supportive of private enterprise, appears a necessary adaptation: a mechanism for psychological survival, as it were. It also reflects the reality in many developing countries where cultural adaptation typically lags behind economic change. When the country reaches the stage at which cultural and economic norms are less at odds with one another, individual entrepreneurship can emerge outside the security of the group. This commonly takes place first in the urban, modernizing context; here, inter-group interaction catalyzes change and some measure of assimilation, perhaps ultimately producing a modern entrepreneurial class based less on ethnicity than on free occupational choice. There is evidence, particularly in Kathmandu, that such a class is beginning to take shape, even if the present-day entrepreneurial community remains overwhelmingly divided along ethnic and caste lines.

Our case-studies suggest that when socio-economic organization and cultural norms are mutually reinforcing, a particularly vigorous form of entrepreneurship manifests itself. The Marwaris and the Thakalis illustrate this point particularly clearly. Both have internal lending systems which function on the basis of trust, solidarity and optimization of economic opportunity for as large a proportion of the community as possible. Both have demonstrated the ability to maintain their cultural identity in the context of physical dispersion and to adapt to changing market circumstances. Interestingly, as the Thakalis' cohesion as a community has diminished somewhat in recent years, so has their single-minded pursuit of private enterprise.

The Newars and the Sherpas present a rather different picture. While it would be misleading to assert that these communities lack a strong internal definition, they do appear to place certain limits on business pursuits. In contrast to the Marwaris and Thakalis, these groups tend to subsume economic priorities under social requirements in an effort to avoid internal conflict. Indeed, Newar culture, with its strict adherence to group norms, and Sherpa codes of social reciprocity require that economic partnerships within the community be avoided. This inevitably increases the risk to the individual entrepreneur, perhaps setting him in competition to other community members. Despite this, both communities reveal facets that are supportive of entrepreneurship: Sherpa skills at 'impression management', for example, and the general Buddhist endorsement of the acquisition of material wealth. But in general, the balance these groups strike between social and economic priorities tends to work against the optimization of economic opportunity.

It is interesting to note that while the Tibetans and Sherpas have moved from trade to an alternative single occupation (carpet-weaving and tourism respectively), and while the Newars continue to rely on 'safe', localized, more-or-less traditional forms of commerce, the Marwaris and Thakalis have diversified into a range of new economic activities. This ability to respond to new openings appears linked with the question of community identity and self-definition, although the relationship requires study in depth.

Nepal's Brahmin and Chhetri communities offer several points of contrast. To begin with, neither community has a specific geographic focus or homeland. And community identity appears to rely less on internally defined objectives and norms than on lineage relationships. While the minority communities we have examined all exhibit a strong communal identity, Chhetri culture (which can to some extent be seen as synonymous with Nepali culture in general) reveals a strong thread of individualism. Indeed, it has been unnecessary for Brahmins, Chettris, or even Newars to focus on group identity as a route to entrepreneurship: all three communities have had access to power, resources and prestige as centre-stage players. Business therefore becomes for these communities an extension of political control; it appears somewhat removed from entrepreneurial activity in the sense of risk-taking and innovation.

Religion. With the exception of the Marwaris and the non-Uray Newars, all of Nepal's entrepreneurial communities are rooted in Tibetan Buddhism. While this places them outside the mainstream culture of a Hindu kingdom (although it can be argued that Hinduism and Buddhism have intertwined to a significant degree in the hills and valleys of Nepal), it appears to have encouraged a more open approach to such questions as the acquisition of wealth, inheritance patterns, father-son relationships and the position of women.

In general, Nepal's majority Hindu culture would seem to place definite restrictions on upward mobility, innovation, and the accumulation of wealth. For the Hindu, occupation is still ascriptively defined through the mechanism of caste. We saw that for the Chhetri Ranas, for instance, political power was justified on the basis of caste; indeed, they attempted to restrict commerce to what were considered the appropriate castes. Even today, caste considerations exert a powerful sway. The choice of a business career for Brahmins and Chhetris is still considered a step down; government service and agriculture remain the preferred options for sons. On the other hand, as we shall see later, members of untouchable castes have begun entering the ranks of small-scale enterprise, most commonly in the urban context. However, such individuals often face severe obstacles in securing bank loans and other facilities, given their lack of clout. Caste thus remains a major constraint on entrepreneurship within the Hindu framework.

In contrast, Buddhism would appear to place far fewer restrictions on upward mobility and actually encourage the pursuit of profit. Tourism, for example, has opened up opportunities for the entire Sherpa community and not only its rich and powerful constituents. Likewise, internal systems of co-operation among the Thakalis, the Tibetans and the Managis—systems based on the Buddhist principle of equal opportunity—have helped significant segments of these communities to improve their lot.

While Buddhism demonstrates a greater degree of pragmatism in relation to business pursuits, it is important to remember that Hinduism developed in an earlier era; the Hindu caste hierarchy appears to have been central to the functioning of that society. Buddhism, a later arrival, diluted these structures in large measure, weakening caste divisions and allowing greater play to the individual. Today, when the high-caste Hindu voyages into the foreign terrain of business, the transition involves a degree of cognitive dissonance. For the Buddhist—at least in theory—all occupational avenues are fair game.

Family structure. The family remains the most pervasive organizing structure for businesses in South Asia; indeed, in the early stages of economic development, the family is the main source of labour, management and capital. While some scholars have argued that economic development works to weaken the viability of the extended family as an economic unit, the examples from Nepal do not all bear this out. Certainly for the Marwaris, the most commercially evolved of the communities under discussion, the family remains the cornerstone of business organization. The other groups we have examined reveal a range of family structures, from Sherpa nuclear families at one end of the continuum to Newar extended families at the other. It is noteworthy that Brahmin, Chhetri and Newar enterprises mirror the Marwari pattern: all these communities base their businesses on the extended family, with the oldest male at the head. Why, then, do some continue to operate and expand as family businesses while others (particularly Newari businesses) disband with the death of the patriarch? In separate interviews, a Newar and a Marwari recounted a similar incident: how, in each case, the respondent's son had approached him to get permission and funding to launch a business venture significantly different from the one in which the father was currently engaged. In the Newar case, the father's reaction was sharp disapproval: the son should follow in his footsteps—an argument that led to the son's breaking away from the family. The Marwari father, on the other hand, sought to keep his son within the family fold; he gave him the support and funding he required, trusting that his basic business skills would see him through. The father felt, furthermore, that by keeping the son within the family he could ensure their mutual economic success.

Within the Newari family system, norms of deference and obedience to elders appear to have a dampening influence on individual mobility and risk-taking. In the Marwari case, on the other hand, there is an interesting interwining of social and business norms. Individual innovation is accorded recognition and is actually encouraged in the context of the family. Furthermore, whereas sons in the Newar system work directly under their fathers in single-business operations, the Marwari family allocates the pioneering and management of new enterprises to all capable adult males. The Marwari pattern therefore allows greater scope for individual initiative within the structure of the family.

The role of women and child-rearing. The exclusion of women from the business domain in the case of Nepal's Marwari community runs against the conventional wisdom that commercial communities in modernizing societies tend to be ahead of other groups in terms of the emancipation of women. However, in communities with a less substantial capital base, women do appear to have played a significant role as entrepreneurs in their own right. In the short run, at least, women's involvement in business appears inversely related to the availability of adult males and of capital.

In Chapter I we hypothesized that where mothers were economically mobile, the mother-child relationship would be less restrictive than that characteristic of traditional societies, allowing the development of innovative individuals. While no specific studies on child-parent relationships in Nepal are available, research on the status of women suggests that women in Buddhist communities are in general more emancipated than their Hindu counterparts: they are given recognition for their income-earning potential and appear less confined to the domestic sphere. From this, one would expect significant variations in child-rearing practices between Hindu and Buddhist communities.

The trading tradition. Our case studies reinforce the view that expertise in trade—whether long distance or localized—is a crucial precondition for the emergence of entrepreneurship. All the communities under discussion relied to some degree on trade historically, and most continue to do so today. This reliance necessitated the development of marketing and investment skills which set these communities apart from the agricultural and administrative strata of the society and prepared them to take up new opportunities in the private sector.

Long-distance trade, in particular, appears to have played a key role in the evolution of Nepal's entrepreneurial communities. With the exception of the Newars, all the communities we have examined, from the Sherpas of the high Himalayas to the Marwaris, were at some stage involved in long-distance trade. The toughening impact of distance and difficulty is captured by von Fürer-Haimendorf's observation that 'long distance caravan trade makes great demands on the stamina and personal courage of the operators, and in both these qualities the Thakalis of the older generation surpassed the basically urban, comfort-loving and perhaps somewhat timid Newars.' (1975, p. 292)

Long distance trade also brings traders into contact with other cultures, exposing them constantly to new markets and new products; it also requires more planning in the manipulation of capital than does localized trade. The special advantages conferred on a community by a background in long distance trade seem illustrated by the case of the Uray segment of Newari society. The Urays, one-time traders with Tibet, have in recent years performed significantly above the rest of the Newari community in business endeavours.

Reciprocity and internal co-operative systems. Reciprocity is an important theme in discussions of traditional societies. One strand of scholarship has suggested that reciprocal forms of organization tend to diminish as economies modernize and individual entrepreneurship emerges (Mauss, 1954; Levi-Strauss, 1969). From our case-studies of Nepal, however, it is apparent that in the early stages of industrialization this is not always the case. Indeed, internal lending systems such as the *dhikuri* function as mechanisms of social reciprocity, equalizing resources at the community level. Such systems give the individual economic and psychological support, reducing the element of risk and sharing out community-based capital and business contacts. However, not all Nepali entrepreneurial communities exhibit such mechanisms; indeed the Brahmin and Chhetri communities appear to eschew any organized form of economic co-operation and reciprocity. It becomes difficult to draw conclusions from what appears to be very complex picture.

Access to ruling élites: 'marginality' re-examined. Each of the minority communities we have examined has been able to advance itself by building links with Nepal's ruling circles. In the case of the Marwaris, this has been achieved through the establishment of joint ventures as well as through the medium of bribery, while the presence of foreign partners has helped the Sherpas build such vital alliances. The Tibetans have been given scope to develop the carpet industry because of its value to the ruling élite as a source of foreign exchange and its employment potential. The Thakalis have chosen the path of cultural assimilation, while the Managis, and other groups involved in contraband trade, also contribute to the national economy and, more specifically, to the coffers of individuals in key positions with whom they share their takings.

This reality suggests that while social marginality is an important element in Nepali entrepreneurship, its importance is only relative and should not be exaggerated. In a pluralistic society like Nepal, no minority group is very far removed from the prevailing Hindu-Buddhist cultural framework. Indeed, the Newars and Thakalis have made it a point to move closer to the mainstream Chhetri culture in order to facilitate their business ventures. The Sherpas have come in by the back door, forging partnerships with expatriates whose links with larger markets—and Western culture—have given the Sherpas an enhanced measure of acceptability. The Marwaris have built on their historical alliances with Nepali rulers and have capitalized on the growing links between the economies of India and Nepal. Social marginality—or, rather, minority status—has not prevented Nepal's entrepreneurial groups from co-existing quite successfully with the powers-that-be.

Chapter Four

Private Enterprise and the Public Sector

> *The biggest contribution of the private sector to economic development is its very existence, regardless of the structure of the society in which it operates ... If nation states are to grow, to regenerate, and hence to endure, the individual citizens of these nations must have some sanctuaries where personal idiosyncracies will be allowed to flourish. This will not only allow entrepreneurial trail-blazers to appear, and enable initiative and creativity to prosper, but will also create a society in which a charismatic leader will be able to promote unpopular ideas without endangering his job.*
> —Aharoni, 1977, p. 310
>
> *An elephant has two sets of teeth—the long beautiful ones on the outside, which are for show, and the sharp ones, hidden inside, which are for chewing.*
> —Nepali saying

When static systems of political and economic domination of the few over the many are forced to change, a redistribution of power and control naturally takes place. The developing nations of the post-war world have, in many cases, demonstrated the relevance of Durkheim's assertion that 'many aspects of social life formerly ruled by unthinking custom or habit become the subject of intervention on the part of the State.' (cited in Giddens, 1971, p. 102) Ruling élites—holding state power—now find themselves in the critical spotlight of outside opinion—at the very time that new international realities compel some measure of economic reorganization. Some form of élite redefinition now seems in order to guarantee survival; the role of the private sector as a vehicle for economic development seems inextricably linked to this process of redefinition. Like it or not, ruling élites must allow at least a breathing space for an entrepreneurial class which seems part and parcel of national economic survival. Granting the breathing space, of course, means that at least a modicum of resources be allowed to pass from central control to wider segments of the population.

This redefinition is not without its price, both for ruling élite and for upcoming entrepreneurs.

In this chapter, the aim is not to judge the objective value of this transition but rather to delineate the process of economic development as it is experienced by the entrepreneur. Through the analysis of successive policies and case-studies of specific industries, our study will seek to illuminate some of the tensions in the relationship between Nepal's public and private sectors; one desired outcome would be the re-establishment of a balance more conducive to the cultural and economic goals and requirements of each. But this is not necessarily a rational process in which supply and demand reinforce one another in a perfect market-place. It is a far more complex process, dependent on human beings whose consumption patterns, production activity, relationships, and individual rights may be rather different from those found in Western capitalist societies.

Our discussion focuses on a microcosm: a small country in which innovation and change are neither linear nor predictable. It is well to remember that this process is merely a minor drama being enacted on the sidelines of more complex relations between multinationals, aid agencies and giant national economies—in relation to which Nepal is but very minor fry. While at home entrepreneurs and political élites may battle fiercely, they share an underlying nationalism and an overall commitment to the goal of national survival.

The portrait that follows of Nepal's private sector has been built up from interviews undertaken by the author with more than two hundred entrepreneurs and a dozen or so senior civil servants. They include the perspectives, individual stories, and slices of the life histories of people who have pioneered not only new industries in Nepal, but also the very concept of entrepreneurship. It is, of course, easy for any business-person in a given context to point out external problems and blame others for what might be their own shortcomings. But it is surely significant that in my interviews, similar tales surfaced and resurfaced, cropping up in a range of industries, in different locations and among different ethnic groups. These results point to definite trends in the overall situation, trends which deserve serious examination. These are, in turn, reinforced by the case-studies, which are intended to provide the reader with a feel for some of the very acute and trying challenges facing all entrepreneurs, whether big or small, in contemporary Nepal.

Many of the entrepreneurs I interviewed were willing to place their frustrations on record—in particular, their frustrations regarding

Nepal's bureaucracy. The fact that they were prepared to do so in a society where such criticism is difficult to voice openly must be taken as a sign of the emerging strength of the private sector, even if it has a long way to go in matters of basic organization. It is to be hoped that the private sector will muster sufficient cohesion to lobby for some positive responses to the problems and frustrations it faces—and that real change can be brought about in the not too distant future.

There is, then, a thread of criticism running through this chapter; but the aim is to give voice to those who for their very survival can only vent their frustrations in the privacy of their own families, or to a disinterested foreign observer. What is not intended or attempted here is a detailed critique of national policy; nor will I recommend specific steps to improve policy or policy implementation. The aim is rather to voice the perspective of the private entrepreneur and, on this basis, to make some suggestions as to how this perspective might figure more prominently in the decision-making process.

NEPAL'S INDUSTRIAL SECTOR: A REVIEW

By no account has industrialization been an easy proposition for the kingdom of Nepal. Nor have the country's relative dearth of natural resources and rapid population growth facilitated the process. With Asia's two economic giants, India and China, for her neighbours, and dependent on a notably high inflow of foreign aid (75 per cent of the national development budget in 1986) Nepal faces constraints to industrialization which are to some extent beyond her control. Her largely uneducated and unskilled population, stagnant agricultural sector and burgeoning national debt would seem to rule out any rapid industrialization in the medium term. But while these constraints should not be underestimated, it can be argued that the pace and nature of industrialization since 1951 has been based on somewhat more controllable factors in the socio-political environment. It is these factors which are explored in the discussion that follows.

As we have seen, Nepal entered its new era of 'democracy' and development only in 1951. Given the legacy of élite control over the country's limited productive activities, the evolving relationship between state and private sector promised to be anything but smooth. Indeed, as Figure 4.1 indicates, industrialization was to have only a limited impact on GNP: by the early eighties, industry still did not

FIGURE 4.1

Nepal: Sectoral Distribution of GNP (1981/82)

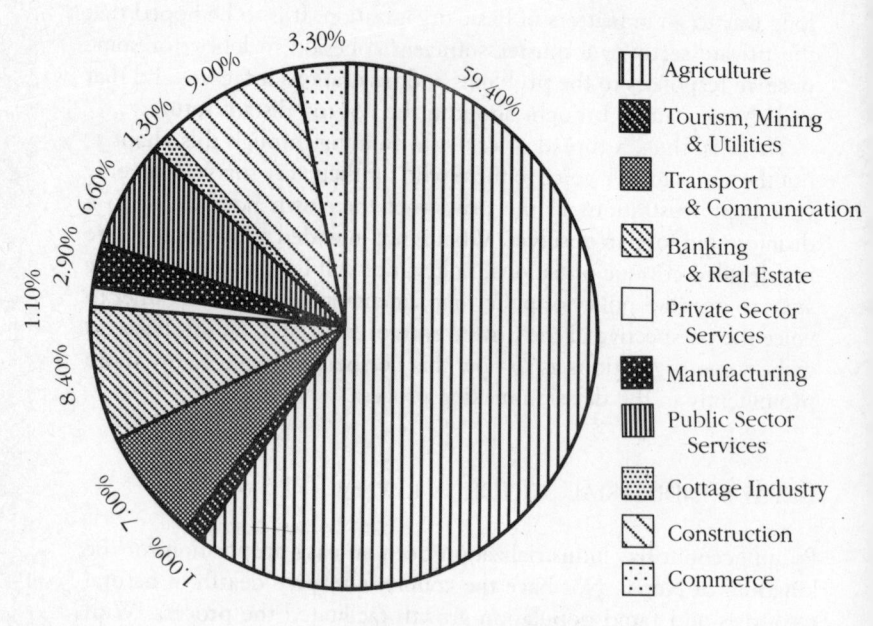

- Agriculture: 59.40%
- Tourism, Mining & Utilities: 3.30%
- Transport & Communication: 9.00%
- Banking & Real Estate: 1.30%
- Private Sector Services: 6.60%
- Manufacturing: 2.90%
- Public Sector Services: 1.10%
- Cottage Industry: 8.40%
- Construction: 1.00%
- Commerce: 7.00%

SOURCE: Statistical Pocket Book, 1984, CBS, Kathmandu.

contribute on a significant scale either to GNP or to employment; if 'private services' are included, industry in 1981–82 could be said to contribute less than five per cent of GNP and account for barely two per cent of national employment. The contribution of manufacturing to GNP was in 1981–82 only 0.9 per cent higher than it had been in 1947–75, underlining the extremely slow pace of industrial development in modern Nepal.

Table 4.1 provides an overview of the types, numbers and comparative efficiency of various Nepalese industries. These figures indicate that agro- and forestry-based industries dominate the industrial sector in terms of number, employment and value added. In the case of the cigarette and bidi industry, and the yarn and textile sector, a large proportion of their raw materials is imported from India or from third countries. Both public and private enterprises are involved in these

TABLE 4.1

Basic Statistics Concerning Various Industries in Nepal (1981/82)

Type of Industry	(1) Number of Industries	(2) Labour as % of total	(3) Value added as % of total	(4) Capacity Utilization
Animal Feed	15	0.7	3.2	
Bakery Products	53	1.8	1.1	
Bidi, Cigarettes & Matches	87	13.9	22.0	62
Bricks and Tiles	191	19.9	1.4	52
Cement and Cement Products	7	0.6	0.7	63
Caps	8	0.5	0.04	
Carpets and Rugs	67	3.3	3.1	
Distilleries	15	0.6	0.7	106
Drugs and Medicines	7	0.1	0.2	
Fruit Canning & Bottling	10	0.4	0.7	
Footwear & Tanning	14	1.2	2.5	68
Furniture	245	4.4	4.7	
Ice and Ice Cream	36	0.3	0.03	
Jute Processing	8	7.4	3.8	78
Jewellery & Curios	4	0.2	0.04	
Knitting Mills	30	1.4	1.1	
Metallic Vessels	29	1.0	0.9	
Oil & Grain Mills	3532	20.0	37.2	
Paper & Printing Press	141	3.2	1.7	
Plastic & Rubber Products	15	0.2	0.3	
Polythylene Pipes	9	0.3	1.8	
Repairing Works	26	0.4	0.1	
Sugar Refineries	11	4.5	4.2	92
Saw Mills	63	1.2	2.6	
Soaps	19	0.4	0.7	
Tea Packing	17	3.5	0.2	
Yarn & Textiles	145	4.8	0.9	
Iron Products	60	2.4	1.2	
Milk and Milk Products	6	0.9	0.9	
Activities	35	1.4	1.9	
Total	4903	100.0	100.0	

NOTE: This somewhat dated data was the most recent available at the time of writing. The absence of the garment industry is notable. The total quantum of labour for column (2), including permanent, contract and family labour, is estimated at 81,050 persons (an average of 16.53 persons per establishment). In column (3), the total value added for all industries was estimated at Rs 2,361,292,000 (equivalent then to about US Dollars 200 million). Information for column (4) was incomplete.

SOURCE: Statistical Handbook, 1986, CBS, Kathmandu.

In 1955, just before the First Five Year Plan was drafted, twenty-four out of a total of sixty-eight previously registered firms were dissolved owing to lack of capital. Thirteen more were liquidated, fifteen were operating at a loss, and only the remaining handful were showing some profit. Of Nepal's seven public sector enterprises at that time, only two were in manufacturing.[1] Infrastructure was extremely limited, with most transportation still undertaken by foot. Communications, too, were underdeveloped, while other industrial prerequisites, such as power and water supply, were inadequate and unreliable. In addition, the country was undergoing quite far-reaching political change; this, too, had an impact on industrial policy.

The First Five Year Plan, launched in 1956, stressed the quality of life and laid down certain employment and production objectives.[2] Cottage industries and 'productive enterprises' were given priority, and the government promised to provide *suveida*[3], or undefined 'necessary facilities'. However, the Plan failed to clarify the role and target areas of public sector *vis-à-vis* private sector industry, creating problems which have persisted right up to the present time.

During the Second Plan period (1962–65), emphasis was placed on the expansion of employment as a means to greater economic stability. The government raised its allocation to industry from 7.5 per cent to 17 per cent of the national budget.

The 1966 Trade and Transit Treaty with India, forged during the Third Plan period (1965–70), exempted Nepali transit goods from customs duties in India and provided warehousing space in Calcutta. This was a significant gain for Nepali industrialists, allowing them to import raw materials more freely from third countries and to develop export-oriented industries dependent on sea transport. Foreign aid also bolstered industrial growth directly (through loans, joint venture support and technical assistance) and indirectly (by its contribution to

---

[1] As we have already seen, these industries were initiated largely in response to shortages created by World War II. They lacked a clear policy framework and adequate infrastructure.

[2] Much of the data and information for this section comes from: *A Study of Non-Agricultural Enterprises in Nepal*, Development Research and Communications Group, Kathmandu, 1984 and Radhe Pradhan, *Industrialization in Nepal*, NBO Publishers' Distributors, New Delhi, 1984.

[3] *Suveida* is Nepali jargon for incentives, exemptions, services and similar help provided by the government to industries. This could include, for instance, tax holidays, rebates and foreign exchange concessions.

the development of national infrastructure). Industries producing sugar, metal utensils, matches, textiles and biscuits were established; a hotel construction sector arose; and the country's first rolling mills appeared. Of the 1257 new industries established during the Third Plan, 60 per cent were small rice mills. The largest investment was in stainless steel and synthetic textile factories, both of which depended upon imported raw materials and were focused primarily on the Indian market. These industries flourished because of facilities offered by the government. But they proved short-lived; India objected to the perceived threat to her indigenous industries, at that time carefully protected.

The Industrial Act of 1974, under the Fourth Plan, was the first attempt by the government to formally define industries by size as well as licensing requirements, banking procedures, and sales, excise and income tax regulations. Tax holidays were accorded to cottage industries, those sectors working for import substitution, export-oriented industries, the tourist sector, and industries using indigenous raw materials.

As a result of the policies of the seventies, many of the industries established during this period came to be dependent upon imported raw materials. While this was perhaps inevitable, given the dearth of indigenous raw materials, the industries which evolved tended to cluster around a few products rather than attempt to fill obvious gaps in the industrial sector. Licensing was, and remains, ad hoc, conducted without reference to any clear set of national priorities. As a 1972 World Bank report comments:

> Like the previous plans, the Fourth Plan includes a long list of industries that ought to be established. If during the Third Plan, the private sector did not meet expectations, it is hard to understand why the Fourth Plan again expects the private sector to play a leading role, especially since no clear effort is being made to engage its participation in new industries.

Nepal is now paying the price for this lack of planning and co-ordination in industrial and raw material import licensing; foreign exchange has become extremely short. Many industries are forced to run below capacity; others close altogether in the absence of an adequate supply of foreign currency. No concerted approach to balanced import substitution and export promotion has been established to rectify this situation.

The Fifth Plan, which included the most recent Industrial Act of 1981, sought to right some of the imbalances created by the previous Act and to stimulate further industrialization. Under the Act, industries were reclassified into four categories based on the fixed investment assets shown in Table 4.2:

TABLE 4.2

Classification of Industries under the Industrial Act, 1981

Industry	Investment in fixed assets	Investment in machinery/ equipment
	(in Rs 100,000s)	
Cottage	up to 5	up to 2
Small	up to 20	more than 20
Medium	20–100	—
Large	above 100	—

The Act established an industrial promotion board to grant licenses to medium- and large-scale enterprises; cottage industries were to be delicensed (exceptions were to be defined by the government). Applications were to be processed within set time limits: 30 days for the cottage- and small-scale sector; 60 days for medium enterprises; and 90 days for large-scale industries. In addition, the Act set out strict sector-wise periods of tax exemption, as Table 4.3 clarifies.

Another concession to industrialists under the 1981 Act was the reduction to one per cent of customs duty on imported machinery and equipment, spare parts, and raw materials used directly in the manufacturing process. Cottage industries won a five-year excise tax holiday and small, medium and large industries a three-year one (extendable by one year for industries located in backward regions). No excise duties at all were to be levied on exported goods or on industries set up in export promotion zones. And the Act listed a series of exemptions from sales tax: cottage industry products; imported machinery, spare parts and raw materials; and goods produced for export.

The 1981 Act, then, sought to promote industrialization by making investment more attractive. Implicit in it were certain clear policy priorities relating to the use of indigenous raw materials and the promotion of balanced regional development. If not entirely new, the

TABLE 4.3

Details of Sector-wise Tax Exemption Under the Industrial Act of 1981

Type of Industry	Exemption	Remarks
Cottage industries	6 years	—
All sizes, using local labour and raw materials	5–10 years	Depending on the extent of value added
Industries producing essential goods	Additional 2 years	—
Energy and mining industries	6–12 years	Depending on the extent of value added
Tourism industry	5–7 years	Depending on the location
Service industries	3 years	
Industries located in export promotion zone*	10 years and 50% concession for another 5 years	
Agro-based special industries	10 years	
Industries located in backward regions	3 additional years	

* The proposed export promotion zone has never materialized.
SOURCE: DRCG 1984, pp. 104–5.

facilities it introduced were more strictly defined than they had been before. In addition to listing these specific incentives, the Act sought in general terms to encourage greater foreign investment.

For our purposes, it is noteworthy that the Act proposed to pursue a policy of 'disinvestment' in favour of the private sector. It stipulated that the public sector restrict its activities to industries of national importance where the private sector could not take the lead because of high investment costs or because it lacked sufficient technological sophistication. The reality, however, was to prove rather different. Far from withdrawing from industries in which the private sector was establishing itself, public sector corporations have remained stolidly in place, often competing with private concerns for raw materials and markets.

While the 1981 Industrial Act sought to stimulate employment via training programmes (in particular, those relating to the cottage sector), the results have proved far from satisfactory. Training programmes, which have absorbed considerable inflows of funds from foreign countries and a good deal of administrative energy, have demonstrated (with few exceptions) only limited success in generating employment for Nepal's urban and rural poor. Nor has the Act effectively streamlined bureaucratic procedures; entrepreneurs argue that these are even more cumbersome today than they were in the past.

Part of the problem appears to be the short life accorded to legislation such as the Industrial Acts of 1974 and 1981. Neither was to remain untouched long enough to provide a real basis upon which industrialists could plan for the future. Unpredictable change seems built into the Nepali policy-making process; as one observer put it, 'The basic problem that entrepreneurs have with the government is that every time the cabinet changes, the policies change. And even if they remain, the interpretation varies depending upon which official you deal with.' Or, as a private Kathmandu-based research organization commented, in perhaps the first comprehensive survey of Nepal's private sector, 'There is also an inherent tendency of governments to use ad hoc decisions with complete disregard for the commitments made by previous governments and the likely consequences of such decisions on the future role of the private sector, including the credibility of the government before the private sector.' (DRCG, 1984, p. 254)

It is, of course, difficult for entrepreneurs to keep track of such changes and to estimate how long-lived they are likely to be. As a result, a great deal depends on the personal relationships individual entrepreneurs and civil servants manage to establish. This has engendered among entrepreneurs a general feeling of scepticism or disbelief (the Nepali phrase is *biswas hundaina*); few expect policies to be implemented, however attractive to the private sector they may appear.

To complicate matters further, there is a serious lack of co-ordination between departments and ministries which serve the private sector. Indeed, contradictory procedures confuse and confound even the most experienced businessperson. The entrepreneur is confronted with a labyrinth of official pathways; not surprisingly, the end result is a questioning of government motives, understanding and good will.

The failure to make industrial headway is further indicated by the size of Nepal's export deficit, which in 1984-85 stood at Rs 3,539 million, an increase of 377 per cent over the 1974-75 figure (World Bank, 1985). Several factors have contributed to this alarming growth. One is the rising domestic demand for imported consumer and luxury goods by Nepal's middle class. The courtry's flourishing black market trade with India and beyond has also had an impact. The failure of the indigenous manufacturing sector to escape dependence on imported raw materials must be taken into account. Recent changes in Nepal's foreign policy which have sought to reduce links with the Indian economy in favour of diversified trade with third countries appear relevant, too. Incentives provided to third-country exporters during the last decade successfully raised the quantum of exports to third countries from two per cent under the Second Plan to 25 per cent in 1975–76 and to 63 per cent in 1984–85.[4] One result, however, is that Nepal now lacks sufficient Indian currency to purchase much-needed inputs from India and is forced to divert valuable foreign currency to buying Indian rupees. And, according to one senior official in the banking sector, 'Primary commodities that could be more profitably exported to India also got diverted to overseas markets under the lure of various incentives provided by the government from which individual exporters stood to gain while the economy suffered a direct financial loss.' (Thapa, 1982)

The experience of Nepal's trade in the recent period provides a fresh illustration of the contradictory nature of official planning. Loans and licenses intended to stimulate investment in manufacturing units have, in practice, become tools in the hands of private operators adept in the arena of quick-money trading. In the process, money and resources have been diverted from more productive, industrial use.

THE PUBLIC : PRIVATE SECTOR RELATIONSHIP: PROBLEMS AND TENSIONS

Industrial policy formulation (and implementation) in Nepal has followed a course of trial and error, reflecting the inspirational biases of successive administrations. It has suffered as governments have attempted to balance issues of national economic development and human and natural resource allocation against Nepal's fragile geopolitical position or against more immediate political concerns. The trial and error method of stimulating industrialization has been a fundamental, and costly, determinant of the development of entrepreneurship.

---

[4] The major exports to third countries are ready-made garments, carpets, and hides and skins.

The private sector—embryonic, disorganized, and culturally and politically marginal—has been involved in policy formulation in only very limited, informal ways. Individual entrepreneurs are able, through their personal contacts with officials, to plead their cases on a situation-by-situation basis. But the private sector as a whole lacks an effective mouthpiece for putting across the problems which beset large numbers of entrepreneurs. Local, regional and national chambers of commerce, designed to provide a forum for dialogue between entrepreneurs and relevant government bodies, are disorganized and largely powerless because of internal factionalism and the absence of any real political clout. Involved in internecine grappling for limited resources and government contracts, the private sector has been unable to organize itself into an effective political lobby.

Unfortunately, Nepal's judicial system hardly comes to the help of entrepreneurs who have not received officially promised incentives and facilities. Litigation is expensive, time-consuming and graft-ridden. There is also the fear of official vendettas. As one legal advisor told me, 'Very few industrialists have taken the government to court. They are afraid, particularly with tax issues, that if they make the matter public, the next time the tax officials will take it out on them.'[5]

Not even those who stand to gain from a successful courtroom battle are likely to support (at least in public) the maverick who dares to take on the government. By and large, entrepreneurs are compelled to tackle each obstacle as it comes and to work within loosely defined patronage networks in which 'source and force' reign over national development concerns. Nor has the legal system been utilized to prosecute those entrepreneurs who misuse governmental incentives (aside from a few token cases). The result is that officials and entrepreneurs coexist in a state of mutual suspicion that hardly promotes healthy interaction between the public and private sectors. The implicit rules of the game are that civil servants and entrepreneurs alike try to benefit as best they can while using the rules and regulations as a general guideline to justify official delays or private sector misutilization. The system works because both have something to gain, not because policies are well conceived and properly implemented. In essence, then, this is a system of collusion, a system that takes a serious toll of

---

[5] About a dozen cases involving industrial policy have appeared before the Supreme Court. In one case, some industrialists got together to fight a new regulation which revoked certain customs duty concessions on synthetic yarns; they were successful.

national economic stability and whose ultimate victim is the ordinary Nepali consumer.

This overview of Nepal's industrial policy-making and its shortcomings provides an entry-point to a more detailed examination of relations between the public and private sectors. As we have seen, the public sector still functions largely on the basis of patronage networks, in an environment where the speedy, rational decision-making typical of capitalist industries has no place. We now turn to case-studies which highlight specific aspects of the problem.

To begin with, how do Nepali entrepreneurs define the problems which beset them? Tables 4.4 and 4.5, based on my own field research, provide some insights.

TABLE 4.4

Perceived Problems of Nepali Entrepreneurs

Problem	Size of Industry				
	Large/Medium	Small	Micro	Total	Rank
Obtaining raw materials	4.5(18)	6.5(26)	7.0(27)	18(25)	I
Obtaining import license for raw materials	3.5(14)	3.5(14)	0	7(10)	IV
Competition with imported raw materials or goods	4.5(18)	3.0(12)	0	7(10)	IV
Competition with public or foreign firms	2.0(8)	0.5(2)	0	2.5(4)	VII
Working capital	1.5(6)	4.5(18)	9.5(37)	16(23)	II
Skilled labourers (technical), finding/retaining	3.5(14)	2.0(8)	4.5(17)	10(14)	III
Market outlet	0	2.0(8)	5(19)	7(10)	IV
Inconsistent government policy	4.5(18)	1.5(6)	0	6(8)	V
Government controls	1.5(6)	1.5(6)	0	3(4)	VI
Totals	25.5	25.0	26.0	76.5	

NOTE: Percentages are tabulated by columns to reflect priorities for a particular size of industry.

Respondents were asked to list three problems. Problems ranked first and second were combined, and weighted, the secondary problem given 50 per cent of the weight of the first, to give a larger critical mass of responses. In all, twenty types of problems were cited.

SOURCE: Laurie Zivetz, Field survey, 1985–86.

As Table 4.4 indicates, the problem of obtaining raw materials is the greatest headache for entrepreneurs, irrespective of the size of their undertaking. While industries dependent on external raw materials face major difficulties, even industries which rely on domestic raw materials encounter obstacles. For large- and medium-scale entrepreneurs, inconsistent government policy is an equally powerful irritant and constraint, while for small- and micro-industrialists the more immediate issues appear to be those of working capital and market outlets. Lack of skilled labour appears to afflict the entire spectrum of industry. The findings set out listed in Table 4.5, derived from a much larger sample, provide a more detailed breakdown:

TABLE 4.5

Problems of Industrial Entrepreneurs and Managers

Problem	Frequency of Response
Working with government	137 (11)
Influence management: source and force	121 (10)
Delegation of responsibility/supervision of staff	118 (10)
Staff motivation	112 (9)
Training and staff development	107 (9)
Inventory management	106 (9)
Marketing: strategies and research	97 (8)
Knowledge of govt. rules and regulations	95 (8)
Manpower planning and recruitment	87 (7)
Technology: choice, procurement, maintenance	84 (7)
Production planning	76 (6)
Self confidence	70 (6)
Total	1210 (100)

NOTE: The data is derived from interviews with 800 industrial entrepreneurs and managers from all sizes and types of industry. The critical incident method was used to gather this data, and skill deficits imputed therefrom.

SOURCE: Laurie Zivetz, *Training for the Private Sector: The Demand and the Supply*, Management Support Services, Kathmandu, 1987.

These findings display a considerable degree of internal overlap; for example, problems with inventory management obviously relate to 'source and force' and 'working with government' as far as imported raw materials are concerned. Four major areas of difficulty are highlighted: obtaining necessary facilities from the government; recruiting and managing staff; marketing; and obtaining and maintaining improved technology. Let us now examine some of these problems from the entrepreneur's perspective.[6]

Raw material availability. An important constraint on industrial expansion and diversification in Nepal is the availability of raw materials. Table 4.6 indicates the source of raw materials for a cross-section of industries. Interestingly, this data, which is based on the only available statistics on the source of raw materials according to type of industry, in some cases contradicts the impressions I formed during work on this study. In my assessment, reliance upon third

TABLE 4.6

Use of Raw Material by Types of Industries (1981/82)

Type of Industry	Domestic	Import from India	Import from Overseas
Rice & Oil Mills	99.71	0.29	0.00
Food & Beverages	52.17	46.92	0.91
Bidi, Cig. & Matches	61.22	8.21	30.57
Saw Mills	99.81	0.19	0.00
Furniture	92.14	7.86	0.00
Paper, Printing Press	92.44	7.56	0.00
Drugs & Soaps	34.11	24.22	41.67
Repair Works	79.09	19.83	1.08
Bricks & Tiles	100.00	0.00	0.00
Jewellery & Metal Vessels	4.56	11.02	84.42
Yarn, Textiles, Footwear	18.65	21.00	60.35
Others	54.56	12.35	33.09
Average	86.28	5.38	8.34

Source: Field Survey, 1983; *A Study on Non-Agriculture Private Sector Enterprises in Nepal*, Development Research and Communication Group, Kathmandu, 1984.

[6] The case studies and quotations cited here involve real individuals. Because the private sector in Nepal is so small, and criticism of government bureaucracy so sensitive an issue, real identities have been disguised. Names have been deleted and sometimes the nature of industries altered to protect the individuals who shared their concerns with the author. Likewise the civil servants who presented their candid views remain anonymous.

country raw materials, and even Indian raw materials, is significantly understated in Table 4.6—although hard data to support this is lacking. The paper and printing industry, for instance, utilizes both Chinese and Japanese raw materials to some extent; however, the available data indicates that all imported raw materials for this sector come from India. (At the time that the study was conducted, Nepal had no paper producing factory of its own: the first was opened in 1986). Likewise, although the data indicates that bricks and tiles are produced exclusively from indigenous materials, there is in fact a significant reliance on imported cement from India and Korea. In addition, two of Nepal's major export industries—ready-made garments and hand-knotted woollen carpets—rely exclusively on imported raw materials from India, China and, more recently, Australia and New Zealand. These caveats aside, the following point is clear: if agro-based industries are omitted from the above statistics, the average percentage of raw material imports from third countries may be as high as 25 per cent.

As we have seen in Table 4.1, Nepal's manufacturing sector is still dominated by agro-based industries. Industries which utilize indigenous raw materials include food processing, leather products and wood products (the last now threatened by dwindling supplies of this natural resource). But as the industrial sector develops and diversifies, it seems inevitable that imported raw materials will play an ever-growing role in the economy. For this reason, the difficulties experienced by industrialists call for closer scrutiny.

Because foreign exchange and licensing are tightly controlled by it, the Nepali Government has been in a position to set priorities, to determine who gets what, and when. This has the more general effect of controlling the growth (and even the survival) of specific industries and firms. The criteria by which licenses for raw material importation are allocated between different industries (and between firms within a given sector) are typically neither clearly articulated nor adhered to, while the procedures for granting licenses (even to bona fide applicants) are lengthy, time-consuming and vulnerable to change. Moreover, because licenses tend to be allocated to those with the 'source and force' necessary to obtain them, and because the black market for raw materials in Nepal and India offers lucrative, quick and sure returns, those entrepreneurs with access to raw materials are in a position to profit handsomely. As a result, many industrialists (particularly those from smaller concerns) are forced at some stage or other to pay higher prices for their raw materials on the black market. This is especially difficult for small-scale industries which are generally short of the working capital needed to stockpile raw materials and pay 'incentives' to the relevant bureaucrats. The marginal difference in the price of raw materials as well as fluctuations in availability make it difficult to forecast production, prices, profits and personnel requirements. One large-scale entrepreneur summed up the situation thus:

> The method of determining licensing encourages misuse, as people can register a firm, get their license, import raw material and sell it on the black. This is especially detrimental for small entrepreneurs who cannot get their own licenses and must buy at higher prices. So their products are less competitive, and some are forced out of business. If licensing was deregulated, the raw materials would be more competitively priced. Right now there are two sources of raw materials—black and straight—so those with direct access get it cheaper. This encourages what many of us call the 'Marwari monopoly'.

A new entrepreneur who assembles copybooks complained to me that he had to 'bribe people at each step of the way to get my license to import paper, and had to borrow from the money-lender, even though I already had a bank loan, in order to subsidize the "incentive" costs.' A senior member of one of the largest business firms in the country defined the problem in these terms: 'The import of raw materials is difficult because the government doesn't give licenses on time, and the amount is not enough. So our factories run at less than optimal capacity. I think the import situation is too controlled.'

Until 1982, the importation of raw materials and technology from third countries was administered under what was known as the Open Generalized License (OGEL) system. Importers were able to go to the bank and open a letter of credit without an import license. In addition, as the Industrial Act of 1981 made clear, industrial importers of raw materials were entitled to a concessional one per cent customs tax. Rebate systems were also instituted whereby some industries received foreign currency rebates for exported items. All these regulations were vulnerable to misutilization, however. By the early 1980s it was becoming clear that Nepal's foreign currency reserves could no longer support the rising level of private sector demand for foreign currency (some of which was being used for non-manufacturing purposes). The government began allocating raw material licenses to specific firms on the basis of their past production performance. One senior official rationalized the new restriction thus:

When we had to terminate the OGEL system because of foreign exchange constraints, we gave the industrialists what had been their utilization or consumption under the OGEL system. We told them we could not give them more than what they imported previously under the OGEL system. If their performance increases we have been giving them additional foreign exchange allocations over and above the performance of the OGEL system. And now there is a clamour for additional foreign exchange from the side of the industrialists.

He then proceeded to make the following interesting observation:

But if you look across the industrial spectrum of Nepal you will find that on average the capacity utilization is 45–50 per cent. It is not above that. And the reason is not that there have been constraints on foreign exchange from the side of government, but it is the market. Despite our population of 16 million people, we don't have the buying capacity, and we have restrictions on exports to India. So it is the buying capacity, not the availability of raw materials, that limits industrial growth.

While very few industries manage to run at maximum capacity, it is perhaps simplistic to place the blame solely on the size of the market. Surely no industrial investor is likely to sink resources into an industry for whose products demand seems insufficient. As a medium-scale industrialist commented to me, 'We are stuck in the bind of never being able to increase our capacity because the government allocates licenses on the basis of capacity utilization. How can we grow?'[7] This remark illustrates yet again the gap that separates Nepal's public and private sectors. As a result of recent policies, many industries were officially registered and provided with bank loans in line with national priorities and the ability of the country to furnish them with the raw materials necessary to run at the capacity proposed in government-approved project schemes. Subsequently, however, many had to function below capacity because they were unable to get enough raw materials.

Ironically, export industries—which are in a position to augment internal hard currency reserves—have been similarly afflicted. As we shall see in the case-studies of the carpet and garment industries presented later in this chapter, the absence of a consistent, predictable

[7] This particular industrialist, who depends upon imported iron, further bemoaned the fact of Nepal's dependence for such requirements (very small by international standards) 'on Indian indentors who play the Nepali buyers off against one another and profit in the process. There should be a policy to help organize this sector and protect us.'

supply of raw materials has become a serious problem for the export sector.

Not only does tight government control limit production capacity, but it also wastes the time and working capital of the entrepreneur. A universal complaint among small-scale producers making machinery, steel furniture and other metal products to meet specific orders is the time-consuming nature of official procedures. As one small-scale producer put it, 'Each time we get a new order to make something, we have to get a new license to obtain the raw materials. This consumes time, energy and our limited stock of working capital. In the end we are rarely able to deliver our orders on time, and cannot reasonably forecast our production or manpower in advance.' A smaller producer outside Kathmandu, who uses imported metal in his cabinet- and furniture-making industry, commented bitterly that he would never again venture into a business dependent on imported raw materials because of the difficulties he faced getting licenses and bringing the raw materials into the country.

As for the tax concessions promised in the Industrial Act of 1981, they are not always forthcoming, and often depend on the whim of the customs officer. As one small entrepreneur complained, 'We are only supposed to pay 1 per cent customs on our raw materials, but to get that facility we have to hang around different HMG Departments for a long time. It's so time-consuming that I gave up and paid the regular 4 per cent customs duty last time, just to get the raw materials in faster.'

Where policy is concerned, what is feasible at any given moment in Nepal is always vulnerable to change. The availability of raw materials is a case in point. In more recent times, certain types of raw material have been auctioned by tender to commercial bidders who then become responsible for local marketing and distribution. While this appears to go some way towards curbing black market operations, industrialists still have their complaints, as this representative of their community makes clear:

> Synthetic yarn has no other value except in industry, but its importation is allowed under commercial import license facilities. The opinion of the Nepal Textile Association was that the importation of raw materials should not be allowed on a commercial license. That means business people should not be allowed to import industrial raw materials.

However, this informant went on to admit that synthetic yarn was not totally consumed by local industries; it had a market elsewhere.

In addition to the tender scheme which applies to certain types of raw materials, wholesaling 'boards' for such basic commodities as metal, wool and cotton thread have been established. These boards are run by government or semi-official associations. Through its proximity to a specific industry, each board is supposedly in a position to distribute on the basis of real needs and genuine utilization. But this attempt to resolve foreign exchange shortages and meet the needs of small industries, while laudable on paper, has offered opportunities for illegal 'profit sharing' for the individuals who run the boards. Very few of the entrepreneurs who buy through these boards are able to meet their raw material demands solely from this source; they must supplement by buying on the black market. A coppersmith from the Terai explained the situation thus: 'I cannot get the metal I need from the board oftentimes, though I have to travel all the way to Kathmandu to get it. I can't keep going back every time, so when I am in Kathmandu I buy from other sources, even though it's more expensive. What to do?'

Meanwhile, the government appears to be taking few steps to punish those misusing its concessions to industry. On the contrary, it has recently withdrawn tax breaks on the importation of raw materials from small and cottage industries in almost all categories—hardly the major culprits in the game of misutilization. The recently introduced passbook system appears to be aggravating the plight of small producers. Under this system, a lengthy process involving five different offices has been set in motion to ensure that import facilities are being advanced only to genuine manufacturing units. The plight of a small entrepreneur in Pokhara (a nine-hour bus ride from Kathmandu) who attempted to get permission to import the raw materials necessary to run his business highlights the human and capital resource burden which this system—designed to protect the entrepreneur—has imposed. This entrepreneur described the passbook process thus:

> First I have to get a recommendation from the Department of Cottage and Village Industries [DCVI] in Pokhara saying I am a genuine industrialist. Then I go to the Commerce Department to get an import license, which I take to the Rastriya Bank [Central Bank] for a foreign currency recommendation. Then I go to the commercial bank which, on the advice of the Rastriya Bank, opens a letter of credit for me. I have to deposit 10 per cent of the amount for the letter of credit. When the goods come to Calcutta I am informed and I usually have to go to the customs office at the border [another six- to eight-hour bus ride] to clear the goods. When I finally get

the raw materials to Pokhara they must be inspected by the DCVI and I must get a letter of quantity inspection, otherwise I will not be able to get the next shipment.

This man's factory utilizes 120 tons of raw materials a year if it runs at full capacity. Owing to foreign currency shortages, the government has allocated this industrialist only 70 tons per year; he is entitled to request only one third of this total at any given time. The whole lengthy process, involving an average of two trips to each office (assuming all goes well), has to be performed three times a year. Perhaps two months out of every twelve have to be devoted to the supposedly simple task of procuring raw materials for a single small factory.

If officialdom is aware of the handicaps such policies place on entrepreneurs, it seems unwilling to admit as much. An official who co-ordinates the dispensing of incentives gave me the following picture of the process:

> We give import licenses for raw materials. Every four months you have to submit an application for raw materials. It won't take long. Even if you live outside the Valley you can send in your application by post. You have to send the application along with the bank account, import license and other verifying documents. They have to come for our recommendation. It takes two to three days here and two to three days in the Department of Commerce. It is the same for everyone, even if you know someone.

However, this individual was rather more candid on the question of monitoring the utilization of raw materials. 'We have no mechanism for monitoring,' he told me. 'For monitoring it is very necessary that they should come to us with their stock and production records. They couldn't lie because excise people stay in their factory.' However, these excise people, like tax collectors in most realms of the bureaucracy, remain relatively unmonitored themselves. Even under this system of tightened control, then, opportunities exist for individuals involved in the process to profit, or to effect delays.

Another mechanism for supplying raw materials to small entrepreneurs was instituted under a World Bank-supported multi-million dollar project to promote small industries. Here, small manufacturing units—in particular those producing handloom cloth, knitwear, carpets and metal objects—have been provided with bank loans at the concessional rate of 11 per cent (against the normal 18 per cent) to purchase technology. A 'performance contractor' is identified as the supplier of raw materials. This person receives a loan as well as concessional rates on raw materials; he is responsible for distributing raw materials to small producers, collecting their finished products and marketing them. The profit margin to the producer is determined by the bank in consultation with the performance contractor. While in theory this approach removes several constraints on cottage industry development—for example, inadequate supplies of material and poor marketing outlets—the scheme has been plagued by an absence of adequate monitoring. Problems between the performance contractor and his assigned producers have been legion. In one case, the producers complained that vital raw materials had reached them only on the very eve of the peak selling season. They suspected that the performance contractor, who also ran a shop, was investing his loan money to increase the inventory of goods in his shop. In another case, a producer said he had never received any raw materials from the performance contractor at all. Such examples illustrate the inability of the government to monitor schemes so as to prevent the private sector exploiting loopholes in them.

Nepal's economic relations with India appear to add to the woes of honest industrialists and entrepreneurs. Many entrepreneurs maintain that raw materials imported from Southeast Asia, Europe and Australasia are cheaper and of better quality than those imported from India. Machinery, metal, cement, and even cotton thread are cases in point. The lower price—unexpected, given the high cost of transportation from third countries, as well as steep F.O.B. prices—is due in part to taxes and tariffs in India which inflate the price of raw materials from that country. It should also be remembered that India, too, relies upon third countries for several raw materials which are duly taxed in the process of being re-exported to Nepal. Because of Nepal's limited access to hard currency, many of its entrepreneurs are forced to purchase raw materials and technology from India rather than from third countries. This puts them at a disadvantage in terms of the quality of finished goods they can produce, weakening their competitive edge vis-à-vis comparable imported products. As one small producer of metal works for bridges complained,

> In the scheme that I submitted during registration I had not put in any provisions to ask for foreign exchange to import raw materials from third countries. But from the last year we have seen that some of the raw

materials are almost 50 per cent cheaper in third countries than in India. The government corporation gets these raw materials from third countries, and I have to compete with them. A few years ago I requested 360 tons of raw materials. After going after them for a whole year, they allocated me 10 tons. I told them, 'Give me 150 tons or I am not taking it.' They didn't give it to me, so I didn't take the 10 tons on principle!

Needless to add, this small industrialist faced considerable economic hardship that year.

Even those industries which can manage with indigenous raw materials face problems in procurement and supply. Grain and sugar mills, as well as industries utilizing these staples, report they are forced to buy their raw materials at a price fixed (and sometimes subsidized) by the government. When the price in Nepal is lower than that prevailing in India, the raw materials gravitate southwards. These producers also maintain that their products compete with Indian processed flour and sugar in a situation where, more often than not, the Indian price is lower because of economies of scale and greater efficiency. The existence of Nepali government subsidies for foodgrains and sugar adds to the problem of leakage across the Indian border.

Agro-based entrepreneurs have been slow to capitalize on the significant opportunities for converting locally grown cash crops and livestock into commodities for the tourist industry. Despite the fact that tourism has become an important source of foreign exchange for the country, it relies almost exclusively on imported raw materials. Buses, aeroplanes, hotel furnishing and construction materials, and, in the case of first class hotels, food items which are not available in the quantity or quality demanded by this sector are all imported. One hotelier I interviewed estimated that out of every US dollar spent by overseas tourists in Nepal, only 16 cents went to benefit the local economy; the corresponding figure for India was, he thought, in the order of 99 cents! 'This does not have to be the case,' he told me. 'We can rely more on our own agricultural products if the producers can supply the quality we need in first class hotels.' This hotelier resorted to importing chickens from India when he discovered Nepali farmers trying to cut corners by raising their animals on inferior feed and injecting them with water to increase their weight. Finally, the hotel decided to open its own poultry farm in Nepal, much to the dismay of feed and poultry producers in the country.

Raw materials often enter Nepal illegally at unpatrolled points along

Nepal's long open border with India. While large-scale traders make 'arrangements' with the concerned authorities, small-scale operators are sometimes caught. The trade flow from Nepal to India is generally of luxury items from third countries, while raw materials such as iron, steel, and Indian-made manufactured goods cross from India into Nepal. Raw materials from third countries are also re-exported to India, particularly if they are 'protected' (hence in high demand) there. As we have already seen, grains, sugar-cane, oils and other agricultural products flow in both directions, according to the respective price in the two countries. Those who are able to bring raw materials into Nepal find a market among those industrialists who cannot adequately meet their production capacity through legal channels.

Although the black market appears to function as an economy unto itself, and as a conduit which siphons entrepreneurial talent and resources away from industry, it has also provided an outlet for select manufactured goods from Nepal from time to time. Black market trade has therefore contributed some seed capital for those engaged simultaneously in industry and trade. In addition, while the black market does not contribute to the national coffers directly by way of tax revenues or measurable productive inputs that are reflected in GDP, it enhances the incomes of a significant number of individuals.

Nepal's bureaucracy has grown markedly in the recent period. With it, a new consumer market for the goods and services introduced by both Western and Indian influences has taken root in urban areas. Low government salaries have combined with opportunities for material gain based on position to breed corruption. Simultaneously, there has been a growing availability of 'extra' capital, whether from foreign aid sources or from business revenues. As a result, corruption has escalated to the point where, for donors, businesspeople and bureaucrats alike, it is an expected, accepted way of life, a part of the cost of doing business in the country.

In the Nepali context, bribery has become a mechanism of sorts for redistributing wealth. The average civil servant in Nepal, managing on a salary of roughly US dollars 75 per month, expects, and indeed requires, a supplementary income to maintain a minimally decent urban standard of living. While the private sector generates the major portion of indigenous capital, the public sector uses its control mechanisms adroitly for a share in the profits. When an official gives an industrialist a license to import raw materials—commodities which can be resold in Nepal or India to other industrialists who do not have access to the license—the official expects a share in the potential profits. When a customs officer closes his eyes to the import or re-export of luxury items, he also expects some remuneration for his trouble. The handsome profits to be made in contraband goods (whether luxury items or raw materials) are beneficial both to the entrepreneurs involved in procuring and marketing them and to the officials who sanction the import and sale of such goods.

In many ways, Nepal's black market functions as a free market. Government protectionist and price fixing programmes, which are easily, even wilfully circumvented, protect no one. It is the small-scale producer and the small consumer—compelled to buy on the black or pay bribes as the situation warrants—who bear the ultimate burden. In this way wealth circulates among the prosperous few, and the majority pay the price. It is little wonder, in this context, that goverment jobs are so highly sought after.

While the problem of raw material supply to industry continues to plague both the public and the private sector, neither has been able to settle on a workable solution. The government, from its side, has been unable to allocate scarce foreign exchange rationally and on a priority basis to the industrial sector. Indeed, the registration of new industries dependent on imported raw materials reflects no systematic long-range planning at all. Nor has the government proved capable of monitoring the abuse of civil service privileges. The private sector, for its part, remains divided between those able to profit from loopholes in policy and those who suffer as a result of such misutilization. In such a situation, characterized by unstable policies and general uncertainty, many potential entrepreneurs are deterred from entering the manufacturing sector altogether.

The raw material problem is unlikely to disappear. In fact, the demand for imports in this category seems likely to increase as Nepal's manufacturing and service sectors grow and diversify. Ultimately, no doubt, the government will have to evolve a policy which serves the needs of the private sector, is capable of being implemented, and addresses national priorities as well as foreign currency constraints.

Incentives and loans. As we have seen, Nepals 1981 Industrial Act offered entrepreneurs an attractive array of facilities and incentives. Small industries and those deemed especially relevant in to Nepal's development goals were given special attention. In addition, development projects (such as the World Bank scheme described above) appeared tailor-made to stimulate small-scale industries, offering such inputs as training, loans and marketing assistance.[8] Rebate systems designed to stimulate export-oriented industries have also come and gone. In retrospect, however, it is clear that despite such efforts the private sector has been able only to inch its way forward and that many of the initial objectives of such development programmes have remained unfulfilled.

A comprehensive analysis of the scope and ramifications of Nepal's development effort is beyond the ambit of this discussion. However, it appears relevant to explore the role played by Indian business elements in Nepal's private sector. Subsequent discussion will also touch on certain psychological aspects of the relationship between the public and private sectors in the search for explanations for the obvious discontinuities between policy formulation and policy implementation.

We have already seen how economic development has brought Nepal into closer proximity with the Indian economy—a reality which our study of the Marwari community underlined. Given India's industrial strength and headstart, entrepreneurs from that country could be expected to be on the look-out for opportunities in their small mountainous neighbour. As the Nepali Government devised its various incentive packages, Indian entrepreneurs were to play a key role in shaping their content and mode of implementation. One example of this came in the mid 1960s when Nepal, in an effort to promote its jute industry, offered jute manufacturers 60 per cent hard currency rebates on the export of jute to third countries; these rebates were applicable to the importation of raw materials and consumer items from third countries. Across the border in India, jute manufacturers were facing high protective tariffs on exports. As a result of Nepal's new policy, Indian jute began finding its way across the border, thence to be re-exported to third countries. Indian and Nepali businessmen alike profited by this scheme, which, for obvious reasons, aroused considerable consternation in Indian Government circles and proved short-lived.

Incentives offered to Nepali industries on the import of raw materials from third countries also stimulated the growth of the stainless steel

---

[8] The Small Business Promotion Project, funded by the German Fund for Technical Assistance (GTZ); a variety of efforts under the rubric of the United Mission to Nepal; and various Integrated Rural Development projects have all addressed private sector concerns, with varying degrees of success (see Zivetz, 1987).

and synthetic textile factories which flourished along Nepal's border with India in the late sixties and early seventies. In fact, these factories were established mainly to supply the Indian market (where similar products were subject to high excise taxes). In 1969 alone, the Indian Government seized as contraband Nepalese stainless steel and synthetic textiles worth six million Nepali rupees (*Matribhumi Weekly*, July 15, 1969, cited in Gaige, 1975). However, most of these factories have reduced their capacity, or closed entirely, in recent years.

In 1966, the Nepali Government introduced a gift parcel scheme which allowed Nepalis to receive packages below a specified value from abroad. Luxury items such as radios, watches and cameras were mailed to Nepal from Singapore and Hong Kong, thence to be smuggled into India by Nepali or Indian traders or 'tourists'. During the main Hindu festival season of 1968, Indian visitors were estimated to have carried ten million rupees worth of such goods out of Nepal (*Nepal Times*, July 30, 1968, cited in Gaige, 1975).

While such schemes may have had some intrinsic merit from a policy point of view, the inability of the government to prevent their misuse caused them to backfire. Was the problem one of policy-makers' poor understanding of the workings of the private sector? Or were vested interests deeply involved in the policy-framing process? The gift parcel scheme, in particular, appears to have been designed to provide exactly what it did: a conduit for black market trade with India. And as the example of the border industries which exported goods to India illustrates, when senior officials stand to profit from industries in which they are, directly or less obviously, involved, the entire process of framing regulations becomes suspect. It is surely revealing that it was only when such illegal practices provoked the opposition of the Indian Government that the Nepalese authorities acted to abolish the incriminating regulations—no doubt to save face and protect their relationship with India.

Once the gift parcel system reached the level of a national scandal, the government, in an effort to shrug off responsibility, blamed Indian businessmen who, they claimed, had 'infiltrated' Nepal with their 'black' hard currency, and 'connived' to smuggle goods into India (*Samiksha Weekly*, Kathmandu, October 9, 1969, cited in Gaige, 1975). Nepali businesspeople in the Terai, even today looked down upon because of their cultural and geographical closeness to India, also felt the brunt:

> An unfortunate side effect of the gift parcel scheme has been an increased resentment expressed by some hill people toward the plains people. Particularly the business-caste groups among the plains people suffer from the grossly overgeneralized reputation for crafty and unscrupulous business dealings. By permitting unscrupulous Indian businessmen to operate in Nepal on a particularly large scale during the gift parcel scheme period, Nepalese government officials unwittingly reinforced the stereotype. (Gaige, 1975, p. 56)

As a small, land-locked country dependent on Indian transit facilities, Nepal cannot afford to jeopardize her working relationship with her powerful southern neighbour. Indian foreign aid, Indian markets and the strength of the Indian economy in general are realities that Nepal can disregard at her peril. At the same time, the Nepalese Government cannot appear to condone illegal activity. As the following comments from a senior government official in Kathmandu make clear, the government is not above a little judicious scapegoat hunting; and the obvious scapegoat is the Indian trader-cum-smuggler:

> We made the policy to help the genuine industrialist. He is not the one who smuggles in from Hong Kong or Abu Dhabi and smuggles out to India or China. He is poor, self-employed, using indigenous raw materials. We withdrew the facilities to those industrialists who are smuggling raw materials ... Bad things are never good. Do you think stealing is good? We have already gone through that stage with a very bad experience. We are not neighbours with India for just four or five days ... To be frank, the truth is most of the smugglers of raw materials are from India. They get the tax holidays from us and take away their earnings to India. I don't say every one of them are Indians. Nepalis have also learned the tricks of smuggling art. Fifty years ago if you left this watch on the street no one would pick it up. Once we opened our borders from 1951 all the vices of the world have entered. We learned both good and bad things from the outside world. If you do the right thing no one notices, but if you do bad things everyone notices. You are being watched. People of the world are good people but certain unnatural circumstances make them bad.

As this same respondent noted, Nepali entrepreneurs have not hesitated to join hands with Indian business interests to make a quick, if illegal, profit.

In general, most industrialists complain that promised incentives are not forthcoming, and that to extract them from the government entails several visits to the relevant office. As Pradhan (1984) comments:

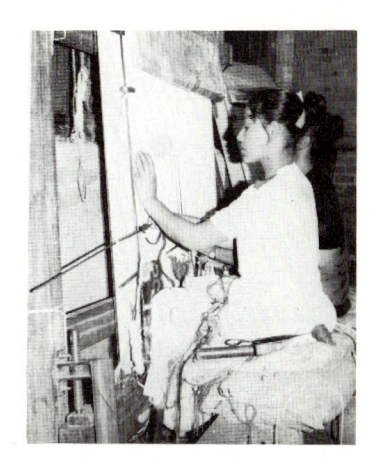

1. (left) and 2.
At work in Nepal's carpet industry. An important source of foreign exchange, the carpet sector provides employment for many through its labour-intensive organization.

3. The garment sector, troubled by a variety of problems despite bouts of heady growth, constitutes an important modern arena of employment.

4. Tourism, very much a growth industry in Nepal, offers plenty of opportunities for the creative entrepreneur, large or small.

5. The kerbside cobbler, a familiar sight throughout South Asia, applies his own entrepreneurial skills within the informal sector.

6. An Indian immigrant hawks fruit from his bicycle: a commonplace event in downtown Kathmandu and other urban centres.

7. A cane furniture maker applies traditional skills: a wayside enterprise typical of small ventures in Nepal.

8. Inside a food-processing factory: a sector ripe for expansion in the new Nepal?

9. Roadside repair services against a backdrop of political graffiti: what will democracy mean for these micro-scale entrepreneurs?

'Industrialists themselves have to try to interpret the industrial facilities and convince government departments to make such facilities available to them.' While I was conducting the research for this book, a new and potentially promising facility for industrialists was announced. When I asked a large-scale entrepreneur whether he had gone to get the facility, however, he responded thus: 'I went to the office, and the staff said they had not been instructed to give it yet. I don't believe it will ever happen, so I'm not bothering.' In a slightly less cynical frame of mind, one medium-scale entrepreneur not far from Kathmandu told me:

> If the Department of Industries acts quickly, I guarantee that we can industrialize our country in the span of ten years. But if the Department of Industry is willing to help and the Department of Taxation raises obstacles by not providing the facilities that are there to be provided, how can we work? We often have to remind them that it's a lot of trouble and time-consuming for us if we have to go to Kathmandu for every small thing; how can we run an industry? I can get what I need most of the time [i.e. he has friends in the right places], but everyone cannot act in the same manner. That is the reason other people are afraid to start an industry.

An exporter I interviewed had a similar lament: 'Every time I want an export license I have to go through the same long procedure. They don't trust us. Why don't they make a list of "clean" firms and let those of us who have proven ourselves get through the process faster?'

Bank loans are, of course, vital to entrepreneurs attempting to start, run or expand their businesses. While the banking sector has matured significantly in the past thirty-five years, (and now reaches a much higher percentage of the population than it once did), it is beset with a familiar range of procedural problems and openings for abuse. The Nepal Industrial Development Corporation (NIDC), one of the country's oldest lending institutions and a public corporation, was established with the specific objective of lending to the industrial sector. But as one entrepreneur told me:

> The best way to get a loan is to hire an officer from the bank. That you could do by giving him Rs. 20,000–25,000, plus all the details. He prepares a garble called a project report and in that garble he is bound to write it so that NIDC will give you the loan. Then you negotiate. You say, 'Why don't you help me in securing the loan, since you prepared the project report?' So he talks with his colleagues and then you pay 1–1.5 per cent of the capital. At least it works!

Small entrepreneurs, who more generally borrow from local branches of the Nepal Bank or the Agricultural Development Bank, also have complaints. Many avoid taking bank loans altogether. Describing the pitfalls involved in securing start-up capital, one industrialist commented:

> There is a premium to get your money. Usually if you know the people very well and they know you, it's 0.5 per cent of the capital. If you are not that good in English, it's 1 per cent of the capital and if you are just a newcomer but you are ready to receive their 'assistance', it's 1.5 per cent of the capital as a bribe. All right, if the system is corrupt, you are not doing anything corrupt by paying them a bribe for legitimate work.

What recourse do entrepreneurs have when promised incentives are not forthcoming? The answer seems to be: not much. A dozen or so cases involving industrial incentives have thus far appeared in the Supreme Court. Protesting against a new regulation which revoked customs duty concessions for imported synthetic yarns, some of the industrialists concerned took the government to court and won their case. These are very much the exceptions, however. By and large, entrepreneurs are compelled to tackle each obstacle on a case by case basis and work within loosely defined patronage networks in which 'source and force' loom larger than national development concerns.

Two Nepali proverbs appear apposite here. Popular among critics of the workings of the civil servant is the saying: *Sarkarko kam kahile jaala ghaam* ('the government's work can wait until the sun goes down.') If one takes this ditty literally (imagining a rural environment where there is no electricity), it suggests that the work will never get done! At a more figurative level, it suggests the civil servant's disdain for prompt, efficient work, his faith that his salary will come, irrespective of whether he works or not. The proverb also conveys the idea that if an individual bureaucrat tries to reach beyond the norms of civil service practice, he somehow threatens 'equalizing forces' which keep the system going (albeit at lowest common denominator level). Nepali intellectuals, conscious of this last point, like to tell the story of some boxes of frogs which were shipped from all parts of the globe to the United States. When the boxes arrived, most were empty: the frogs had escaped. The exception was the box from Nepal, which still boasted a full contingent. Why was that? Because they kept pulling at each other's legs (*kuta tanne*) so that no single frog could advance his prospects and escape. The concept of *kuta tanne* is important in understanding how modes of equalization of resources (and status) perhaps originating in the agrarian context re-emerge in the upwardly mobile strata of Nepalese society. The person who succeeds or innovates—whether in business, academic life, or government—typically becomes an object of suspicion and envy; an attempt will be made to 'pull his legs' to keep him in line.

There are additional aspects to what might be described as the psychological barrier between bureaucrat and entrepreneur in Nepal. At one level, of course, the problem boils down to the suitable dispensing of bribes: if a bribe is expected and not forthcoming, an individual bureaucrat can procrastinate for weeks, even months, making feeble excuses as to why papers are not being processed, pleading his helplessness in the process, and intimating that 'things could be done' to expedite the process. But there is something more subtle at play here, something which pervades the public sector and throws light on the mutual dependency that links Nepal's public and private sectors. One large-scale entrepreneur summed it up thus:

> There is a feeling of terrible competition in our psychology, in particular of the person in the government who sees a successful businessman. He thinks: 'Why is this person rising up so rapidly, and I can't?' So he consoles himself by telling himself, 'But I am the person to give all the licenses and permissions.' So, for instance, if I am an officer and I know that your problem is genuine, if I sanction your file immediately I am afraid of what other people are going to say. They might think you bribed me. So instead I will sit back and take my time. I will be very careful. This is the case that still exists today.

This situation is played out day after day in the halls of government offices; it represents what, in psychological terminology, might be termed passive aggressiveness. While a Nepalese civil servant commands high social prestige, he does not necessarily enjoy a very lucrative salary. Furthermore, his post, and his promotion, are often only loosely related to performance. When a government worker encounters an individual who is visibly prospering as a result of his own hard work—and perhaps earning far more than himself—this naturally arouses envy and anger. The two individuals are juxtaposed by the very nature of the system and the culture of *kuta tanne*; there are few incentives, beyond bribery and kinship, which can prod the one to help the other. National priorities, even the threat of administrative censure, take a back seat to personal gain and personal power in an environment where both are scarce commodities.

It is important to note, however, that increasing numbers of government officials are becoming involved in the private sector on a 'sideline' basis. Some may be silent shareholders in an industry run by another family member; in such cases, the individual in government service can open the door to further official contacts. Other officials sell their services to donor projects or to private consultancy firms, in some cases to perform tasks which legitimately fall within the purview of their official work. Here, a government position provides the base for new income earning activities. Such practices, while they may provoke the raising of eyebrows, are rarely punished; they therefore proliferate. In Nepal, holding a public sector position provides prestige, while working in the private sector provides an income.

Meanwhile, the misuse of incentive schemes continues. In the course of my research, I came upon several registered 'small-scale' industries that in fact employed more than 300 workers apiece; their 'small-scale' status qualified them for tax breaks and licensing concessions. One industry registered as 'small' employed about a hundred people and was reported by its owner to be worth one crore rupees! Unable to control such blatant abuse of its concessions, the government has retaliated by withdrawing facilities from almost all small-scale and cottage industries. When questioned on the implications of this move for genuine small-scale businesses, a senior civil servant proved defensive in his response:

> What you have heard is not right. We have not withdrawn any facilities from cottage industries. The truth is big industrialists snatched away the facilities given to poor people in the name of cottage industries. One of the industrialists even exchanged foreign currency worth Rs two crore in the name of cottage industries. We cannot do anything because the government has given them facilities; there's a public notice and we can't punish them in court. If I don't withdraw the facilities by public notice I can't do anything.

But this withdrawal of concessions has hurt not only the 'big industrialists' mentioned here but also virtually the entire small-scale sector, 'poor people' very much included; claiming its inability to prosecute the guilty, the Nepalese Government has perhaps thrown the baby out with the bath water. While this may appear politically expedient, it has the effect of making the innocent pay for the sins of the guilty. And a further casualty, of course is the credibility of the government—whether in the perception of the private sector or in the eyes of the public at large.

Direct competition between the two sectors. According to the Industrial Act of 1981, Nepal's private sector 'will be given the first opportunity of promoting the development of industry through investment.' The Act continues: 'As a principle, His Majesty's Government will not establish industrial enterprises under its ownership except when large-scale investment is involved and private sector investment is inadequate.' These directives represent a radical departure from a series of Plans in which the public sector was given priority in establishing industries in the country. The 1981 Act was promulgated at a time when the emergence of a growing, more capable, private sector coincided with the recognition of profound inefficiency within public sector corporations. Despite the disorganized condition of the private sector and its many problems, the profit motive—absent from the functioning of public corporations—was now to be encouraged. This step was seen to be both expedient and essential.

Figure 4.2 compares public and private sector industries in terms of their value-adding capacity and their employment generation. The fact that the value added per employee is higher in public sector corporations reflects the relative technological sophistication of this sector. The aggregate statistics for the private sector include cottage and small-scale industries; these vastly outnumber those using sophisticated machinery, and hence tend to depress the averages for this sector. The data provide an indication of the size and employment contribution of the two sectors when subject to direct comparison.

The number of public sector enterprises in Nepal has grown from a baseline of one under the First Plan to 73 under the Sixth Plan. Nearly one third of these are in the manufacturing sector; they produce sugar, cigarettes, tea, jute, textiles, cement, drugs, bricks, timber, leather, shoes and other items. Electricity generating, transport, agricultural inputs and marketing, trade, and, of course, banking corporations make up the rest.

How do these enterprises, stretching across so broad a spectrum of economic activity, actually perform? Figure 4.3, based on data collected in the early eighties, indicates a mixed picture.

The relatively poor performance in the trading arena appears to

FIGURE 4.2

Public vs. Private Manufacturing Enterprises:
Value Added and Employment

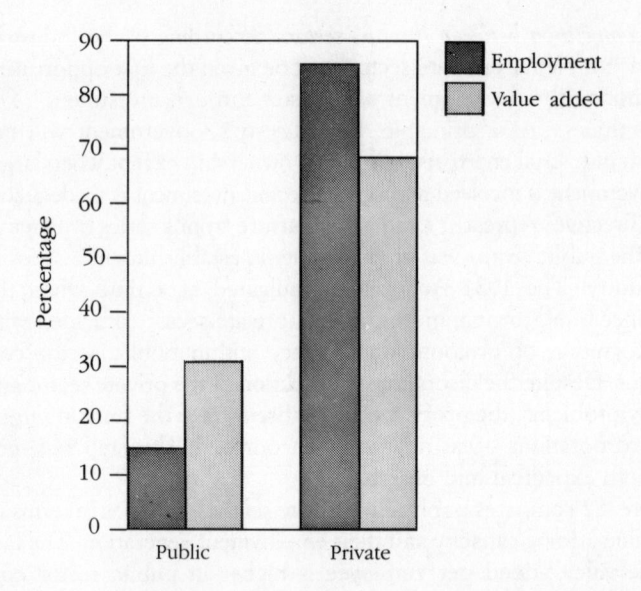

Sources: 1. CCU/HMG, *Performance Review of Public Enterprises in Nepal.*
2. ISC, *Industrial Sector Plan Study (1980/81–1990/91)*, Kathmandu.

reflect mismanagement: the commissioning of products which have no market; the purchase of subsidized but unmarketable commodities from countries such as China under the lure of concessional rates; an absence of aggressive marketing and distribution strategies; and, of course, the search for kickbacks on imported items.

The contribution to GDP of the public sector as a whole—and of manufacturing enterprises specifically—has been almost constant since 1975 (DRCG, 1984). This would seem to indicate a picture of relative stagnation. As an editorial in *The Rising Nepal*, Kathmandu's leading—and government-controlled—English language daily points out, 'some corporations, even operating under monopoly or oligopoly, have run into losses while the adequacy and quality of services and products provided by them have not often provided any reasonable degree of satisfaction.' (April 18, 1986)

FIGURE 4.3

The Performance of Public Enterprises
(1982/83)

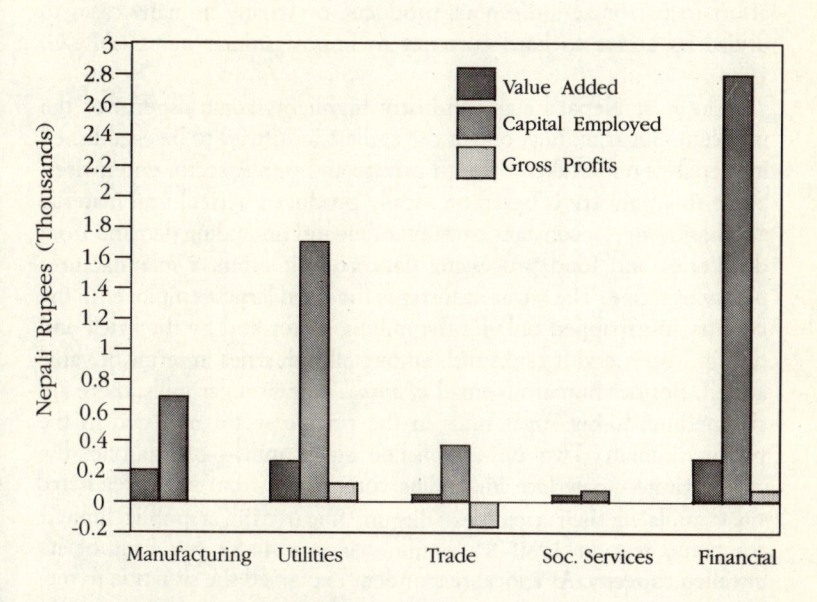

[Bar chart showing Value Added, Capital Employed, and Gross Profits across Manufacturing, Utilities, Trade, Soc. Services, and Financial sectors, measured in Nepali Rupees (Thousands).]

SOURCE: CBS, Statistical Handbook, 1986.

Despite repeated government resolutions to improve the administration of public enterprises by making their management more accountable, and to privatize certain industries (or at least sell a proportion of the shares of public enterprises to private concerns), little appears to have been accomplished. The government has continued to license new public corporations even in areas where the private sector has already staked its claim; Pradhan (1984), in a study of industrialization in Nepal, recorded public sector competition as the third most serious problem facing private industrialists.[9] Given government control over certain types of raw materials and licensing, and government subsidies to public sector industries, the private sector is

---

[9] Lack of initiative within the private sector was, significantly, the most outstanding problem identified by Pradhan's respondents. Second on their list was the tendency of entrepreneurs to get lured into trade (as distinct from manufacturing) in the quest for quick profits.

clearly at a disadvantage here. A further complaint is that public trading firms such as National Trading Limited import raw materials and manufactured products which directly compete with indigenously produced items. Indeed, the public sector is seen to have made little effort to patronize indigenous products, preferring in many cases to utilize its access to hard currency to import similar items (DRCG, 1984).

A look at Nepal's sugar industry highlights some aspects of the problem. Sugar milling, one of the earliest industries to be established in Nepal, is undertaken by both private and public sector enterprises. Since this industry is based on locally produced agricultural material and has to meet a constant consumer demand (including demand from distilleries and food processing concerns), it offers a manufacturer plenty of scope. The sugar industry is the third largest employer in the country, outstripped only by the milling sector and by the brick and tiles industry; and it ranks fifth among all industries in terms of value added. Besides numerous small *khansadi* or raw sugar mills, there are six medium-to-big sugar mills in the private sector and two in the public domain. Two old-established sugar mills—one public, the other private—now face impending competition from newly registered sugar mills in their vicinities. Birgunj Sugar Mill, a public limited company, was in 1980–81 running at just 44.89 per cent of its installed capacity. As a local respondent explained the situation to me:

> The Birgunj Sugar Mill has the production capacity of 1500 tons per day. But it cannot work at capacity because the cane is not available in enough quantity. It might run only for the next twenty days [this season]. Moreover, as it's a government undertaking there are many loopholes. Management is lax and people don't work with interest. There is always a labour problem. They let it go as it's not on their personal risk. If the Birgunj Sugar Mill was in India they would run it with 500 staff, but there are 1700 staff at the mill now! Still, they will not go bankrupt—the government will make it run, whatever the situation is.

By 1984–85, the Birgunj Sugar Mill had boosted its activity to the point of running at 73.33 per cent of installed capacity. Significantly, the government then issued a license for a private sector sugar mill in the next district. Since much of the sugar-cane feeding the Birgunj mill comes from that district, the chronic shortage already facing the Birgunj mill may well be exacerbated once the new mill goes into production.

The Mahendra Sugar Mill Private Limited, which opened 20 years ago in Bhairahawa, has faced similar raw material shortages in recent years. In 1985, for example, the mill was able to run at only 50 per cent capacity because of sugar-cane shortages. The owners blame insufficient sugar-cane production in the area. But they also point out that when the government fixes prices for Nepalese cane far below the going price in India, local cane will naturally gravitate across the border—to the detriment of domestic industry.

Several years ago the government decided to build a public sugar mill with Chinese assistance in a locality which currently supplies the Mahendra mill and on a site more accessible to cane growers. Part of this land was purchased from a prominent politician (indeed, some farmers claim their land was simply confiscated). When questioned about the decision to open a public sector mill, an official explained: 'If the owner of the present mill [i.e., the Mahendra mill] is king in his area, he can exploit the farmers. It is good to have competition. Since no firm came forward from the private sector to open a mill in the next district, the government had to step in and open one.' Or, as another civil servant put it:

> The government fixes the minimum price of sugar-cane. And we have found that only in those areas where there are government industries those rules are observed. If there is more than one industry in an area, ultimately it is the farmer who benefits. Mahendra Sugar Mill has another advantage. It can draw its raw materials from the Indian border. When you talk of industries in the Terai region you have to take that aspect into consideration. There are certain areas where we supply from our side to the Indian sugar mills. There are some sugar industries in India which are fed by our raw materials. At times, we even close our eyes when some of the sugar-cane from India is brought into Nepal.

At the time of writing, the Mahendra Mill's new public sector competitor had not been completed. However, the fate of the private sector mill appears only too predictable.

Several questions arise from these brief case-studies. Can Nepal afford to establish new units within a given industry when existing units are already facing shortages of raw materials? Does not the establishment of public sector enterprises such as the Mahendra Mill's unwanted competitor go against the Industrial Policy of 1981, which appeared to promote private sector industries? If a public sector unit such as the Birgunj Sugar Mill is ailing as the result of mismanagement, might it not be better to privatize the unit rather than start all over again with a completely new enterprise? If the Mahendra Sugar Mill is short of raw materials, would not direct intervention in that specific industry be more cost effective than erecting a new public sector unit nearby? For will not the same problems be bequeathed to the fledgling enterprise?

A similar situation exists in relation to imports; here, the government brings in manufactured items and raw materials which are often subsidized and in fact compete with locally produced goods. For example, one plant producing machinery for small- and medium-scale oil and grain mills faces competition from government-imported machinery from China. Such machinery enters Nepal as part of an aid package and, thus subsidized, can be sold at a lower price. Despite making repeated complaints, the owner of this plant has been able to convince the government neither to stop importing such machinery nor to raise the price of the Chinese machinery to a level comparable with that of his product. The textile industry, which depends on India for most of its raw materials, is in a similar situation. By its own admission, this industry is not as efficient as its Indian competitor, nor does it produce cloth of the same quality. Even allowing for this, however, the odds seem unfairly stacked against the Nepali textile producer, as this respondent makes clear:

> In India you can get trained workers much cheaper. They have special units for spinning, dyeing, and finishing the fabric. We have to do much of this ourselves in our own factory and it's not as efficient. We have to import all of our machinery, spare parts, and even mechanics from India. Most of the thread comes from there. But imported cotton cloth from India comes in untaxed. When the King was here, I asked him to protect our industry, like they do with cigarettes.

A small candle manufacturer in Birgunj made much the same complaint:

> There used to be one hundred candle-making industries in this town. Most of them collapsed because we could not compete for raw materials; now there are only three or four. The government required us to buy our raw materials from National Trading [i.e., the government trading corporation]. They sell Chinese raw materials. Indian raw materials are cheaper, but there is a quota and it's mostly taken by the big industrialists. Since we are so close to the border, we can't compete with Indian candles . . . We wrote a letter to DCVI [the Department of Cottage and Village Industries]

asking them to put a stop to bringing in Indian candles. They did it for some time, but then they stopped. So I had to try hard in establishing myself. The others went out of business, but I have been able to get my raw materials from India by one way and another, and I also bring some Indian labourers from India.

The case of the candle manufacturer underlines the paradox inherent in many policies designed to protect the small-scale entrepreneur. The government imports subsidized raw materials from a third country but does not pass the subsidy on to the manufacturer. And, while the importation of low-priced *raw materials* from India may be somewhat restricted, the importation of competitive Indian *products* is not. The entrepreneur responds, first, by appealing to the government through established channels, seeking the protection that would enable him to obtain his resources through legal channels. When this fails, he opts for the only alternative available to him: smuggling the less expensive raw materials in from India. For the entrepreneur, this is a simple matter of survival.

The Nepalese Government represents the largest organized potential market for the kingdom's fledgling industrial sector. Although some government agencies make an attempt to stimulate private sector manufacturing by offering competitive tenders for Nepali goods and services, this practice is not yet widespread. For example, the government constitutes a major potential customer for stationery items; unfortunately, however, 'preference is stronger for foreign products in the name of quality, but primarily because of the possibilities for greater commissions and kickbacks.' (DRCG, 1984, p. 20) The same appears true of the construction industry, where indigenous entrepreneurs complain of 'being underbid by foreign firms, and since price is the only criteria they use, and the foreign firms are ready to lose money just to get a foot in the door, we are losing contracts to them. How can the construction industry grow?'

A quick look at the Nepalese shoe industry reinforces these observations. In 1963, a private sector shoe factory was opened in Kathmandu's industrial estate. Three years later, a public sector shoe factory, with approximately three times the production capacity, was established. Because of raw material, quality, management and price constraints, both factories came to depend primarily on Nepali governmental and military agencies for their market. (Ordinary consumers prefer shoes imported from China and Hong Kong, which are cheaper and more fashionable.) The owner of the private shoe company (who also happens to be a senior member of the Chamber of Commerce) describes his situation thus:

> I used to buy leather at Rs 5. Now I have to buy at Rs 53, and the quality is never consistent. But since I am forced to buy from the government leather corporation, I have no say in this. The public sector shoe factory gets this leather at a reduced rate, and I told them they should also give me this concession, but they have not . . . Two years ago I needed a special chemical to treat the leather which is imported from Africa. I had to wait eight months to get the chemical, so all of my staff were on overhead. If the public factory faces such delays, the government subsidizes, but I had to pay this myself. Furthermore, I am competing with the public factory for the market. I supply 50 per cent of the police with shoes, even though I could fill the whole order at Rs 34 per pair less than the public factory's price . . . Once I had an order from an office to supply shoes at Rs 50 per pair. The government factory stepped in and took the order away from me because they sold the shoes at half the price. They could afford the loss, but how can I? My factory runs more efficiently, and I could supply the whole market, but they are controlling the market and can support their inefficient management. How can we develop in this kind of a situation?

While public corporations, by all accounts, continue to operate inefficiently, they offer generous employment scope for political appointees and, of course, kickbacks for managerial staff. While the financial costs of such inefficiency would seem to demand that public sector enterprises 'clean up their act,' the political will to do so appears limited. By continuing to support public sector corporations—even in the face of legislation such as the 1981 Industrial Act—the government ensures a large measure of control over industrial raw materials, markets—and profits.

Protectionism: mixed opinions, mixed policies. In the first stages of industrialization, many countries have found it imperative to protect infant domestic industries with high tariff walls and internal price fixing mechanisms. In Nepal, opinions vary within the private sector on this issue; predictably, it is those who face the stiffest competition from imported commodities who have come out loudest in favour of protectionism.

Nepal's two giant neighbours and role models—India and China—have both made use of protectionism at various stages of industrialization. For Nepal, entering the world market at a much later stage and highly vulnerable to foreign competition, the actual scope for protectionist measures appears limited. The issue is an important and complex one which policy-makers and entrepreneurs seem likely to debate for some time to come. What are the principal perspectives within the debate?

We have already seen how private industrialists in Nepal (for example, those in the textile, candle and sugar industries) face competition from imported raw materials and finished items. Where there is an opportunity to sell Indian items, often superior in quality and more cheaply priced, in the Nepali market, the trading community has taken advantage of the situation, whether it has to circumvent government regulations or not. The Nepalese authorities have found it difficult in the past to monitor such practices along Nepal's lengthy open border, and transgressors have been punished only sporadically. Given this thriving, internal network of traders bringing competitive products into the market-place, political will and administrative efficiency seem the sole protective mechanisms for indigenous industries.

The following comments from two of my respondents illustrate the strength of feeling in favour of some kind of protectionism. A major producer of feed, poultry and eggs had this complaint:

> There are 50 producers of feed, 12–15 hatcheries and 8–10,000 farmers raising chickens in Nepal, so this is an important source of income, even for the farmers. We face two problems: we cannot get the molasses we need from sugar refineries, even from public firms, because they divert it to distilleries. Then, we cannot compete with Indian eggs which are 10 paise cheaper. We petitioned the government, and they put up a five paise tariff per egg. We complained that this tariff was not high enough, so the government lowered the tariff to one paise per egg! Now there is no longer a tariff. This is especially hard on us in the summer when there is a surplus of eggs in India and they are willing to sell at a lower price.

Even the general manager of a public corporation feels the pinch. As he told me, 'We need protectionist policies to protect our businesses. Even our public shoe factory is forced to compete with Chinese shoes which are effectively dumped in Nepal when they come in through Tibet. The Chinese don't have a pricing policy, so when they reach their quota in their own country, they sell them outside.'

However, the private sector is far from unanimous on the need for protection. One large-scale entrepreneur in an industry which already enjoys protection from competition with imported products thought not all local units worthy of this shield: 'If they are inefficient, they should not be protected. The public sector enterprises are the best example.' But a senior civil servant gave a different assessment:

> For industrialization we have to pay a little heavy price. If you don't give some amount of protection to the local industries, and expose them to competition with large firms in India or South Asian countries, they can't stand really. In India at one time they followed this protectionist policy. But now, after the coming of Rajiv Gandhi, they opened their economy and they are much more competitive. Had they opened their economy in the beginning, they might not have reached this stage.

However, this same respondent noted that 'There are certain areas where we supply [sugar-cane] from our side to the Indian sugar mills. There are some sugar industries in India which are fed by our raw materials. At times we even close our eyes when some of the sugar-cane from India comes to Nepal.'

The negative side of protectionism was also noted. As one of my interviewees pointed out, 'Protectionism is okay for infant industries, but after that it becomes a vehicle for institutionalizing corruption, because the industrialists are operating in an artificial environment.' In fact, the issue of protectionism shares similarities with other areas of industrial policy: while it exists on paper, it has posed serious administrative problems. Many Nepali industries (particularly small industries) lack any real protection—either from exploitative elements within the country such as black market traders or from legally imported items (for example, those brought in through public corporations).

While protectionism has been used in adjacent countries to nurture infant industries, Nepal's attempt at achieving a similar pattern of insulation has been hindered by her long open border with India and by her trade relations with India and China. Decades behind India in terms of industrial and entrepreneurial development, Nepal functions at a distinct disadvantage.

Human resources. The limited availability of skilled labourers and managers is another factor which plagues every sector and size category of Nepalese industry. This issue goes to the core of the cultural framework in which the business culture functions, reflecting not only the very real human resource constraints facing Nepal (obliging it to turn to Indian labour to fill the gap), but also the inability of the private sector adequately to develop and motivate local skills and talent. The growing dependence on expatriate labour (and the implications of this trend) will be addressed here, while the fundamental issues of motivating, developing and retaining manpower in the context of specific firms will be taken up in the next chapter.

Nepal relies heavily upon Indian workers—administrative, skilled, and unskilled—to sustain existing levels of industrial production, as Figure 4.4 makes clear:

FIGURE 4.4

Non-Nepalese Labour in Nepal by Type of Industry

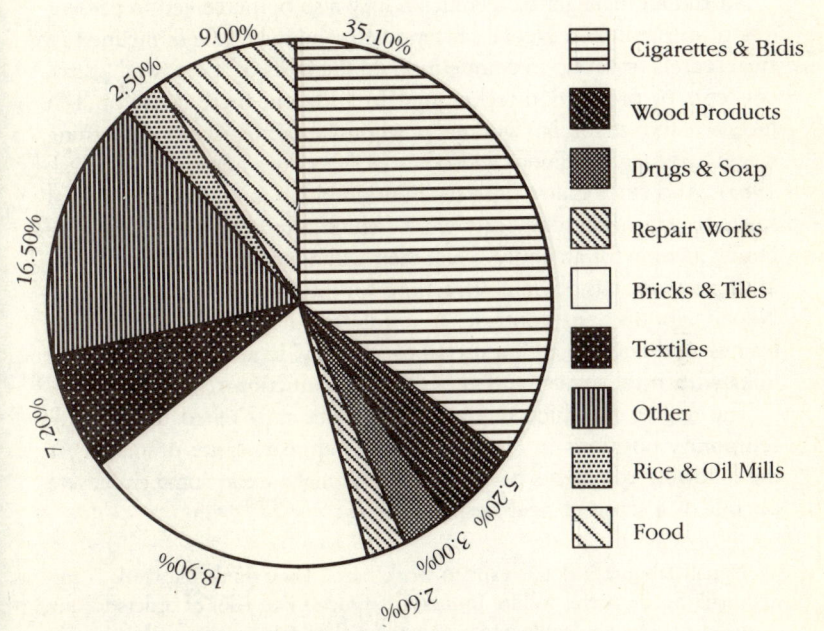

- Cigarettes & Bidis: 35.10%
- Wood Products: 16.50%
- Drugs & Soap: 7.20%
- Repair Works: 18.90%
- Bricks & Tiles: 2.60%
- Textiles: 3.00%
- Other: 5.20%
- Rice & Oil Mills: 2.50%
- Food: 9.00%

NOTE: 'Non-Nepalese' here refers exclusively to Indian labour.
SOURCE: DRCG, Field Survey, 1983.

Although the scale of employment of Indian labour varies from industry to industry, the overall dependence of Nepal's industrial sector on Indians in both unskilled and skilled positions is pronounced: Indian workers constitute more than a quarter of the entire labour force. Whatever the reasons (and these may include a late start in vocational training and national education programmes),

Nepal faces real limitations in the number of trained personnel available to industry. Lack of training, however, does not account for Nepal's current dependence on outside labour. The social prestige attached to jobs in the government sector has contributed to a mini brain-drain within the country, to a diversion of the nation's skilled personpower to the bureaucracy. Another factor may be the practice, among Nepali managerial cadres and skilled workers, of moving from job to job. This, together with the absence of a strong, traditional work ethic within the Nepali labour force as a whole, has given Indian labourers (rated more highly skilled and more diligent in their work) an edge in securing employment.

An Indian manager or technician may also be perceived to present less of a threat to a Nepali entrepreneur: he may be less inclined to steal secrets or set up in competition on the basis of 'borrowed' ideas, concepts or production techniques. In addition, there is the built-in incentive to hire foreign workers to whom labour legislation governing wages, working conditions and other facilities does not apply (Agarwal, 1983). And since many expatriate unskilled labourers come to Nepal solely to engage in temporary work (which often constitutes the only family income for an entire year), their willingness to work long hours at short notice has obvious attractions for the Nepali industrialist. The Nepali labourer, in contrast, has still to adjust to industrial time frames, and develop an 'industrial psychology' in a situation where his links with rural society and agricultural production remain strong.

The degree to which migrant Indian labour is relied upon to fill temporary positions in Nepali industries appears quite dramatic. As the following comments from industrialists make clear, some employers act out of a sense of near-desperation:

> Nepali labourers don't want to work hard. They think the work is too small. So we prefer to hire Indians . . . Once I had a lot of orders for my product. I had a deadline to supply them. The next morning when I came to the factory to tell them to produce so much, I was surprised to see no one here. They did not come because they said they were unhappy with the management. Such events happen every now and then when there are local festivals, harvest seasons or cultivation seasons . . . We have a hard time getting trained people, especially technical and management. We give them training but they run away. So it's better to bring people from India. Also the Nepalese steal our secrets: we cannot feel free to share important information with them because they lack loyalty to our firm and will take any chance to run away with it. They prefer to join the service of the government corporation.

The existence of a substantial expatriate workforce has obvious implications for Nepal's domestic employment situation—implications which are not lost on the government. There is also a loss to the national exchequer through repatriated earnings. But in the short run no workable solution save indirect expulsion (as we shall see in the case of garment industry) has emerged. Given Nepal's delicate economic relations with India, its long open border, and the treaty agreement which for many years has granted reciprocal passage and employment facilities, the government has few alternatives. It may try to exhort domestic entrepreneurs to 'hire Nepali' but this may well make little economic sense. A further possibility is government intervention to upgrade national training programmes so as to bring them more in line with the needs of the private sector.[10]

Further problems: fluctuating policies, weak co-ordination. Industrial entrepreneurs in Nepal often complain that a situation of constantly shifting policies makes it difficult for them to effect long-term planning. They also point to a lack of co-ordination between offices involved in licensing, loans, taxation and other crucial areas. This has led to what has been aptly termed the 'credibility gap' separating the private and public sectors (DRCG, 1984). Policies which are initiated by one administration may be discarded, reinterpreted or reinvented by the next in what appears a never-ending process of trial and error. The lack of continuity from one administration to the next confounds both the civil servant—who must implement a succession of new policies—and the entrepreneur—who must constantly readjust his priorities and production plans. As one mill owner put it, 'Sometimes I cannot sell rice or *dal* (lentils) in Nepal because of competition with India; but sometimes I cannot export my goods, even when the price is lower here, because the government won't let me. It's never the same.'

New policies are greeted with scepticism and suspicion, for everyone knows that before the ink is dry a new set of rules is likely to be promulgated. This reality, added to the fact that implementation of regulations and procurement of incentives is ultimately a very personalized matter, makes it difficult for entrepreneurs to equate

---

[10] See Zivetz, 1987. USAID intends to invest considerable funds over a five to ten year period to assist the Nepalese Government in providing training in appropriate management and technical fields for the private sector. My report discovered that, with few exceptions (notably the SBPP project, and some of the technical schools run by the United Mission to Nepal and SATA), most vocational and management training in Nepal is highly theoretical and tends to be focussed on public sector employment.

change with improvement. Because government policy changes so often, many entrepreneurs find it less risky invest in trade, where profits are quickly realisable and often more reliable; indeed, most large industrialists bank on trade as their economic mainstay. For such a strategy to work, however, resources and personpower may be spread more thinly in an effort to minimize risk. This is hardly an option for the small-scale industrialist with only limited access to capital.

Commenting upon the lack of co-ordination between ministries, one entrepreneur told me, 'The rules are so vague and open to interpretation that I can go to one office where they tell me I am exempted for five years from tax, but then I go to another office where they tell me to pay the sales tax because I am registered.' Such confusion is especially perplexing to the small industrialist who may not understand, let alone master, the intricacies of bureaucratic functioning.

The government is not unaware of the problem of poor co-ordination and contradictions between the policies and approaches of different ministries. A study recently carried out by the National Planning Commission investigated such problems in an effort to rectify them.

THE PUBLIC : PRIVATE SECTOR RELATIONSHIP:—
TWO CASE-STUDIES

Two of Nepal's major export industries—hand-knotted Tibetan-style carpets and ready-made garments—reveal many of the problems we have examined. They highlight not only the constraints facing the entrepreneur but also the complex issues the government faces as it attempts to promote export-oriented industries.

The carpet industry. In the period since the mid 1960s, hand-knotted carpets have become Nepal's second largest export commodity. While 10,458 square metres of carpet (valued at Rs 2,479,000) were exported in financial year 1972–73, this total had swollen to 329,518 square metres (valued at Rs 376,414,000) by 1985–86 (Trade Promotion Centre, 1986). Today, this sector employs an estimated one million people, or one-sixteenth of the entire population of the country, most of them on a part-time basis (*Gorkhapatra Sansthan*, March 21, 1986). The industry is in many ways ideally suited to Nepalese conditions: it is labour-intensive, offers farmers employment in the off-season, requires only rudimentary skills and a minimum of sophisticated technology, and is a good earner of hard currency. However, the success of the carpet industry has not been achieved without cost and difficulties—many of which still exist today.

For a start, the fluctuating supply and price of raw materials is a universally acknowledged handicap. The carpet industry has traditionally depended on wool from Tibet, and indeed it is this special type of wool that makes the Nepali carpet unique. Tibetan wool is imported by a few traders (most of them Newars) belonging to the Trans-Himalayan Traders Association. A senior member of the Tibetan business community explained the situation thus:

> In the old days the carpet producers were very few. At that time there was a time in the year when they [i.e., Trans-Himalayan Traders] used their monopoly power, and there was another time for us to use our monopoly power. So it was balanced. When there was an over-supply, we could say 'we are not buying', and we could stop buying until the price came down. Now that there are so many more carpet producers, the situation has changed. Now the monopoly is only in the hands of Trans-Himalayan Traders. So the shortage is permanent.

The Tibetans in Nepal, because of their refugee status, are not in a position to approach the Chinese directly. 'It's like an iron curtain,' commented one Tibetan producer. 'The Trans-Himalayan people have the right contacts, as they are the traditional traders.' As a result, the wool suppliers are able to realize very high margins; one producer talked in terms of 110 per cent profit margins on the sale of wool, although this was probably an exaggerated estimate.

But even for the prospering Trans-Himalayan Traders, business brings its own problems. China exports its high quality Tibetan wool on a barter basis; 70 per cent of the wool must be paid for in Nepalese goods, only 30 per cent in cash. For the Traders, this arrangement generates seemingly endless hassles:

> Now we are supplying soap and matches. About 80–90 per cent of our trade is agricultural products. The Tibetans want Nepali sugar, but sometimes the government doesn't want to supply sugar. Sometimes too they levy a heavy custom's duty so that our relationship with the Chinese becomes unworkable. We told them: 'If you want this wool supply to continue, you have to help us. You have to distinguish between this and

overseas trade, Indian trade, and even trade with mainland China.' Sometimes they listen, sometimes they don't.

By the early 1980s, it was apparent that expansion was being hindered by the uncertain supply of wool from Tibet. With World Bank support, the Nepal Wool Trading Company was established in 1983 to import wool from New Zealand and Australia. This was to be blended with Tibetan wool. The new trading company was owned by 27 shareholders, including carpet producers and government representatives. While it overcame initial difficulties in obtaining the necessary import licenses, the company proved open to abuse by those in its inner circle in a position to divert imported wool to the black market. As one carpet producer told me, 'You can always get wool. If Trans-Himalayan and Nepal Wool Company won't provide it, you can buy it at a higher price on the black.' The Nepal Wool Trading Company has also run into difficulties in persuading the government to release licenses and foreign exchange so as to ensure a steady flow of imported wool. One official explained government obduracy thus: 'We didn't give the license because we wanted to keep the ratio of New Zealand and Tibetan wool constant, and not flood the market.' This may represent the government's perspective, but such action hardly helps producers running well below capacity because of wool shortages. As one carpet manufacturer put it:

> Sometimes the government also has a lot of problems with foreign exchange, and importing New Zealand wool means using foreign exchange. But we are not accepting that. We are saying: 'Please give us one dollar of wool and we will bring you seven dollars on our export.' We usually discuss with the Commerce Secretary and the Industry Secretary. They are very understanding, but there is always a constraint, and things sometimes move very slow.

Several years ago, in an effort to encourage exports, the Nepalese Government established a rebate system whereby a percentage of the hard currency earned in exports was to be returned to the exporter after the order had been dispatched. This resulted in over-invoicing by carpet producers, and the scheme was eventually abandoned. The promised rebate was never paid.

Today, Nepali carpets appear to be facing increasing competition from Indian and Chinese machine-spun and hand-knotted carpets (which are of similar quality but less expensive).[11] Within Nepal, this industry has faced problems no less severe than those faced by other sectors. Yet in spite of these problems and limitations, carpet exports have managed to grow. If the carpet industry is to continue to provide Nepal with employment opportunities and hard currency, its welfare will have to be carefully monitored.

The garment industry: a missed opportunity. The Nepalese ready-made garment industry resembles the carpet industry in that it relies on imported raw materials (in this case from India), and, requiring only basic skills, offers significant employment opportunities. It, too, has shown significant growth over the last twenty-five years. In financial year 1972–73, Nepal exported garments equivalent to 10,458 square metres of cloth and valued at Rs 2,479,000; these were primarily handloom garments for the West German market. By 1985–86, the exports had grown to 329,518 metres, valued at Rs 376,414,000; a large proportion now took the form of garments made of Indian cotton, mainly destined for the United States (Trade Promotion Centre 1986). Today garments represent Nepal's largest export item to countries other than India.

In several respects, however, the garment industry differs from the carpet sector. For a start, it was initiated primarily by Indian entrepreneurs and, until recently, relied heavily on expatriate labour. Furthermore, because of the quota system imposed by the US Government in 1985, Nepalese governmental involvement in this sector has been more far-reaching. The expansion of this sector is tied directly to the ability of its entrepreneurs to acquire American quotas or to identify products and markets which fall outside the US quota system.

The rapid growth of the Nepalese garment industry began in 1983, when the United States reduced its quota for Indian garment imports, and Indian entrepreneurs began to move into neighbouring countries to take advantage of the absence of quotas there. They established factories in Bangladesh, Pakistan, Nepal and Sri Lanka, importing raw materials, machinery, managers and workers from India. These industries produced garments and also operated (covertly) as clearing-houses for garments produced in India, labelled in the exporting

---

[11] Several prominent carpet producers told the author they had been approached by American buyers. Because of raw material shortages and the quantities required by the buyers, the negotiations never got off the ground. The major buyers of Nepali carpets today are West Germany, Great Britain and other Western European countries.

country, and shipped out to the United States. While it is difficult to estimate the exact volume that was re-exported in this manner, there is no question that a sizeable proportion of the exports, particularly in the early days, was not produced in the country of ostensible origin.

In Nepal, the impact of these developments was highly visible. Large empty mansions in Kathmandu (many of them palaces from the Rana era) suddenly sprouted signboards proclaiming them to be garment factories; inside, lights burned all night to facilitate round-the-clock production. Certain parts of the city were suddenly populated by newly arrived Indian labourers. Customs buildings bulged with shipments of garments bound for the United States, while government offices busily registered new companies. Most of the new garment concerns were registered as small-scale, though whether in fact they met such criteria is doubtful. By law they were compelled to register in the name of a Nepalese national. It was common practice, therefore, for Indian entrepreneurs to engage a sleeping partner. This individual was generally paid a flat fee for his name, and was often only peripherally involved in running the business. One observer estimated that while a sleeping partner might receive Rs 5000 per month on average, his Indian partner might well be clearing Rs 500,000 per month, much of it to be banked in India.

The rapidly conceived nature of these partnerships led, in many cases, to discord between Nepali and Indian partners. As one observer expressed the problem, 'The Indian partners intended to run the factory as a cottage industry for five years and then run away to leave the Nepali partner to pay the taxes.'

Some enterprising Nepalis also took their cue from the Indians, and opened their own factories. But Indian domination of this sector continued: of an estimated 145 firms that were operating at the height of the sector's production in the mid 1980's, roughly one hundred were estimated to be under *de facto* Indian control.

In September 1985, the United States imposed a quota on many of the items being exported from Nepal, imposing quotas on the other countries of the region at the same time. Nepal reacted by requesting the United States not to impose further quotas.[12] However, these were imposed on other items, and by the end of 1986 only about one-third of the originally registered factories were still functioning (most of

[12] While the President of Bangladesh went to the US in person to deliver a similar message and negotiate, Nepal sent a letter inviting US government officials and garment importers to visit the country, which they did in January 1986.

them far below capacity). The bulk of the Indian workers had fled back home or to other countries, and the export of ready-made garments from Nepal dropped far below even the allotted quota. What lay behind this sudden collapse?

After the quotas were imposed, the Nepalese Government had held back their distribution to eligible firms for three months as it attempted to sort out some method of allocation. One senior official I spoke to described governmental thinking thus:

> When we got the quota we had a hard time deciding how to allocate it. The firms were all so different from each other that we could not find any common parameters. So we said, all right, let us just give them ten per cent of their installed capacity, and then we released that much. Now we think that those Indians who have come to Nepal to make fast money will not be staying here any more. Once this quota has been allocated to them and is exported, they are sure to leave the country. Then the Nepalis, and even Indians who have come to Nepal with a long-term investment interest, will remain. From 1987 onwards, we expect their share of the quota will be much higher. And in the meantime we will try to explore ways and means of exporting non-quota items to the US and finding European markets.

While the government was deciding how the quota should be allocated, things went from bad to worse from the producers' perspective. In a confusing and sometimes contradictory attempt to 'encourage' Nepali employment and entrepreneurship in this new industry, the government issued a rush of new rules requiring the replacement of Indian workers by Nepali labour in the garment sector. Quotas were to be allocated quarterly on this basis as well as on past production capacity. In the event, producers lost money when they were unable to meet delivery dates stipulated in the letter of credit arrangements they had made with their American importers.

The labour issue became a very sensitive aspect of the rapid rise of this industry. In 1984, only nine per cent of the labourers in garment factories were Nepali. Ethnic conflict erupted in the capital as a result of the visible presence of Indian labourers; the government was also disturbed by the outflow of wages to India. In 1985, the government developed a formula whereby the ratio of Nepali to Indian employees was to increase every year and twenty per cent of the machines in any factory were to be set aside for the purpose of training Nepali workers. By 1986, 60 per cent of all labourers in garment factories were

Nepali.[13] But success in this area was counterbalanced by the fact that insufficient quotas were limiting the employment capacity of even the largest factories. As one entrepreneur recalled, 'I trained 279 Nepali workers, mostly women, but now I have only 59, as I don't have enough work and many have run away to other factories. What's the use of making those rules if we can't employ the labourers?'

On top of this, the government meted out quotas for garments in an arbitrary, haphazard manner (with 'source and force' playing their customary role) and in so doing drove all but the largest manufacturers out of the industry. While the effort to induce Indian entrepreneurs and labourers to leave Nepal was effective, many Nepali entrepreneurs suffered as a result. One Nepali entrepreneur described his plight thus:

> The quotas are issued at four month intervals, and we never know whether we'll get it the next time or not. How can we plan? How can we make commitments to our buyers? My overhead has been high because sometimes I have cutters, tailors and machines sitting idle, but if I send them away what am I going to do if the quota comes in the next quarter?

With inventories piling up in Kathmandu factories and orders undelivered in New York, Nepali manufacturers began to lose their credibility abroad, and orders tapered off. Many of the Indians who had sunk capital and time into the industry in Nepal moved on to other countries where conditions were most favourable.

In addition to the confusion over quotas, manufacturers were plagued by a taxation structure which, affecting imported raw materials and exports alike, raised the F.O.B. price of garments to uncompetitive levels. To take one example: Nepal had enjoyed real advantages over India in the export of garments made of rayon; for a start, its US quota was more generous. In 1985, in a bid to reap its share of this profitable segment of the industry, the government decided to tax the import of rayon fabric from India. It imposed a seven per cent import tax, a 20 per cent sales tax, and an export tax. Together, these served to price the finished products out of the market; the export of rayon garments from Nepal has virtually ceased. The frustration suffered by entrepreneurs in this sector is evident in the following comment:

---

[13] The figure comes from a personal conversation with C. Tiwari, who cited a study done by the Commerce Department.

There is a lack of co-ordination between ministries. The Department of Industry says: go ahead and develop your industry; but it withholds the quota; then the Ministry of Finance slaps on a high tax for our raw materials, so we cannot keep our prices competitive. Then we face a lot of red tape at customs because they don't want to follow the rules. I need a full-time person just to run around for the government work.

One large-scale Marwari industrialist (whose father was in the cloth trade with Nepal) presented the problem differently: 'Other countries like Korea, Taiwan and Hong Kong have successfully built up their ready-made garment industry based on imported cloth. Why is His Majesty's Government so nationalistic? They are more concerned about socio-political issues than economic development.' It appears that what this industrialist termed 'nationalistic' concerns—the effort to reduce the visibility of Indian entrepreneurs and labourers—may have overruled economic considerations. In the process, many Nepali entrepreneurs without the resources to sit out the storm were squeezed out along with the Indian investors. The government used quotas as an incentive to encourage the employment of Nepali labourers; the private sector established and supported training courses to augment the supply of skilled indigenous labour. But poor administration and counter-productive taxation regulations diminished the scope for Nepali entrepreneurs to employ such labour; intra- and inter-ministerial inconsistencies and contradictions compounded the problem, placing brakes on the development of this industry.

Recent statistics indicate a six per cent fall in the export of ready-made garments between 1983–84 and 1984–85. However, the figures for 1985–86 showed a 34 per cent rise (Trade Promotion Centre, 1986). Today, most of Kathmandu's garment factories are owned by wealthy, established business people, many of them from the Marwari community. What seems to have happened is that those with access to 'source and force' have cornered the quota; it can be anticipated that the growth of this sector will continue as long as the quotas and the current continuity in regulations hold. Even so, the situation is hardly a healthy one. According to one garment manufacturer I spoke to, most factories in this sector are able to function for only two months out of every twelve, and many remain dependent on Indian labour.

CONCLUSIONS

While our discussion has not attempted to present a complete picture of the politico-economic environment in which Nepalese industrialization is taking place, it has voiced some of the perceptions and concerns of the private entrepreneurs involved in the process. To that extent, it has reflected a certain bias in favour of the private sector. An attempt has also been made to throw light on the relationship between the private and public sectors in Nepal, and to relate this to geopolitical and socio-cultural factors—some immutable, others part of Nepal's historical inheritance, and yet others amenable to change.

As the quotation cited at the beginning of this chapter argues persuasively, the private sector offers a context in which creativity, innovation, and leadership can emerge. In Nepal, this can be seen to be taking place, albeit painfully, and at the expense of traditional modes of behaviour. The uneasy relationship between traditional patronage networks employed by the ruling élite and the demands of 'rationalized' capitalist modes of production has given rise to a situation in which the two main actors in the drama—the public and private sectors—seem unable to synchronize their efforts. The flourishing black market, large-scale smuggling and corruption appear to be unfortunate by-products of what is, ultimately, a tussle for control. But while such tendencies may have the short-term impact of holding industrialization back, they are perhaps necessary evils which may eventually push the process forward towards acceptable solutions.

The major issue facing industrial entrepreneurs in Nepal today is access to raw materials—particularly imported ones. In addition, entrepreneurs protest that government policies keep changing; that promised facilities are meted out on the basis of 'source and force' and ad hocism rather than on the basis of elementary justice. The government, for its part, has reacted to diminishing reserves of foreign currency by allowing the registration of a disproportionate number of industries dependent on imported raw materials; it has also placed obstacles in the path of export-oriented industries which could be expected to open up new sources of foreign exchange.

The official standpoint is that the government has extended quite attractive incentives to entrepreneurs, only to see these exploited and misused. From the entrepreneur's perspective, however, such misutilization is part and parcel of 'entrepreneurial' spirit in action: the natural tendency of the enterprising individual to locate loopholes in rules and thereby enhance his profits. To expect otherwise is perhaps naive.

While Nepal's evolving industrial policy has certainly clarified the respective roles of the public and private sectors in achieving national economic goals, it is evident that crisis management, rather than consistent, rationalized planning, has dominated government thinking. When one set of policies appears to be failing because of misutilization, the government typically changes the policies rather than punish the guilty; in the process the innocent, too, are made to suffer. Given these realities, industry hardly emerges as an attractive career option for the generation of better-trained men and women entering Nepal's job market today. It is small wonder that a secure job in government continues to be the first choice of such individuals, despite the lure of higher incomes in the private sector and the country's pressing need for a stronger entrepreneurial corps. Government posts, however, are becoming increasingly scarce in a situation of budgetary constraint, and a certain inflow of young people into business is evident, particularly in the capital. This trend cannot but help to strengthen the industrial sector—and improve its standing at home and abroad.

What steps might the Nepalese authorities take to improve relations between the public and private sectors and ease the lot of the private entrepreneur? The problem is clearly compounded by a business culture still defined in large measure by traditional élite perceptions and behaviour. And, of course, it is Nepal's ruling élite which has the most to lose from radical change. Perhaps the public sector holds the key to the problem; perhaps basic change in its relationship with private industry hinges upon the degree to which it is prepared to show flexibility. As one spokesman for the private sector put it:

> They are trying to control us and hold us back because they think the pie is so small, and if they give us too big a share, what will they have left? But I told them: 'Give us a bigger piece of the pie now, and you will see that in time there will be a bigger pie for all of us, with more to go around.'

For this to happen, however, those in positions of political authority should be willing to relinquish some of their powers and join hands with the entrepreneur. The ruling élite should also avoid creating circumstances in which the untrustworthiness of the business community becomes a self-fulfilling prophecy. The same private sector spokesman described the dangers inherent in creating 'a generation of young people who must learn first and foremost how to grease the system. If they know how to do that, they will be successful. What kind of a business ethic is that?' Such attitudes, of course, are not changed through legislation alone. In a sense, the pioneer entrepreneurs of today (whatever methods they might employ) are establishing precedents for the future internal development of the industrial sector and its relations with the government. But this they cannot do independently. Only when the private sector is widely perceived—both within the government and outside it—as a partner in the development process rather than as a corrupting influence can industrialization be expected really to take off.

At another level, beyond the divisions that separate public and private sector, there exists a subtler dimension of converging interests. If the government promulgates policies but closes its eyes to those who misuse them, who, in this situation, is the villain, and who the victim? It is hard to say. What is clear is that civil servants certainly give the nod to corrupt private sector activities. Under the circumstances, change will not come easily; inefficiency and red-tape provide plentiful opportunities for personal gain—whether by private entrepreneurs or by civil servants. The element of collaboration between bureaucrat and private businessman should not be overlooked in a discussion which has focussed primarily on the factors that separate them. As long as the political will to clamp down hard on profiteering is weak, those in positions of power (in both sectors) will continue to profit while others—small-scale entrepreneurs, consumers, the national economy in general—will continue to pay the price.[14]

---

[14] At the time of writing, the Nepalese Government was negotiating a multi-million dollar 'structural adjustment loan' with the World Bank. Among other things, the loan promised to increase the quantum of foreign currency available for the purchase of overseas raw materials. Whether the loan will function as a stick or a carrot within the parameters we have been examining will be interesting to observe.

Chapter Five

The Entrepreneur and the Enterprise

The reasonable man adapts himself to the world. The unreasonable man attempts to adapt the world to himself. Therefore, all progress depends on unreasonable men.

—George Bernard Shaw

In Chapter III the socio-cultural and historical roots of entrepreneurship were examined in terms of the emergence of various entrepreneurial communities. This approach assumed the existence of identifiable organizing principles within specific ethnic groups which provide inhibiting or catalyzing substrates upon which economic behaviour is based. We shall now take a closer look at a cross-section of industrial entrepreneurs and their enterprises in an effort to deepen our understanding of these substrates and how entrepreneurs have responded to them.

Western role models of management have been exported wholesale to many Third World countries. In the past, this transfer was effected through colonial ventures; today it is achieved (more subtly perhaps, but with a similar impact) through foreign-sponsored projects, advisors, contracts and private investors touting 'transferred technology' in the name of economic development. Such technology also requires transferred management practices. Since these interventions are externally derived, they are often inconsistent with, and foreign to, indigenous modes of production. Aharoni (1977) suggests the following analogy: while in a developed country context, the innovator may simply add one brick to a wall, in the case of a developing country, the entrepreneur is faced with building a brick wall where none existed before, with labour that has never seen bricks.

In Nepal, the indigenous culture has only limited reference points to inform the structuring and operation of modern industries. Traditional modes of production and exchange offer only partial behavioural antecedents for entrepreneurship and management based on modern technological and organizational principles. As we have already seen, productive activity in Nepal's primarily agricultural economy was based on reciprocal, kinship, barter and patronage relationships involving some equalization of resources at the community level. Economic innovation was considered deviant and, as a result, has been confined to minority or socially marginalized communities. Not surprisingly, the relationship between the private sector and Nepal's ruling élites has been characterized by tension between the traditional forms of economic relationship and those required by capitalist modes of production.

Broehl (1982) suggests a paradigm which, in its attempt to explain management practices among developing country entrepreneurs, is useful for an understanding of the management styles of Nepali entrepreneurs. According to Broehl, the entrepreneur has three options when he makes management-related decisions. One alternative is for him to allow his cultural background to dominate business decisions, often with less than satisfactory results. Or he can mix traditional and modern management practices, in the process rendering himself vulnerable to indecisive or inconsistent decision-making. A third option before him is to switch over completely to modern management strategies. The last choice raises further problems, among them that of coexisting with bureaucratic institutions and tradition-bound indigenous labour. There are inherent contradictions (or at least conflicts) between the entrepreneur's culturally ascribed belief and behaviour systems and modern (i.e., Westernized) management practices. Because existing socio-cultural codes appear strongly at odds with those required by efficient, modern industry, it becomes quickly apparent that industrial entrepreneurship is not simply a process of technological, market, or product innovation. It is also about a process of cultural redefinition. Just how this conflict can be resolved is revealed in the operational and management styles of entrepreneurs themselves. Management styles can be examined on a continuum which extends from the traditional to the modern. No matter where the entrepreneur falls on this continuum, his relationship to technology and management is unlikely to be free of tension. Nor is an 'optimal' management style readily identifiable.

Broehl's model, or continuum, is also helpful in describing the factors that influence an individual to become an industrial entrepreneur. At one end of the continuum, such a choice may be made because of a tradition of family involvement in business. In this case, real industrial entrepreneurship is measured by the individual's ability to adapt to new markets and introduce new modes of production or marketing. At the other end of the continuum are those individuals for whom the choice of industry represents a break with the past: the decision to become an industrialist is, here, a totally new and unfamiliar one.

This model is not invoked to suggest a 'no-win' scenario, although the facts indicate that there are limited victories to be had in industry, at least in the short run. Rather it is employed as a way of classifying and understanding the range of choices and management strategies before industrial entrepreneurs in Nepal. Occupational choice and management styles will now be explored in more detail, utilizing Broehl's continuum as a guide and reference point.

The discussion which follows is based on figures I derived from interviews with sixty-six Nepalese industrialists representing a cross-section of the entrepreneurial community. This data spans industries of varying sizes and types, located in different geographical settings and owned by individuals (both men and women) of varied ethnic origin. Given the smallness of my sample, my generalizations will have to be made with caution. It is hoped, however, that the data will provide some useful insights, and act as a base for future research.

In the organization of the data, size of industry is an important criterion. The Nepali Government's stipulations regarding size categories of industry (discussed in Chapter IV) are followed here.[1] To qualify for government benefits, industries must be registered; there was a total of 4884 registered private sector industries in Nepal at the time of the 1980 National Census (CBS, 1984). Non-registered industries, including micro- and some small-scale industries, may well have numbered as many as four hundred thousand (ADB, 1984).[2]

The data presented in these pages can usefully be compared with findings from other developing countries. Several recent studies of

---

[1] Since small industries have received generous tax and importation concessions in the past, many industries which in fact exceeded governmental parameters for a small industry were registered as such. All industries employing over 25 permanent labourers, even if registered as small, have been reclassified as medium for our purposes.
[2] While an industry may possess the stipulated fixed assets to be classified as a small industry, the owner is required to register it only if he needs government assistance. There is, therefore no way of counting the exact number of cottage industries in the country; these numbers are in fact informed guesses.

interest include the research on personal entrepreneurial characteristics carried out by McBer and others (1987) in Malawi, Ecuador and India. There is also the overview of small enterprises in select Asian countries conducted by Sharma (1979). These may provide interesting points of reference for the data from Nepal.

THE ENTREPRENEUR: CHOOSING A BUSINESS CAREER

While business may be the occupation of choice for an increasing number of individuals in the developed world, many small and micro industrialists in the developing world, and Nepal in particular, appear to arrive at their station in life by default. In an environment where the risks are high, the rewards uncertain and the family the only cushion against disaster (a family which itself is often dependent on the self-same business for employment and sustenance), what motivates an individual to engage in business—and in industry in particular? In Nepal, the entrepreneur ventures forth into unknown territory, inspired by few role models, and with unclear signposts guiding him to his raw materials, technology, technical expertise and market. There is also a labyrinthine bureaucracy whose rules and regulations shift according to the whims of individual bureaucrats and administrations. Under the circumstances, successful entrepreneurship depends on a combination of serendipity, creativity, profitable kinship links and an ability to work the system; indeed, these factors appear just as vital as access to modern management practices and technical expertise.

As we have seen, business avocations are perceived in Nepal to offer far less security than does traditional agriculture.[3] Nepali peasants generally prefer the security of land ownership (no matter how small the unit) to non-agricultural entrepreneurship or industrial employment; given their poor access to capital, peasants can hardly be blamed for their caution. Traditional artisans, who tend to come from the lowest castes, lack the confidence, information, and status necessary to expand their ventures or contend successfully with the bureaucracy. The trading community, who represent a small critical mass of business expertise in the country, have, to a large degree, chosen to expand their trading networks rather than invest in the manufacturing sector.

---

[3] An estimated 93 per cent of the population of Nepal comprises subsistence farmers. These may produce basic household necessities such as cloth, furniture, and simple implements for their own use, although increasingly such items are purchased from local bazaars and markets.

What factors, then, act to push an individual away from 'safe', inherited occupational tracks and into industry? The opportunities opened up by development aid; the extension of transportation; the expansion of the bureaucracy; a rising tourist sector: these are some of the influences which appear to be at work, opening new markets and possibilities. At the same time, the reality of increasing landlessness and unemployment in rural areas has acted as a stick, compelling the creation of a number of first-generation entrepreneurs.

Non-agricultural employment in Nepal has traditionally focused on jobs in the civil service. Common wisdom has it that an important reason for educating children—particularly sons—is to secure them a government job. The status and security of such employment (not to mention the potential for 'earning' on the side) has made this route preferable to the risky one of entrepreneurship. Except in the case of families who have built their wealth on business, a son from a landed rural or otherwise upwardly mobile family who fails to secure a government job may then be set up in business—but very much as a second choice. Under such circumstances, it is considered desirable to have at least one family member inside the government to help promote the fledgling enterprise.

Figure 5.1 provides a breakdown of the responses of my sample of sixty-six entrepreneurs to the question, 'Why did you go into industry?' These responses indicate that both 'push' and 'pull' factors are at work. The discussions which followed the posing of this question revealed, in most cases, either that the entrepreneur had inherited the business or that he had chosen it as a result of dissatisfaction with his previous employment. The majority of the entrepreneurs who said they preferred business to government employment had held positions as teachers, civil servants, or traders before taking up their current enterprise. Frustrated with income levels, the bureaucracy, their boss, or the lack of acknowledgement they had received, these entrepreneurs were united by a common theme: the desire for more individual freedom, more recognition and a larger income.

Two of my informants had been teachers before starting their businesses; they had felt frustrated by the salary levels and wanted more recognition for their efforts—recognition they believed would flow from a new business career. Another respondent, the manager of the largest knitting concern in Pokhara, made the point that when he died, 'People will remember that I was the one who started this industry in this town, that I gave employment to so many people.' Yet

194 / *Private Enterprise and the State in Modern Nepal*

FIGURE 5.1

Reasons for Entering into Industry by Size of Industry

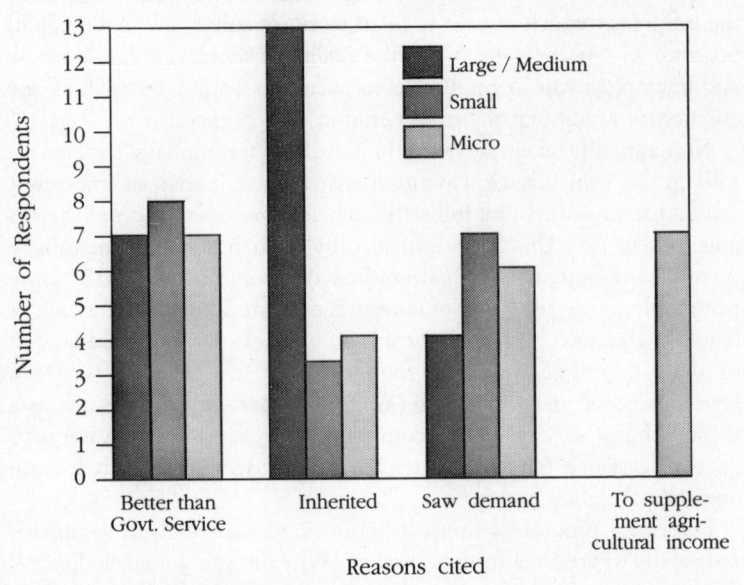

another complained bitterly that when he had been in the government, his boss simply could not understand his commitment and dedication to the job: 'Not only was he [the boss] not technically competent, his real objective in the job was to line his pockets and advance his position.' Now settled in business, this respondent felt he had more freedom: 'No one can tell me what to do, and I feel I am really helping the country in my work.'

Another industrialist who, unusually, combined his business career with a post as a highly placed civil servant, told me he had started his agro-based industry 'to help the farmers'. This individual clearly relished his maverick status as one able to play both sides of the game and exert leverage by virtue of his dual occupation.

There certainly appears to be a measure of cognitive dissonance in these responses. Feeling pushed out of jobs with more social status, an individual attempts to rationalize his decision to engage in business by invoking higher purposes: helping people, or seeking greater personal freedom. These findings are consistent with conclusions reached by

Brockhaus (1982) on the basis of an extensive review of studies made of the factors influencing the decision to go into business. Simply put, Brockhaus concludes that a person out of work or dissatisfied with his current work is the one most likely to make the move into business. Harris' (1981) study of Nigerian entrepreneurs supports this contention. These findings indicate something equally important, however: that non-farm agricultural employment (even in unrelated occupations such as administration, teaching, and military service) can constitute a stepping stone to business.

Those who, in Figure 5.1, entered business as an adjunct to agriculture came primarily from artisan castes. Like many small farmers, these individuals found it difficult to support their families from their shrinking landholdings. Mr Sarki and his brothers, to take one example, had been born into the cobblering caste. They moved to the city and set up adjoining shoe-making units. The family continues to farm; with the additional income generated by the shoe-making business, they can now make ends meet.

Mr Damai, from the tailoring caste, left his brothers to look after his tiny plot of land in the hills and moved his entire family to the Terai, where with the help of a distant relative, he opened a small tailoring outlet. His wife and older children work with him.

Family background. As Figure 5.1 indicates, the majority of large- and medium-scale industrialists are in business because their families are in business. It is interesting to note that many respondents in this category were deferential about their father's entrepreneurial ability ('He is the one who started all of this,' and so forth), even where it was clear that it was the respondent who had pioneereed the industry. Nonetheless, tutelage by the father or family patriarch in the ways of business appears to have fixed the choice of career for most respondents here. For these entrepreneurs, business was for all practical purposes an inevitable occupational choice and one for which they had been groomed since childhood.

The choice to enter into business appears, then, to follow Broehl's (1982) continuum, ranging from traditional or inherited obligatory options to conscious decisions by those for whom industry appears an alternative to an unsatisfactory or frustrating previous occupation. In between are the caste-based artisans, some of whom part company with their traditional trades to move into new fields of business promising new opportunities.

In Figures 5.2 and 5.3 the occupational status of my respondents' fathers and grandfathers is presented. As might be expected, a family

FIGURE 5.2

Father's Primary Occupation by Size of Industry

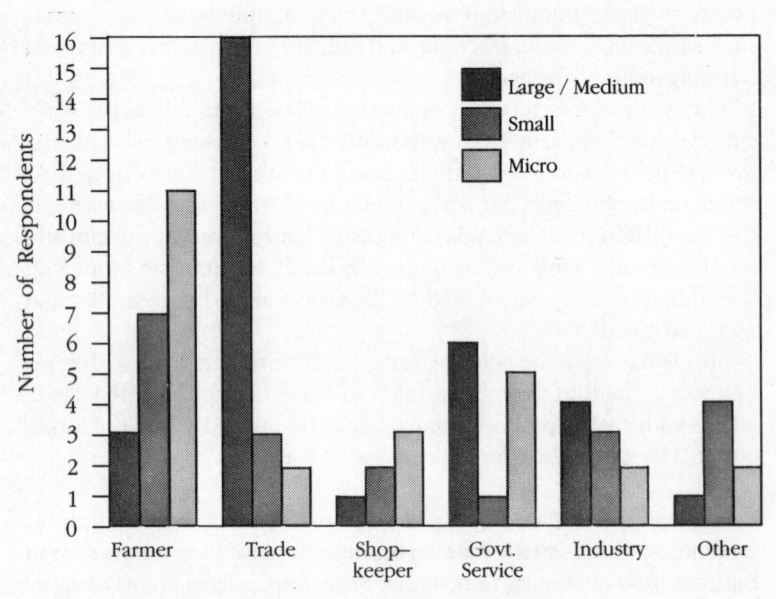

NOTE: 'Trade' includes both internal and external categories.

tradition of trade, industry and shopkeeping (in other words, an extended experience of business-related activities) is positively related to current size of industry. The majority of large- and medium-scale entrepreneurs come from trading families, as do some small-scale businessmen. Micro-level entrepreneurs, in contrast, originate from agricultural backgrounds. Sixty-seven per cent of the large- and medium-scale entrepreneurs in my sample reported trade and industry as their father's primary occupation. Indeed, many were still engaged in trade—although the nature and source of the goods had, of course, changed over the years. Another twenty-one per cent of respondents in these categories reported that their fathers had been in service positions. Many had held prestigious posts which allowed the sons important contacts and access to resources, thereby facilitating the

FIGURE 5.3

Grandfather's Primary Occupation by Size of Industry

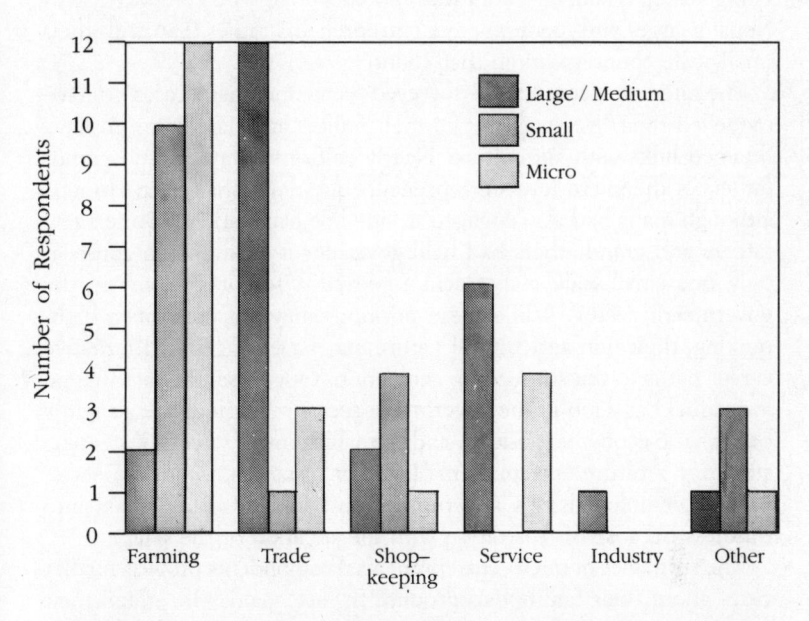

establishment and operation of the new generation's business endeavour. From this it appears, that inherited skills, capital, and contacts may play a key role in the success of large- and medium-scale enterprises.

The occupational background of small entrepreneurs is more varied. The data indicates that most of these come from a background in which there was a slow shift away from agriculture (the primary occupation of over fifty per cent of the respondents' grandfathers and of roughly forty per cent of their fathers) into other occupations. None of the grandfathers of the small entrepreneurs in my sample had been industrialists, but the next generation had witnessed a shift in this direction. Trade, which hardly figures as a primary occupation for the preceding two generations, is the predominant secondary occupation of fathers in the sample. Thus, the factors predisposing small-scale entrepreneurs towards business seem less tied to family traditions than was the case with bigger-scale entrepreneurs.

My findings offer certain points of contrast with the results of other research in this area. Sharma's (1979) study of small-scale entrepreneurs from six Asian countries found most to have come from trading or business families. Benefiting from a longer tradition of private sector commercial endeavour, Sharma's entrepreneurs in Hong Kong, Thailand and India should perhaps be compared with Nepal's large- and medium-scale entrepreneurs rather than with their small-scale counterparts in that country.

The micro entrepreneurs I surveyed seemed, in many cases, to have modelled their lives on those of their fathers and, like them, to have retained links with agriculture. Nearly half of the fathers and grandfathers of the micro-level entrepreneurs questioned had been farmers, although many had also engaged in side-line occupations. Quite a few fathers and grandfathers had held government positions; in contrast, only one small-scale respondent reported a recent ancestor in the government sector. While these positions may not have been high-ranking, their non-agricultural nature may have suggested alternative career paths to the succeeding generation. Of course, the fact that an individual has a job in the government sector might indicate a slightly better socio-economic position, and one which might serve as a stepping stone for a future entrepreneur. In other instances, the micro entrepreneur, employed in a government post initially, had shifted into business because of frustration with the situation or the salary.

The surnames of micro-entrepreneurial respondents provide further clues about their family background. In fact, many who stated their fathers and grandfathers to have been 'farmers' were clearly of artisan caste origin.[4] For such individuals, agriculture was typically the family's economic mainstay. The fathers and grandfathers of these caste-defined artisans—tailors, cobblers, metalworkers, butchers, and so on—would have been engaged in *jajmani* relationships with higher caste clients. (The *jajmani* relationship between local artisans and the landed gentry involved payment by the latter of fixed amounts of payment in kind [usually grain] in return for specific services.) However, the artisan was generally involved in agriculture as well—as a small landholder, sharecropper, or landless labourer.

The spread of capitalist production relations in Nepal's agrarian economy, while very far from complete or evenly spread, has weakened traditional *jajmani* relationships. With their inherited skills, the sons

---

[4] In such cases, respondents often tried to disguise their low-caste status: some had even changed their names.

and daughters of artisans are perhaps more likely to venture into cottage industry than are their non-artisan fellows. The edge these individuals might possess in terms of entrepreneurial skills should not, however, be overestimated. It is only those able to adapt traditional skills to the needs of a rapidly changing market and reconcile themselves to new modalities of exchange who have been able to establish viable businesses. Two small case-studies illustrate the point. They relate to two members of the Tamrakar, or coppersmith caste living in Pokhara. They both took out bank loans under the World Bank scheme (described in Chapter IV) designed to assist small businesses. Mr M. works alone and continues to make his pots and religious ornaments by hand. He complains that it is difficult to get enough raw materials, that the *sahuji* (shopkeeper) so fixes the price that he sometimes sells his goods without compensation for his labour, and that demand for his products fluctuates because people no longer buy metal cooking and water-carrying vessels as they used to. Mr M. seems to regret his move into independent manufacturing—he preferred his former relationship with the *sahuji*, who provided him with his raw materials and gave him orders directly. It made him feel less vulnerable. Mr R., in contrast, invested his loan in machinery. He now uses this to produce brass and copper handicrafts for the tourist market as well as vessels which are still used for ritual purposes. He does not procure his raw materials from dealers (whom both producers decry as exploiters), but recycles used pots and utensils which he buys from households which no longer have use for the heavy vessels. Mr R. has hired four Indian technicians; his sons also work in the business. He has three retail buyers for his products and is doing quite well.

These examples reinforce the point that traditional expertise by no means guarantees successful entrepreneurship. Caste artisans who have successfully ventured into the urban market have done so because of their ability to marry entrepreneurial vision and management abilities with their inherited skills and technical deftness.

Bhattarai (1986) took a detailed look at sixty-six participants in training programmes for small-scale entrepreneurs conducted in Nepal in 1985–86. He found the fathers of the participants to be more or less evenly distributed between farming, government service, business and 'other categories'. These findings suggest that industry may now be a more acceptable, and accessible, option for young entrants from a range of backgrounds than it was in the past.

Returning to my own sample of entrepreneurs, to what extent are family members other than fathers and grandfathers involved in business? Figure 5.4, which sets out my findings, suggests the existence of a role model within the family for roughly two-thirds of my sample.

FIGURE 5.4

Other Family Members in Business

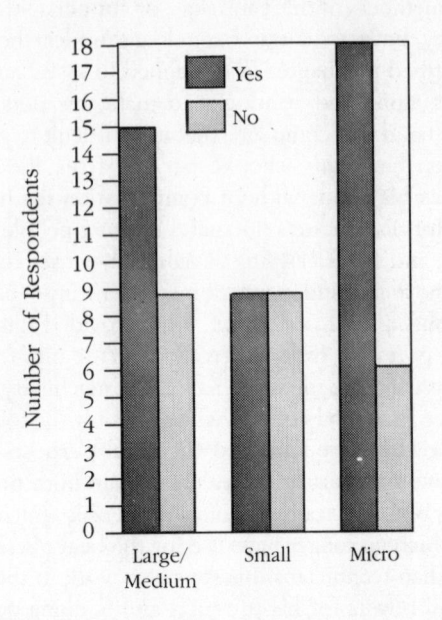

Micro entrepreneurs whose parents may not be in business often receive crucial initial support, encouragement and training from an uncle or some other close relative. An example of this is Mr Nepali, who runs a successful tailoring factory in Bhaktapur. He manufactures jeans and fashionable shirts for the Kathmandu market. Nepali learned his skill from his mother who is a tailor (*damai*) by caste, but he got his start in business with the assistance and encouragement of his maternal uncle, Mr Damai. Mr Damai used to sew clothes for farmers once a year at the *desain* or festival time (when it is customary to buy new garments). In return he received a fixed amount of grain. When imported garments began to flow into his locality, Damai found his services in decreasing demand. Five years ago he decided to move to Bhaktapur and open a small tailoring shop there. When his nephew,

Nepali, married, the young man realized that his land inheritance would not be enough to support his family. So Nepali moved to Bhaktapur and joined his uncle's shop. Nepali worked for his uncle for a few years, then had the idea of opening a small clothing factory. With his inherited skills and the experience gained from working with his uncle, Nepali was able to successfully establish his factory. Today, his unit employs ten people, about half of whom come from his own family.

The findings presented here are consistent with McBer's (1987) data from three other developing countries. Here, approximately 75 per cent of the 161 small-scale entrepreneurs interviewed had other family members who had started businesses. This sample was broken down into 'successful' and 'average' entrepreneurs in an attempt to determine which demographic and personality variables might most strongly account for successful entrepreneurship. The 'successful' entrepreneurs in the McBer sample were more likely than the 'average' category to have relatives or close friends who had themselves started businesses.

An interesting finding highlighted by Figure 5.4 is that more than one-third of large and medium entrepreneurs and roughly half of small entrepreneurs did not have other family members in business. However, discussions during my interviews suggest that the majority of these respondents had at least one relative, however distant, in the civil service. In many cases, the respondent referred to this usefully placed relation as the person who had helped him to start his own business.

Acquisition of skills. Figure 5.5 sets out the responses to the question, 'Where did you acquire the skills to go into this business?' It is revealing that the small and micro entrepreneurs interpreted this question as referring to technical skills, while entrepreneurs from large- and medium-scale concerns tended to include managerial skills in their responses as well. The majority of large, medium and micro industrialists seem to have acquired their skills within a family framework. For the first category, the critical skills are of a conceptual, managerial nature; the challenge lies in assembling the managerial and technical infrastructure necessary to create an industry responsive to new demands. Interestingly, many small-scale entrepreneurs depend on employed technicians. The owner's role here is primarily managerial, particularly in the case of the more sophisticated manufacturing enterprises, where an entrepreneur often does not know how

FIGURE 5.5

Source of Skill Training for Current
Industry by Size of Industry

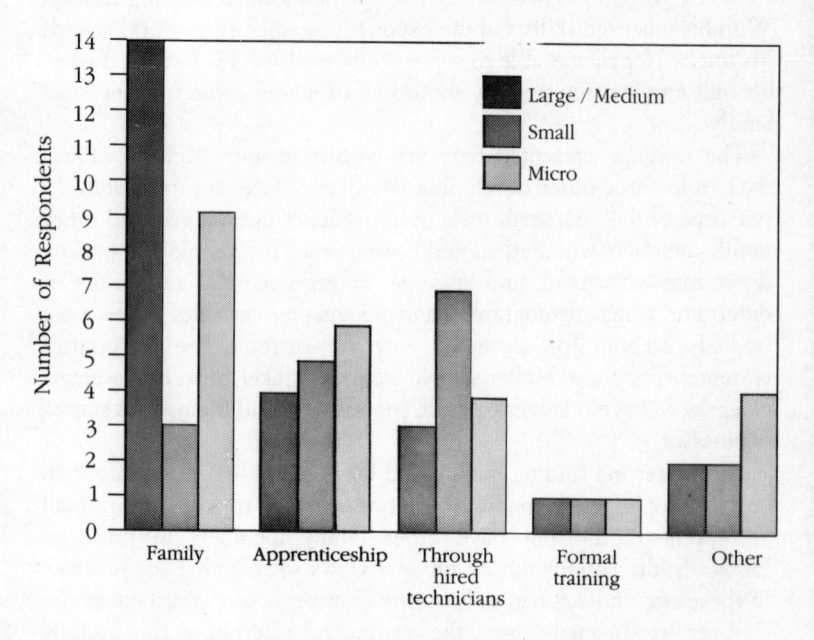

[Bar chart: Number of Respondents by source (Family, Apprenticeship, Through hired technicians, Formal training, Other) for Large/Medium, Small, and Micro industries]

to operate or maintain his own machinery. Economics of scale in small industries, together with a rapid turnover of skilled labour, leaves the small manager-cum-entrepreneur particularly vulnerable; without the support of his paid experts, he can be rendered helpless.

The micro entrepreneur typically doubles as manager and technician. For him, the essential skills are technical in nature, and may include stitching, weaving, carving, soldering and similar skills. These skills may have been handed down, or they may have been acquired during work for another firm. For such individuals, effective entrepreneurship lies in their ability to adapt their existing skills to meet the needs of a constantly changing market—as the case-study of the two Pokhara coppersmiths underlines.

Roughly 25 per cent of the small and micro industrialists I interviewed had gained their skills while working for someone else. Informal apprenticeship of this type appears to be an increasingly important factor in Nepal. Practical experience is clearly a key element in building confidence, contacts and skills; working in someone else's business, an employee gains a chance to observe and learn key aspects of the businesses—at little personal financial risk.

The 'imitative' entrepreneur is, however, no mere copy-cat. Choosing to venture out on his own, this individual is expressing something akin to the daring of the 'innovative' entrepreneur, the individual who launches a first-of-its-kind industry in a specific locality. The decision to set up a fresh venture (even if it is very similar to the one he has worked in) does involve an element of risk-taking; and entrepreneurial ability is essential if the new venture is to succeed.

The data presented in Figure 5.5 suggest that entrepreneurs rarely gain from formal training programmes the insights and practical skills they obtain from friends, relations or their own experience. At least one other study corroborates this impression (Nihan and Jourdain, 1978).

'Imitative' entrepreneurship: opportunities and dangers. In an environment with few entrepreneurial role models and little market information, imitation plays a key role in determining an individual's choice of industrial venture. 'Hari next door seems to be profiting in his soap-making operation; I think I'll try too;' such reasoning seems to be extensively at work. And, as we have already noted, there is the temptation for an enterprising employee to set up a concern identical to that of his former employer.

McClelland and Winters (1969), in a study of Indian entrepreneurs, observed that when deciding to go into businesses, new entrepreneurs tended to overestimate the scope of the market because of lack of information. This point appears even more relevant in the case of Nepal, where the market is smaller and more dispersed than in India and where market information is almost non-existent. Thus, while there may be sufficient demand to sustain one bakery in a town, the addition of a second may not necessarily increase the number of consumers; this is the type of risk which imitative entrepreneurs must face.

Imitative entrepreneurship is also likely to trigger the hostility of existing entrepreneurs. I heard many complaints about imitators; for example, 'One of our active partners left us and started his own factory. After he got practical experience with us, established contacts with customers, got management training through this factory, he finally left us.' Another respondent put the problem thus: 'We have a hard time getting trained people, especially technical and management. We give them training, but they run away, and some start their own businesses. So it's better to bring people from India.' When someone opens an identical industry down the road from an existing concern, the established entrepreneur must fight to maintain his hold on the market. There are several options here: he can improve his product; seek a wider market; lower his prices, or offer his clientele other types of incentive; accept a lower profit margin; or, of course, go under (Harris, 1981). Fear of the imitative entrepreneur may make established industrialists hesitate before hiring non-family labour.

From a national development point of view, however, imitative entrepreneurship appears a positive phenomenon; it indicates an occupational shift away from agriculture. As we noted in Chapter IV, government policy plays an important role in relation to this kind of entrepreneurship, especially among registered industries. The ready—some might say over-ready—distribution of licenses prompted one large-scale industrialist respondent to complain, 'The government is giving out so many licenses [i.e., for his line of business] that there is too much competition for a very small market. I cannot do anything about this, so I am leaving it up to God!' One result is that the more obvious forms of enterprise have become over-subscribed, while others remain untested. The problem is compounded by the fact that technical expertise is highly concentrated in certain skills and in urban localities. A prime example is the tourist industry. With the increase in tourists visiting the country, Kathmandu experienced an explosion of small hotels, restaurants and curio shops during the eighties; and each business appeared identical to its neighbour. Large trekking agencies have splintered; there are now more than thirty competitors offering tours and treks, many of them just scraping by in conditions of intense competition.

The case of Mr Sherpa illustrates the pitfalls of operating in an over-subscribed market where imitators are all too ready to cut in. In 1982, Mr. Sherpa opened a small muesli (granola breakfast-cereal) production unit with the technical advice of some foreigners with whom he had been associated in mountaineering activity. Muesli was in high demand by trekkers, and as the number of tourists coming to Nepal for trekking increased, Sherpa's business flourished. However, over the last two years three other dry-food companies have opened up, two of them with better financial backing, government contacts, and technical expertise. One of the companies has copied Sherpa's label so closely that it is hard to distinguish between them. However, the competitor's ingredients are cheaper, and Sherpa now finds himself being undercut and slowly pushed out of the market. Without legal or financial recourse, Sherpa can only lament the situation, and struggle to break even, while he thinks of other types of product to substitute for muesli. He cannot afford to abandon the technology in which he has invested so heavily.

In fact, Nepal's tourism is full of untapped possibilities. As a rule, trekking agencies supply tourists with porters to carry the foodstuffs, camping gear, kitchen utensils and everything else the trekker needs for up to six weeks in the field. For an innovative entrepreneur, this reality might suggest possibilities: the provision in remote rural areas of better supplies of food, improved housing and other amenities geared to the needs of the itinerant visitor. The problem here involves not only an absence of will but also a lack of information. Certainly more could be done to identify similar untapped areas of economic potential and inform entrepreneurs about them.

The entrepreneur: some conclusions. My findings suggest that the decision to engage in industry is far from random. In many cases it is an established family tradition. In others, the choice to move into industry springs from dissatisfaction with one's current situation; and here a role model in the immediate environment may act as a catalyst. For those who lack any family model or reference point, the decision to go into business is often born of exposure to business through employment. Hence, the element of imitation tends to be particularly pronounced. The small and micro entrepreneur is more likely than his bigger counterparts to have decided to enter business from another, unrelated profession. At an obvious level, wealthy business houses anticipate the next generation continuing the family's entrepreneurial tradition—and have the resources to ensure that the tradition endures, expands and prospers.

These findings may help to explain why the great majority of Nepal's rural inhabitants—even those with little or no land—fail to engage in business. Without role models or family support, not to mention access to investment capital, the Nepali subsistence farmer seems unlikely to venture into the uncertain, risky world of business.

THE ENTERPRISE

The role of the family. As we saw in Chapter III, business in Nepal tends to be a family based affair. As a rule, the senior male member of the family heads the business, and preference is given to family members in employment. Eighty-three per cent of my sample of 66 entrepreneurs reported that they employed family members in their business. The DRCG (1984) study found that, overall, about ten per cent of all jobs in the manufacturing sector are held by members of owners' families. Not surprisingly, there is an inverse relationship between the proportion of family members employed by a business and the size of the business.

The advantages of employing family members include their availability and their greater trustworthiness and reliability. The practice also keeps profits within the family. In micro industries, a business may actually be established to absorb family labour (which might otherwise go waste) and thereby offset the cost of supporting a large number of family members.

However, in larger enterprises or in the more successful smaller ones, family representation may prove a liability as much as an asset. If family members take precedence over outsiders, the entrepreneur may not always get the most skilled or efficient workers; the efficiency of the industry may thus be curtailed. Linton (1964) in fact contends that weaker kinship relations are positively correlated with economic profit. But while this generalization may be substantiated in certain instances, it is by no means universally the case in Nepal. Large corporate structures based on joint family management typify the most successful industrial concerns in the country.

As for non-family labour, a high turnover of both technical and managerial cadres characterizes Nepal's industrial sector. This fact of life further reinforces the preference for family labour. In large industries or multi-industry corporations, family management is the rule. Although the skills of individual family members may be objectively deficient compared with those of outsiders, internal issues of trust and confidence typically override such considerations.

Some comments from entrepreneurs I spoke to underline these observations. For example, a large-scale industrialist explained that 'We cannot delegate jobs relating to financial transactions to our subordinates because this is where leakages occur. So all purchasing and major marketing decisions and transactions are made and overseen by the senior partners.' A small-scale industrialist noted that 'If I hire outsiders and train them, they always tend to ask for advance and run away with the advance; this has happened many times.' And a cottage industrialist was similarly wary: 'I know I could expand my business, but now I'm employing all of my family members and it's enough. Last time I hired someone who lives nearby. He found out how I was doing this industry, and now he is doing the same thing.'

If employment tends to be reserved for family members, partnerships with outsiders are also exceedingly rare. Eighty-five per cent of my respondents reported either that they had no partner or that they were in partnership with a family member.

Within a family business context, decision-making hierarchies are generally maintained on the basis of sex and seniority. The eldest son will commonly have precedence over younger sons in inheriting control over family businesses and resources. In extended families, younger brothers are typically expected to assist their senior male sibling. Figure 5.6 shows the pre-eminent position of first sons in my sample:

FIGURE 5.6

Position of Entrepreneurs in Family *vis-à-vis* Other Brothers

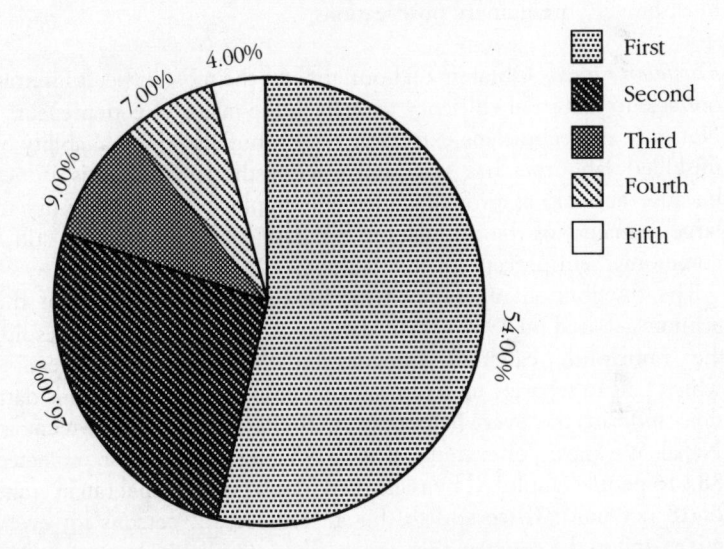

- First
- Second
- Third
- Fourth
- Fifth

First: 54.00%
Second: 26.00%
Third: 9.00%
Fourth: 7.00%
Fifth: 4.00%

Most of the industries in my sample were less than one decade old. As Table 5.1 indicates, there was considerable variation here between size categories, with large/medium concerns registering substantially longer lives than their small-scale equivalents:

TABLE 5.1
Age of Industry by Size of Industry

	Large/Medium	Small	Micro	Total
Average age of Industry (in years)	10.4	4.5	8.3	7.7

Part of the explanation may be that small industries, with their more personalized structure and built-in rigidities, may be less inclined to diversify. The second generation may prefer to set up on its own, leaving the original firm to die with its owner. Only four per cent of my sample had inherited their business, and all were in the large-scale sector.

These findings are consistent with the DRCG (1984) study of a larger sample of industries. Here, 76 per cent of the industries studied had been established between 1974 and 1982. However, given the fact that the industrial sector itself is less than three decades old, these must be very preliminary observations.

The labour force. Obtaining labour appears the most difficult internal obstacle to industrial efficiency (at least in the minds of entrepreneurs). Not only are technicians extremely scarce, but also the availability of unskilled labourers has not kept pace with demand. This is not because agriculture provides adequate employment and security to large segments of the population, but rather because there is still a commonly held perception that it does.

The distribution of employment between various sectors of the economy (based on 1980 census data) is set out in Table 5.2. Despite the unhelpful, catch-all category of 'productive labourers'—which fails to separate agricultural from industrial workers—this data does indicate the overwhelmingly rural character of employment in Nepal. We know, for example, that in 1982–83 there were an estimated 88,616 people employed by registered industries in Nepal (an average of 18 per unit). If we add to this an estimated 2 persons for every micro unit in the country, then the number of individuals employed in the manufacturing sector comes to approximately eight per cent of

TABLE 5.2

Employment of Economically Active Population over 10 Years of Age, according to the 1980 Census

Type of Employment	Number	Percentage
Professional/technical	64,132	1
Administrative workers	6,232	0.1
Clerical workers	49,161	0.7
Sales workers	85,341	1
Service workers	16,430	0.2
Farmers/fishermen	6,259,613	91
Productive labourers*	213,851	3
Other	156,126	2
Total	6,850,886	100

* A very broad category, including both agricultural and industrial wage labourers.
SOURCE: Statistical Handbook, Central Bureau of Statistics, 1984.

the total population over the age of ten.[5] The 1980 census data also suggests that for every two economically active individuals over the age of ten, there is one who is economically inactive—indicating the seriousness of the problem of unemployment. Underemployment is difficult to quantify. One study, based on data for 1976–77, measured underemployment in terms of unutilized days and came up with figures of 63 per cent in rural Nepal and 46 per cent in urban areas (Agarwal and Amatya, 1984).

Unemployment and underemployment are clearly very high in Nepal. It is interesting, therefore, that the industrial sector imports perhaps as much as 28 per cent of its labour force from India, a reality explored in the previous chapter. Nepal's industry clearly has the potential to generate more jobs for indigenous workers than it presently does; my findings indicate that the demand for industrial labour may exceed the supply—at least from indigenous sources.

The slow response to this demand should be understood in the agrarian context of the country and the newness of industry as a source of employment. The fact that the Nepalese peasantry has not

---

[5] My figure for micro-level employment is not available from any formal source. It is based on an estimate of between three and five part-time employees (whether family or non-family) per unit; these may also engage in agriculture. Thus the estimate is equivalent to two full-time persons per industry.

really come forward to meet this demand—even in the face of widespread unemployment and underemployment—perhaps indicates the conservatism of this sector towards alternative sources of employment. It is certainly true that Nepal has not witnessed the rapid urban migration which characterizes many other developing nations. Nor does the admittedly scanty evidence indicate that the unemployed (or underemployed) are converging on manufacturing units. Peasants still cling to the land, even those who can barely scrape a living from it. In the hills, where soil erosion and deforestation have combined with population growth to marginalize increasing numbers of residents, external income sources (in particular, remunerations from serving Gorkha soldiers) provide what some might consider an artificial stability to the economy (Blaikie et al, 1980): Many hill residents have migrated southwards to farm in Terai lands which, until recently, were able to sustain a larger proportion of the population. Today, however, national agricultural production teeters between deficit levels and outright famine conditions. The individual farmer faces the division of his landholding into smaller and smaller segments.

Alternatives to farming are imperative, yet rural Nepalis seem disinclined to seek those alternatives. Even when they do, they find it difficult to adjust to the novel demands of industrial schedules, as the following sample of complaints from employers makes clear:

> Nepali labourers don't want to work hard. They just want their salary. They think the work is too small. During the harvesting, cropping and festival seasons we have high rates of absenteeism. So we prefer to hire Indians.

> Mostly the Nepalese just want the table and chair; they don't want to work and we have a hard time motivating them.

> The day after pay-day most of my workers don't come. But I can't say anything or they may leave me for good.

> Once I instructed the workers to finish a job on time. I had to go out, and when I came back they were only 50 per cent finished. Workers lack a feeling of responsibility.

> We have a problem with the spinners. Most are the wives of farmers or military men who spin in their free time. We need a constant supply of spun wool to keep our carpet production going, but they work according to their whim. We tried making a shed where they could work steadily together but the same problem arose: they would not show up regularly. So we have to make do.

How should we interpret this phenomenon? Linton (1964) suggests that there are built-in disincentives for peasants to work hard for others if experience has taught them that no matter how much harder they work, their surplus will be extracted by the landlord or the tax collector. Sadie (1964) observes that 'work for its own sake is not part of the scheme of things.' In other words, in traditional agrarian settings there may be a preference for leisure over increased material gain which may disincline peasants to take regular labour seriously. Linton (1964) further maintains that it is easier to teach individuals how to work a machine than to persuade them to show up for work every day. Perhaps this is linked to what could be termed the 'farming mentality': the idea that there is a time for hard work and a time for relaxing, and that these times are determined more by the weather than by man-created, arbitrary schedules. When it is time for *pujas* (religious ceremonies), the all-important maintenance of good relations with the gods and the community invariably takes precedence over production schedules. Indeed, religion and social reciprocity seem far more significant than economic imperatives in the values of the peasantry. From their perspective, survival is bound up with the former rather than with the latter. And it is difficult to change one pattern of behaviour (in this case, attitudes towards time and work) when everything else in the environment serves to reinforce the prevailing norm (Mead, 1964).

Furthermore, from the point of view of the household economy—particularly in an extended family situation where labour is interchangeable—there are psychological pressures against an individual working harder at his factory job if his kin are still on the farm enjoying the seasonal slack periods. When the individual's personal income is not linked to his output—for example, in a situation where he must share his earnings—there is little incentive to take a job outside, or, if a job is taken, to perform it well (Bauer and Yamey, 1957). These points provide clues as to why a simulated family environment and use of terminology likely to engender family-type loyalties in workers are an important part of the Nepali managerial frame of reference. As one employer explained, 'In general there has been a tendency for the workers to leave the company when they gain skills. To save myself from it I have hired labourers from my locality. We have a kind of family relation among us.'

Such attitudes, and the behaviour associated with them, are, of course not unique to Nepal. But given the weakness of forces for change within the country, it may take longer here than elsewhere in the developing world to create a modern industrial labour force.

If we return to Broehl's model for a moment, we find that the response of the Nepali labour force to opportunities in the industrial sector falls at the 'traditional' end of the choice continuum. Prospective labourers as a rule prefer what is familiar to what is unknown, despite the economic benefits the latter may offer, benefits not easily achieved in agriculture. Those who actually enter the ranks of industrial labour may demonstrate ambivalence about their responsibilities and roles, vacillating between their old ties to the land and their communal obligations on the one hand, and the demands of their new workplace on the other. The entrepreneur, faced with the problems which this situation creates, is compelled to seek management and administrative strategies designed to nudge employees along the continuum in the direction of 'modern' work ethics.

Management practices. As an agent of change, the entrepreneur is caught between a traditional government bureaucracy (involving old forms of patronage) and a tradition-bound labour force upon which he is dependent to make his industry run. How does this situation affect management practices? Do Western management practices at all fit into the scheme of things? As we saw earlier, when Western models of management are superimposed on traditional systems, they force entrepreneurs to attempt to reconcile the old with the new. In so doing, the entrepreneur may allow his cultural background to dominate his business decisions, producing less than effective results. Alternatively, he may mix traditional and modern management practices in a manner which may make him appear indecisive. A third option is to go over completely to modern practices, a radical step which may alienate him from his own culture. The case-studies which follow highlight the problems associated with all three tracks.

The first story features Mr P., who owns a small weaving factory. He also runs a retail outlet in which he markets his own products as well as imported Indian fabrics. His wife, two daughters, and one son are all engaged in the business, and he employs four other weavers as well. His employees are often late, and, on average, absenteeism is as high as one day a week. Because they work on a piece basis, because Mr P.—who trained them—considers them his 'children', and because he really has no idea of his optimal production capacity, Mr P. becomes concerned about their under-performance only during the festival season (when there is a sudden increase in the demand for his product). Otherwise, he tries to be understanding when his workers are late or absent—because he does not want to lose them.

The second case history is that of Mr T., who bought a plastics production unit when he noted a growing demand for plastic bags and wrappers in the market. He had to take a loan to buy the machinery, and spent a lot of time running from one government office to another to get his machinery into the country and secure a license for the importation of raw materials. He felt frustrated by the procedures, but was helped by the presence of a distant relative in one of the offices.

When Mr T. finally started production, he had two Indian technicians and four Nepali workers in his employ. He did all the liaison with buyers and government offices himself. Mr T. knew that when he was not at the factory, production would deteriorate, but he didn't know what to do about it. The employees would ask him for advances on their wages, which he gave, hoping they would reciprocate by working harder. When that failed to happen, he set targets for the employees to meet, and indicated (as nicely as he could) that he would take action if the workers did not comply. But the technicians knew Mr T. could not easily find replacements for them, so they did not bother to meet the targets. Two of the Nepali workers were distant relatives of the owner, so they were not worried about their jobs, either. Mr T. had no idea of how much he could be producing, and his knowledge of accounting was so rudimentary that he had no way of knowing how much money he was making or losing. But since his was the only plastic bag industry in his locality, he wasn't worried. A short while ago, however, some merchants began wholesaling Indian-made plastic bags to several of his buyers. Now Mr T. is concerned that they may threaten his business.

Then there is the tale of Mr R., from a well-respected business family. He was educated at a prestigious school of management abroad, and when he returned to Nepal from his studies, he introduced many of the concepts he had learned into his business. In particular, he introduced incentive schemes for workers whereby they receive monetary bonuses for improved performance and productivity. He also restructured the management system so as to effect a decentralization of authority; many management decisions which had previously been made by Mr R. or his immediate family members were now reallocated. In general this system worked, although the extent of fiscal mismanagement at the branch level was extremely hard to monitor, given the structure of the system. Mr R. worried that perhaps he was giving up a personal 'family' touch with his managers in favour of a modern system that might be alienating them. Also, Mr R. found himself in conflict with his father when he suggested that the firm demand certain privileges from the government to which it was legally entitled. He also refused to do *chakari* to important officials. As a result, he found himself out of favour with certain individuals in a position to facilitate his business requirements.

These examples capture the plight of the Nepali entrepreneur, caught between tradition-bound bureaucracies and workers on the one hand, and modern technologies and an increasingly competitive market-place on the other. He is constantly juggling opposing forces, trying, through trial and error, to make them work effectively together. It is perhaps this attempt, above all else, that makes the Nepali entrepreneur a frontrunner in the movement for cultural and economic change. Since the country's existing institutions (and individual behaviour patterns) seem intrinsically opposed to the transformation necessary to support modern modes of production the entrepreneur is seeking to introduce, there is a constant need to balance, to pacify, to make do. Many entrepreneurs spend all their time just keeping afloat, just coping with bureaucratic or staff problems, so that there is little energy or will left for innovation.

Patronage and personalized management styles appear essential to the maintenance of that balance, both within industry and in relation to state institutions. It can even be argued that such styles are the most efficient; just as the bureaucrat knows how to respond to the cultural cues of *chakari*, so the labourer understands that he must show deference to his boss above all else. Producer and client likewise enter a situation where price and quality are related to the requirements of their personal relationship, a point which is especially relevant for smaller industries. But what costs do such practices entail as far as private sector efficiency is concerned? The answer seems to be that the costs are heavy: underutilization of new technology; the inability to meet deadlines; marginal, poor or inadequate quality control. For the entrepreneur competing in the international market or importing goods and services, such problems are very real.

However, the fact that Nepali entrepreneurs in most cases do not adhere to Western management practices does not indicate a lack of sophistication. To succeed as an entrepreneur in the circumstances that now prevail in Nepal requires a considerable degree of savvy and vision. In a context where affiliation is more important than profit, where patronage gets precedence over efficiency, and where so much decision-making necessarily relies on hunch, entrepreneurial skills have to differ from the Western management model. As Broehl (1982) comments,

> Business values and business ethics tend to be tradition-bound rather than subject to the maximization concepts of Western microeconomics. The entrepreneur must move back and forth from one value orientation to another, constantly attempting to accommodate role effectiveness to the pressures of divergent values.

Financing. The availability of capital is obviously an important factor for initiating and continuing a business. In Nepal, such seed money most often comes from personal or family savings, as Figure 5.7 indicates. The sources of financing shown here may be skewed slightly

FIGURE 5.7

Initial Source of Funding by Type of Industry

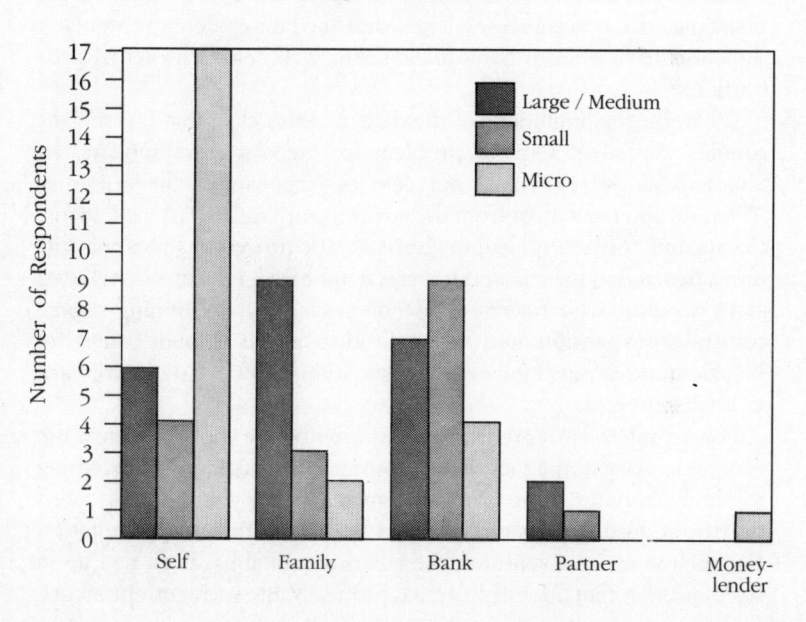

in favour of formal institutions for the small and micro sector; this is because the sample was selected on the basis of referrals from projects, chambers of commerce and other institutions which often had links with banks and perceived 'successful' entrepreneurs to be those with bank loans. Even so, it is clear that a large majority of enterprises are initiated with family resources. National statistics indicate that, on average, less than one per cent of the credit disbursed in the country goes to the cottage sector. This is consistent with findings from other countries: for example, a review by Harris (1981) of 269 Nigerian industries found that 80 per cent of them were self-financed. Likewise, an inventory of studies from developing countries has indicated that most industries begin with personal or family savings (Shapero, 1982).

Once the business is running, entrepreneurs feel more confident about borrowing from institutional sources. DRCG (1984) found that while seed capital most commonly comes from the entrepreneur himself, working capital is more often borrowed from outside institutions or individuals. As Figures 5.8 and 5.9 indicate, once businesses are launched, bank financing becomes more or less on par with other types of financing. Once again, however, we should take into account a certain skewedness in the data: while there appears to be an over-representation here of small and micro entrepreneurs with institutional financing, the percentage of large- and medium-scale entrepreneurs shown as having taken bank loans seems well below the actual proportion.

Whatever the limitations of the data, it seems clear that insufficient running capital is a major problem for Nepal's entrepreneurs. In Sharma's study (1979), 22 per cent of responses to the question, 'What do you need most from the government?' related to bank loans. Complaints focused on lengthy bureaucratic procedures plus the stiff terms demanded for collateral; these, it appeared, effectively excluded many would-be borrowers. The non-availability of running capital constrains expansion and diversification across a wide range of Nepalese industries. However, the situation is not as straightforward as it first appears.

For the micro entrepreneur operating with little capital, often at the economic margin, the fact that his business is contributing something to family earnings is often a sufficient reason for continuing it, irrespective of absolute revenues or alternative investment opportunities. For such minuscule ventures, the fact that capital has been tied up in fixed assets is tantamount to actual profits. Many such entrepreneurs,

FIGURE 5.8

Source of Financing for Running the Business

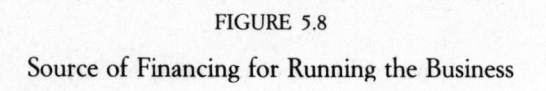

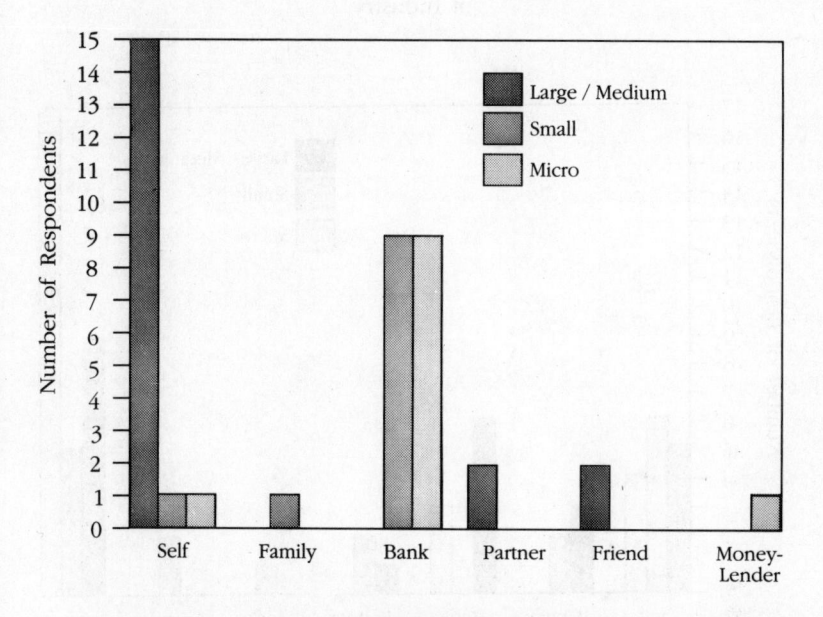

[Bar chart showing Number of Respondents by source (Self, Family, Bank, Partner, Friend, Money-Lender) across Large/Medium, Small, and Micro enterprises. Self: Large/Medium 15, Small 1, Micro 1. Family: Small 1. Bank: Small 9, Micro 9. Partner: Large/Medium 2. Friend: Large/Medium 2. Money-Lender: Micro 1.]

* In many cases the entrepreneur indicated that the business was running primarily on reinvested profits. This response covers this reality, as well as other individually-owned resources invested in the business.

when questioned about sales revenues and profits, had little idea how much they earn, even within a very short time span. None of the micro entrepreneurs I spoke to, and only a few of the small ones, kept any formal accounts. They revealed a general mistrust or lack of understanding of banking procedures, and limited knowledge of other investment opportunities.

Social pressure to observe religious ceremonies and ritual also tends to divert funds away from business; at the same time, such observances secure the entrepreneur a firm place in the community.

Low levels of bank borrowing may reflect deficiencies in the lending institutions themselves as much as popular prejudice against 'using other people's money'. In Nepal, banking facilities verge on the archaic, with lengthy, cumbersome procedures that require applications of the same 'source and force' that is essential elsewhere in the

FIGURE 5.9

Secondary Source of Financing by Size
of Industry

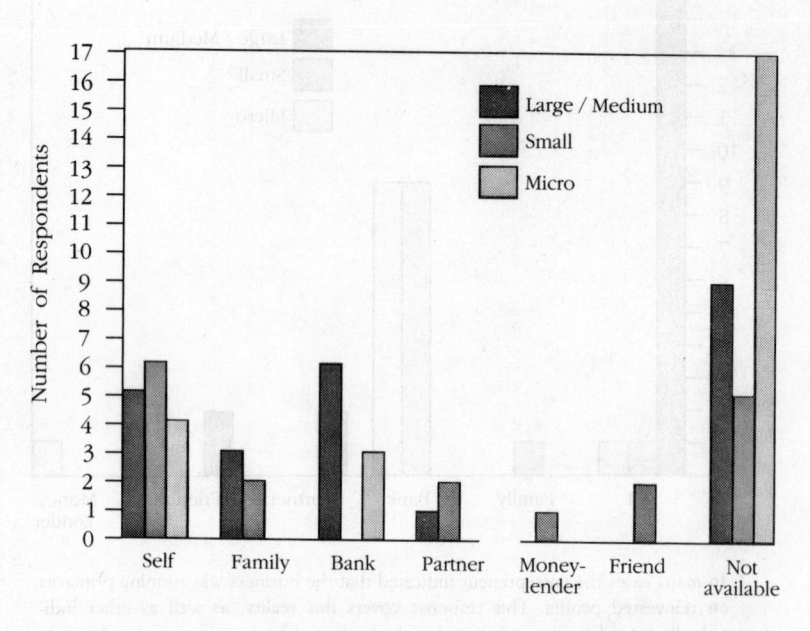

government sector. The following comments from small-scale entrepreneurs reveal the problems they encountered when they turned to the banks for help:

> I needed money to expand my business. So I applied to the bank for a loan. I wasted several months and the effort was useless.
>
> When I applied for a loan in the beginning, the bank was hesitant to finance. Then one foreigner from the Project visited my factory and my loan was sanctioned in two days.
>
> I wanted to get more loan to expand my business, but the manager in the bank is transferred, so I am not sure whether I will be able to get it.

Of the 25 entrepreneurs in my sample who had some comment to make on the banking system, roughly half had uncomplimentary remarks on the quality of service they had received.

From the banker's point of view, of course, loans to small industries present risks and bureaucratic burdens that may be out of proportion to the likely financial returns. A banker in a rural setting, with little motivation to attract more business, may well be disinclined to go out and find new clients, let alone spend time helping someone who may come forward for a loan. Although many projects designed to promote small industries have a component designed to help entrepreneurs gain access to bank loans[6], the inefficiencies of the system, and the inability of many entrepreneurs to work it successfully, have prevented bank credit reaching a wider spectrum of industrialists.

If small industries get short shrift here, even large ones that promise the banks substantial returns are not given priority. Hamal (1972) points out that Nepal's major industrial lending agency, the Nepal Industrial Development Corporation, has concentrated its loans on the tourist sector rather than seeking to promote the country's manufacturing capability. In fact, investment patterns in larger industries reflect the vulnerability of Nepal's industrial sector and place further constraints on capital accumulation. Blaikie et al (1980), examining industries in Nepal's central region, found the following situation:

> In nearly all agricultural processing enterprises in the region there are significant possibilities for capital accumulation, although there is a tendency in practice for the owners to be involved in other businesses as well and to move their capital between different sectors in order to take advantage of particular opportunities (often due to State actions and not 'fundamental' economic circumstances) as they arise. There is a widespread unwillingness to commit funds too inextricably to one form of economic activity, the essence of successful business enterprise being to keep assets as liquid as possible at all times. One consequence of this is that few establishments are maintained with adequate equipment over sufficiently long periods to become firmly established. (pp. 202–3)

The authors cite the example of the local construction industry, which they describe as 'essentially transient in nature, often having no

[6] In 1984, a World Bank project for cottage industries, working through the banks, sanctioned Rs 32,284,000 in loans for this sector. Less than half of that amount was disbursed, mainly because of bank inefficiencies (Agarwal and Amatya, 1984). When Actionaid/Nepal tried to launch a community development project aimed at women (involving loans of up to US Dollars 100 for each woman who wished to start a cottage industry), the procedures proved so cumbersome that after some months of effort, all attempts to attract bank financing were abandoned, and a project subsidy eventually got the project off the ground.

visible existence except on the site where construction is taking place ... [This] represents in the clearest possible fashion, the predominant underlying tendency of industrial production in the region: lack of permanence and no ongoing financial commitment.' (p. 204) These comments aptly describe the investment strategies of large and medium industrialists throughout the country. Industrial entrepreneurs are not immune from the market, political and cultural forces which induce many non-industrial investors to put their money into land, trade—and foreign bank accounts. Spreading one's investments around is, indeed, a rational response to a tricky situation in which government policies change frequently, where the market is limited and where lucrative, short-term investment opportunities (requiring immediate access to capital) inevitably beckon. Once again, there appears to be a need to adapt traditional forms (in this case, investment patterns and lending institutions) to the demands of a changing market-place. There is an underlying conservatism here which must be tackled if the industrial sector is to gain better access to financing.

Technology. Access to technology and technical know-how appears a problem of similar dimensions. Nepal's underdevelopment exacerbates the problem; literacy, for example, was limited to a privileged few until 1951, and even today only 35 per cent or so of the population is literate. In the past, such technical skills as existed were passed down, unchanged, from father to son. Today, even the casual visitor notes the skill of the Nepali craftsperson: a tailor can reproduce a garment from a photograph and guarantee a perfect fit; a carpenter can fashion a highly intricate doorframe using age-old designs. But the ability to modify and update such skills to meet the challenge of a changing market does not seem to have been part of the inherited repertoire of skills. Such ability is, of course, the hallmark of the true entrepreneur. Furthermore, the survival of traditional skills confines the nation's pool of 'technicians' to an extremely limited range of industrial options; as a result, the number of technically trained workers in Nepal is still comparatively small.

Despite the growing demand in industry for trained technicians, technical training is hardly a sought-after option. Eligible students still prefer 'professional' types of education, untainted by the stigma of manual labour. In the short run, at least, many industries will be forced to rely on imported Indian labour to fill gaps in their technical manpower requirements.

Access to technology is further hampered by inadequate information. Since there is no single clearing-house of information on technology, entrepreneurs typically learn about new developments through informal networks (often based in India). As one industrialist related, 'I had the idea for this business while I was visiting friends in India. They helped me get the machinery, showed me the business, and now, if I have problems, I can go to them for help.' Even if new technology is acquired from abroad, its maintenance and upkeep often present problems. Entrepreneurs rarely possess the necessary technical expertise themselves, nor can they always afford a full-time technician to supervise maintenance operations. This is particularly critical for smaller manufacturing units:

> In the beginning, I had a hard time bringing this machinery from India because I needed clearance from the government. Finally, after going to different offices for a year, they let me import it. Last week, my machinery broke down, and since my mechanic had run away, I had to take it to Kathmandu to have it fixed. That wasted a week. Last time this happened, I had to go all the way to India to buy the broken parts and my factory was closed for a month.

> This season, the sale of our *maida* (flour) was lower than it's ever been. This is because the quality was poor which was due to a lack of qualified technicians who could use and maintain the machinery properly.

Nepal's experience in the area of new technology raises important questions about the fashionable concept of 'appropriate technology' (admired in certain Western development circles). At an obvious level, technology, as an external intervention, should suit the context into which it is introduced, and should take account of the available manpower and managerial skills. Aharoni (1977) makes the point, however, that what is seen as 'appropriate' by outside benefactors may all too easily run into serious problems when it is sought to be applied:

> When one goes beyond general admonitions about the desirability of adopting more labour-intensive technologies, one often finds that some of these technologies are quite inefficient. In addition, labour-intensive technology requires a body of managers able to efficiently supervise a large number of workers. In many developing countries, however, such management skill is more scarce than capital. (p. 179)

Nepal's computer sector illustrates this point graphically. If the number of computer training and consultancy firms which have sprung up recently in Kathmandu is any indication, computers are sweeping the kingdom. But if we take a closer look, we find these units typically run by one individual who has had some specialist training, aided by a cadre of 'staff' who have a minimal grasp of how to operate the computer, and even less understanding of its applications. As elsewhere, owning a computer has become a status symbol for both public and private sector institutions. But in Nepal the ability of the buyers to put these highly sophisticated machines to proper use is still limited. The demand for computer technology here has not evolved from earlier dependence on, and knowledge of, the typewriter and the calculator (as was the pattern in Western countries). The computer stands side by side with archaic filing systems in which records are written by hand (on handmade paper) and documents are often fingerprinted to verify the identity of the author. Information, furthermore, must flow through a complex hierarchy of bureaucrats who commit to paper as little information as possible in order to maintain their control over decision-making. Computers appear to be highly inappropriate in such an environment, despite their objective potential for improving information systems and management structures. It seems that when technology oversteps the limits of culture or existing technical expertise, it becomes an end in itself rather than an asset to the society or institution into which it is introduced.

Harvey Wallender (1978), in a five-country study of technology transfer, noted a general inability on the part of managers to identify the moment when new technologies should be applied. This he saw as a key factor limiting technological improvements in developing country enterprises. Imitative entrepreneurship resolves this problem to some extent, since the imitator can capitalize on the informal research (and mistakes) of his mentor or model. Another trend, observable in India among other places, is the growth of a cadre of 'technical entrepreneurs' who appear to be pushing out the traditional industrialist. While this trend has not taken hold yet in Nepal, it appears inevitable. For if Nepal's entrepreneurs are to compete with their overseas rivals, increasingly sophisticated technology will certainly find its way into the country.

Marketing. Nepal's marketing structure provides an additional indication of the localized and fragmented nature of the country's manufacturing sector. Figure 5.10 shows that 76 per cent of small and micro concerns generally sell their products directly to the consumer. Large industries, on the other hand, are typically linked to nationwide (and, in some instances, international) distribution marketing networks.

FIGURE 5.10

Market Outlet by Size of Industry

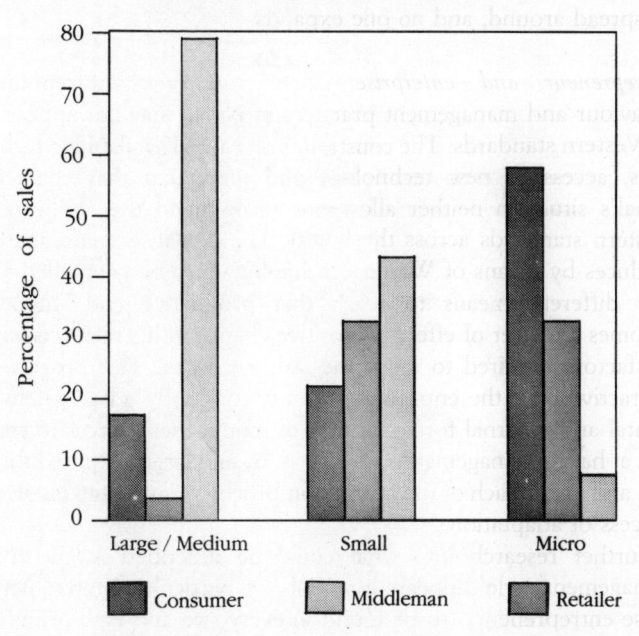

In fact, the actual number of manufacturing units nationwide which market their goods through wholesalers may be lower than this data suggests. The DRCG (1984) study found that 83 per cent of the units they sampled sold their products directly to customers who lived in physical proximity to the industry. Given the concentration of Nepal's manufacturing and service sectors within a narrow range of industries, and the intense competition resulting from this, entrepreneurs commonly rely on personal relationships to establish and maintain their clientele. In many cases a customer will patronize one particular teashop, *kirana* store, jeweller or tailor in the interests of a pre-existing relationship. Such a relationship may depend not only on kinship, ethnicity or friendship but also on such factors as the willingness to extend credit. Traditional rules of reciprocity make it incumbent upon customers to patronize the specific shop (or producer) which has extended them credit. Any bazaar town in the hills boasts two or three *kirana* stores selling exactly the same things: packaged biscuits, cigarettes, matches, kerosene, cooking oil, cheap fabrics, plastic sandals and so on. No one store is obviously prospering more than another—but neither is it going under. No single shop has an advantage in this situation; each has its own clientele. What profits are to be had are spread around, and no one expands.

Entrepreneur and enterprise: some conclusions: Entrepreneurial behaviour and management practices in Nepal may not appear ideal by Western standards. The constraints on capital availability, technical skills, access to new technology and marketing that characterize Nepal's situation neither allow nor recommend the application of Western standards across the board. The Nepali entrepreneur who produces by means of Western technology may be compelled to use very different means to reach that productive end. Innovation becomes a matter of effecting positive change in his relations with all the factors required to make the industry work. This process is an interactive one; the entrepreneur must constantly adapt to environmental and external forces and try to mould those forces to suit the task at hand. Management expertise is, by and large, acquired through trial and error; each of the options on Broehl's continuum involve that process of adaptation.

Further research into what could be described as the 'Nepali management style' appears essential. Of particular interest here are those entrepreneurs (to be found in every size and type of industry) who seem to have stumbled upon a winning formula for dealing with the innumerable constraints and problems built into Nepal's current reality. Upon this small, successful section a great deal would appear to depend.

Chapter Six

Looking Back, Looking Forward: Some Concluding Observations

One commonly noted problem with the social sciences is that the researcher—from whatever discipline—is always on the outside looking in. He or she must necessarily make assumptions about the reasons people behave the way they do in order to explain the behaviour under scrutiny. A second problem is the fact that generalizations are based on observations which are circumscribed by time and space; social scientists assume that situations characterize or pervade a wider population than the one under study. If, on the other hand, the researcher consciously becomes part of the population under study, the problem becomes one of separating himself or herself sufficiently to observe and comprehend with some objectivity.

This study of entrepreneurship in Nepal, conducted by an expatriate researcher who has herself owned and managed an industry in that country, has been open to all these pitfalls. It began as an inquiry into the phenomenon of entrepreneurship in one developing country—a study of the individuals (and communities) who have taken a considerable risk in social and economic terms. The aim was to understand the factors that motivated that decision, to characterize the individuals making it, and to examine their responses to the opportunities and problems they encounter along the way.

The study took this author all over the country, allowing her glimpses of a variety of homes and factories. The data collection yielded not simply hard socio-economic information on Nepal's entrepreneurs but also constantly repeated themes of woe, frustration, impatience, regret, apathy and even (on occasion) guarded optimism and hope. As she listened to these stories, as she learnt how individual entrepreneurs had started their ventures, the author was herself facing problems as she struggled to keep her own business afloat. Inevitably, the writing of this book became an outlet, a chance to vent the very real frustrations encountered in the course of navigating the government, customs, banks, workers, producers, raw materials—in short, every element involved in a business venture.

Nepalis tend to be congenial, positive, pleasant people. As I watched the cynicism grow within me, fed by what seemed an endless stream of obstacles to my own business (an idealistically conceived project designed to offer employment to the jobless and open up previously untapped markets for indigenous products) I marvelled at the relative calm of the many local entrepreneurs who had faced more serious, even survival-threatening obstacles. In the course of time, I was able to see that my frustrations arose in large measure from my own unreal expectations: what I had assumed to be my due—from government, workers and producers alike— was a perception derived largely from an ethnocentric view of reality. For the Nepali entrepreneur (as for the population at large), concepts such as individual rights, productive efficiency, or even frustration seem to be perceived quite differently. Of course, the Nepali entrepreneur, unlike myself, is part of the process, and a product of it. This allows him or her to deal with day-to-day problems with a great deal more calm than I could muster; for such problems are perceived within a very different frame of reference.

The analysis presented in this book is, inevitably, derived from a Western point of view. It has sought to understand process from the perspective of the actors involved in them; at the same time it cannot claim to present a totally fair or comprehensive picture of the insider's position on the situation. The bottom line, to restate a point much debated within the social sciences, is that there is no objective reality; a great deal hinges on who happens to be looking at a problem, be it economic development or cultural change, and from which perspective they make the observations. While Western experts may seek objective, universal yardsticks for measuring 'progress', those whose progress they observe may have very different, even opposing, criteria or yardsticks. Conscious of such limitations, then, this analysis is intended as something of a snapshot: one view, food for thought, but hardly the last word on the subject.

One point deserving of emphasis is that Nepal has come a considerable way along the path of industrialization in the short time this has been a national priority. Given the constraints which faced the country in 1951, the past forty years have seen quite rapid national advance.

What does the future hold? My research suggests that industrialization in Nepal can take several quite distinct directions in the years to come. While the scenario projected in this book may appear bleak, there are also hopeful signs. Viewed as a younger sibling to other developing countries, Nepal has the opportunity of learning from their mistakes as well as their successes. She also has the advantage of imported Indian role models; their presence can be expected to help develop indigenous entrepreneurship. A further bonus is Nepal's access to substantial aid from developed nations; if properly utilized, such aid could provide the infrastructure, capital, training and other facilities essential for private sector development. All this would, of course, strengthen the economy as a whole. Whether Nepal will take advantage of her opportunities to catch up with her more developed neighbours hangs in the balance. For, as we have seen, such progress is not conditioned merely by economic rationality. Culture, history, politics, and, in particular, traditional relations between the rulers and the non-agricultural private sector may play a more crucial role here.

Several questions emerge at this point. Who will be the economic 'winners' in the game of industrialization? What role will ethnicity play? Can the current political establishment deliver on its promises of decentralization and greater support for industry? What role will foreign aid (and foreign influence) play in this process? And finally, given the very real cultural, geographic and economic constraints on growth, is it possible to draw up an optimal set of policy guidelines to stimulate the growth of entrepreneurship?

An enterprise culture is, of course, by no mean universally acclaimed. Critics of the 'trickle down' theory of economic growth, conscious of the need for social justice, tend to regard private entrepreneurship as a system by which traditional political modes of domination are replaced by more far-reaching (and sinister) élite economic control of the masses. Industrialization is here seen as desirable to the extent that it frees developing nations from dependence on richer ones. When, however, élite members of poor nations establish their own businesses (perhaps even joining the ranks of the multinationals), they are seen as turning their backs on their own people. This seems something of an oversimplification. The ability of an admittedly privileged few to enter the ranks of big business (possibly with an international dimension) is predicated on the fact that the country as a whole can support their participation in the global economy. The emergence of a bourgeoisie is a prerequisite for this; such a development is linked to wide-ranging internal transformations which, as we have noted in the course of this study, serve also to open new opportunities to wider sections of the population. These opportunities are not just employment-related; they include the goods and services, educational facilities and general infrastructure essential for industrial progress.

Nepal's entrepreneurs are clearly far removed from membership of any multinational 'mafia'. Rich or poor, large or small, they are, in the main, far-sighted individuals alert to the opportunities in a traditional but changing economy. By tapping such opportunities they are helping to transform that economy. If egalitarianism is an important yardstick for measuring development, it is perhaps fair to say that entrepreneurs are contributing to this by helping along a process which will generate more resources and make them available to a much broader spectrum of the Nepalese people. Not that the entrepreneur perceives his mission thus. From his own point of view, the entrepreneur is concerned with the pursuit of profit. From a national perspective, however, aggregate profit in a dynamic private sector bolsters not only GNP but also employment and national self-sufficiency. It also strengthens Nepal's position within the global economy.

Perhaps even more important than this is the fact that, in Nepal at least, the private sector offers a counterpoint to the traditional ruling élite. The opportunities made available through economic development have allowed resources to accumulate in the hands of segments of the population which hitherto enjoyed little power and which could be regarded as politically and socially marginal. Access to resources, whether financial or political, is still influenced by the play of traditional forces. But serendipity has shown its face in Nepal's unpromising terrain. An example is the rise of tourism in the Khumbu Valley, which stimulated remarkable changes among the Sherpas. Another is the carpet industry, the creation and pride of Nepal's Tibetan refugees— and a godsend to an economy desperate for foreign exchange. There is also the case of the construction industry, which the Thakalis, through their emphasis on technical education, have been able to capture. All this suggests that industrialization has indeed chipped away at the historical monolith of Chhetri-Brahmin control over Nepal's economic resources and political life.

It can be predicted with some confidence that urbanization, and exposure to an expanding range of cultural and economic influences, will weaken the influence of caste and ethnicity, factors which currently define entrepreneurship in Nepal. It would be naive, however, to expect the sway exercised by the Marwari community over the private sector to decrease significantly in the next generation. The entry into this sector of other erstwhile agricultural communities, and the diversification into new business areas by ethnic groups already established in the non-agricultural private sector will depend in large measure on government policy and its implementation. If real opportunities and incentives become available, courtesy the government, more individuals—from a variety of backgrounds—can be expected to move into the industrial sector. This is a major imponderable, however. Much will depend on the willingness of the ruling élite to slacken its grip on resources and power in the larger national interest. From this vantage point, the rationale that underlies income-generating projects and those aimed at building a national infrastructure appears more than justified. Such projects, conceived in the conviction that giving people greater economic power necessarily enhances their political clout and social status, aim to liberate the poorest of the poor from their traditional position at the very bottom of society.

As for Nepal's donor agencies, their role in stimulating industrialization and the growth of an enterprise culture, while clearly critically important, is not by itself a sufficient prerequisite. This study of Nepal has demonstrated that no matter how well-conceived a project may be in theory, it will prove ineffective if it fails to take the existing bureaucratic culture into account. For instance, loan projects which merely provide bureaucrats with more leverage and opportunities for personal gain do little to help the would-be entrepreneur. Training programmes focused on inappropriate skills raise unrealistic expectations among producers while creating markets for goods for which there is no real demand. Even training in entrepreneurship, if conducted in an environment unreceptive to innovation and change (particularly one where newcomers have no access to existing patronage networks), may only create frustration.

Any project designed to develop an existing or potential export market must also address itself to obstacles—in this case, in the area of customs and licensing. If, as the majority of entrepreneurs contend, the primary obstacle is the government itself, foreign aid donors might more productively direct their efforts here, seeking to correct basic administrative flaws in the system before attempting to stimulate further private sector activity. This suggests the need for a broader review of government policy and its implementation before more localized income-generating projects are initiated. For even if an entrepreneur gets the training, finances, technology and market he requires, he will still face a stream of problems in the day-to-day operation of his business. In an environment which remains far from conducive to industrialization, valuable talents and resources will continue to be wasted.

There is a fine line between suggestion and coercion in the relationship between donors and governments. But the role played by overseas donors in the economies of certain developing countries underlines the contribution such aid can make to the shaping of policy and the monitoring of its implementation. An ideal *modus operandi* would be one in which donor and recipient government work as partners towards ends which are clearly articulated in policies. When a donor provides large-scale aid, then turns its back on how that aid is actually utilized, it certainly bears part of the blame for the likely result: distorted development. In fact, a token income-generating project which fails to challenge or change the way institutions operate (including those at the local level) may actually reinforce the inequitable status quo.

The extent to which entrepreneurship can develop in a situation such as that of Nepal depends in large measure on central government attitudes and policy. While a direct, detailed analysis of policy has not been attempted here, certain observations can be made on the basis of the findings presented. If the ultimate objective of Nepal's ruling élite is to expand the national economic pie, then expanding the industrial private sector would be one way of achieving this. As long as the government holds control of the pie close to its chest, for fear of losing it entirely, the economy remains intact, but stagnates. If the government initiates policies designed to stimulate the private sector—for example, easier access to foreign currency, less cumbersome export and import procedures, legal recourse in matters of regulations and personnel, and expanded training facilities—Nepal would undoubtedly witness an expansion of the pie. The government is already under pressure from several donors to effect such changes. Much depends on whether those who now hold the reins will loosen their grip, perhaps even joining hands with the emerging entrepreneurial class to move forwards to a future beneficial to all.

If something as complex as entrepreneurship can be presented as a continuum, or a progression of stages, the following sequence might suggest itself. First comes the phase in which the individual or the community is just breaking ground; a monetized economy is introduced, but without yet threatening reciprocal forms of economic exchange which tend to equalize wealth at the village level (besides sustaining patron-client dependencies). In stage two, production becomes more systematized and increasingly concentrated in the hands of the few who own the means of production, organize workers and select technologies. At this point, factors such as infrastructure, policy measures, and market competition begin to become important. In this phase, too, entrepreneurship and expanding technical expertise become crucial. In the final phase of our simplified journey, the entrepreneur must upgrade his management skills and technical efficiency in order to compete in both local and international markets. At this point, factors such as access to raw materials and technology become critical determinants of the pace of industrialization; as before, government policy is also crucial.

In such a sequence, Nepal would currently appear to teeter between phases two and three. Its entrepreneurial communities have demonstrated vision and a willingness to respond to challenge; but numerous forces, cultural as well as economic, impede their advance. Entrepreneurship in Nepal appears to be in a process of constant trial and error, attempting to reconcile the new with old, familiar and traditional patterns. Because their efforts are seen to threaten existing interests, Nepal's entrepreneurs tend to keep their distance—by choice and design—from the mainstream culture. Their separateness relies, however, on the strength of their links with the government and with larger trends in the international market. If Nepal is to achieve a level of industrialization which will free her from dependence on foreign aid, the social separateness or segregation of the entrepreneur and his community will have to be reduced. Internal forces which currently obstruct the work of the entrepreneur must be overcome. If, as we have argued, Nepal's industrialization must involve close interaction between public and private sector concerns, the ultimate goal of national prosperity should be highlighted. Perhaps the various actors in the process will then come to realize that they have objectives and dreams in common.

Old customs, of course, die hard. Nepal's present-day ruling élite surveys the prospect of sharing power and profits with the peasantry and an upstart bourgeoisie with unmistakable scepticism and disbelief. As one scholar notes, 'The critical dilemma faced by the few remaining ruling monarchs in the world today is whether to opt for political development or political power.' (Gaige, 1975) Although hesitation and ambivalence appear to accompany the choice, the reinstated Shah dynasty, presumably with the consent of powerful political and landed interests, appears to be following the former option. The fate of Nepal's economic future in general, and of its industrious entrepreneurs in particular, rests, for the time being at least, on what further steps the world's lone surviving Hindu monarch takes along this unfamiliar, uncharted path.

Glossary

Ashram. Place of religious retreat

Banian. Indian commercial middleman under the British Raj

Basa. Communal kitchen in which food is generally offered free to members of the same caste or ethnic group

Chakari. Behaviour appropriate for someone seeking a favour (for example, the presentation of small gifts)

Desla guthi. A special social grouping for receiving low-interest loans and credit

Dga-nye. A Tibetan reciprocal exchange system

Dharma. Action conforming to universal order or, more specifically, the rules of one's caste

Dhikuri. A group credit system whereby the first borrower gains access to immediate credit while the last gathers the most interest

Gelugpa. A Tibetan Mahayana Buddhist sect which became prominent at the time of the rise of the Dalai Lamas. It gives emphasis to *sutra* (text) rather than to *tantra* (practice)

Gompa. A religious shrine or pilgrimage point for Tibetan Buddhists, believed to hold the remains of important religious leaders

Guthi. A Newar social organization based on lineage or worship of a common deity

Gwali. Labour given by kinsfolk without the expectation of exact reciprocity

Ijara. Monopoly privileges over trade, manufacturing, mining or tax collection initiated under the Shah rulers and expanded under the Ranas (who received part of the proceeds)

Jagir. A land grant given to civil and military servants in lieu of cash payment

Jajmani. The system of prestations and counter-prestations by which the castes as a whole are bound together in a village. The system makes use of hereditary personal relationships to express the division of labour

Jyapoo. A Newar farming caste

Karma. The idea that a person is born in happy or bad conditions because of his or her actions in an earlier life

Kirana. Basic commodity stores common in the hills of Nepal

Kuta tanne. Pulling at the legs of someone so as to keep him or her from advancing

Larke. A Sherpa co-operative group for social exchange purposes

Mukiya. Headman or leader (from the Nepali *mukh*, meaning 'face' or 'mouth')

Nyingma. Unreformed Tibetan Mahayana Buddhist sect which follows the tantric approach

Sahuji. A shopkeeper-cum-moneylender

Samiti. Organized group or society (usually with a welfare orientation)

Sana guthi. Newar social organization which performs rituals upon the death of a member

Sardar. Sherpa mountain expedition leader

Shakya. Newar Buddhist artisan caste

Shrestha. Newar administrator and merchant caste

Skyid-sdug. Tibetan mutual aid or welfare association

Stupa. A circular, often domed building erected as a Buddhist shrine

Subba. Historically, a Rana appointee in charge of trade. In current use, the headman of a particular Thakali community

Suveida. Nepali jargon for incentives, exemptions, services and similar help given by the government to the industrial and business sector

Thek. Exploitative system of land revenue collection

Thouwu. A ritual friendship relationship between Sherpas and members of other communities (usually Buddhist)

Tshong roo. A Managi co-operative trading organization

Uray. A Newar Buddhist business caste

Vaisya. (Also *Vaishya*) One of the four *varnas* (see below): originally, grazers of cattle, but subsequently comprising a group of castes involved in trade and mercantile activity

Vajracharaya. Newar Buddhist priests

Varna. Originally, the four classes or estates or 'colours' into which ancient Indian society at the time of the Rigvedas was divided. The *varna* comprised three categories of twice-born (Brahmin, Kshatriya and Vaishya) as well as the low-born Sudra. The outcastes were excluded from the *varna* framework. *Varna* should not be confused with *jati*, or caste—a later development. Today, *varna* is often used to denote a group or category of castes

Bibliography

Acharya, Meena, and Lynn Bennett (1981): *The Rural Women of Nepal: An Aggregate Analysis and Summary of Eight Village Studies*, Vol. II, Part 9, Regional Service Centre, Manila, Philippines.

Adikiri, Krishna Kant (1984): *Nepal Under Jang Bahadur, 1846–1877*, Vol. I, Sahayogi Press, Kathmandu.

Agarwal, Govind Ram (1982): 'Domestic Resource Mobilization in Nepal: Paradoxes and Prospects' in G.R. Agarwal (ed.), 1982.

——— (ed.) (1982): *Current Issues in Nepalese Development*, CEDA, Kathmandu.

——— and Udaya Bahadur Amatya (1984): *Rural Industrialization in Nepal*, Centre for Economic Development and Administration, Tribhuvan University, Kathmandu.

Aharoni, Yair (1977): *Markets, Planning and Development: the Private and Public Sectors in Economic Development*, Ballinger Publishing Co., Cambridge, Mass.

Ashe, Jeffry (1980): *Assisting the Smallest Scale Activities of the Urban Poor*, Action International/AITEC, Cambridge, Mass.

Asian Development Bank (1984): *Technical Assistance to Nepal for an Industrial Sector Study* (restricted).

Asian Employment Programme (AEP) (1982): *Employment and Basic Needs in Nepal: A Preliminary Analysis of Problems and Policies*, ILO/ARTEP, Kathmandu.

Avendon, John F. (1984): *In Exile from the Land of Snows*, Michael Joseph, London.

Bagchi, Amiya Kumar (1970): 'Entrepreneurship in India,' in Edmund Leach and S.N. Mukerjee (eds.), *Elites in South Asia*, Cambridge University Press, Cambridge.

Bajracharaya, P.H. (1959): 'Newar Marriage Customs and Festivals,' *Southwestern Journal of Anthropology*, Vol. 15, Winter 1959.

Bauer, P.T. and B.S. Yamey (1957): *The Economics of Underdeveloped Countries*, James Nisbet and Cambridge University Press, London.

Berreman, Gerald D. (1972): 'Race, Caste and Other Invidious Distinctions in Social Stratification,' *Race*, Vol. XIII, No. 4, April 1972.

Bhattarai, Maheshwor Prasad (1986): *Entrepreneurship Development Programmes in Nepal: A Case Study of the Small Business Promotion Project*, (unpublished M.A. thesis), Tribhuvan University, Kathmandu.

Bjonnes, I.M. (1983): 'The Impact of Tourism,' *Journal of Mountain Research and Development*, Vol. 3, No. 3.
Blaikie, Piers, John Cameron and David Seddon (1980): *Nepal in Crisis: Growth and Stagnation at the Periphery*, Oxford Universitiy Press, Delhi.
Brockhaus, Robert H., Sr. (1982): 'The Psychology of the Entrepreneur,' in Donald Sexton et al (eds.), 1982.
Broehl, Wayne G., Jr. (1982): 'Entrepreneurship in the Less Developed World,' in Donald Sexton et al (eds.), 1982.
Burton, Roger V. and John M. Whiting (1969): 'The Absent Father and Cross-Sex Identity,' *Merrill-Palmer Quarterly Behavior and Development*, VII, Spring 1969.
Carstairs, G. Morris (1961): *The Twice-Born: A Study of a Community of High-Caste Hindus*, Indiana University Press, Bloomington.
Central Bureau of Statistics (His Majesty's Government of Nepal) (1986): *Statistical Pocketbook*, Kathmandu.
Chao, Ksang (1975): 'The Growth of a Modern Textile Industry in Competition with Handicrafts,' in D.H. Perkins (ed.), *China's Modern Economy in Historical Perspective*, Stanford University Press, Stanford.
Chuta, Enyinna and Carl Liedholm (1979): *Rural Non-farm Employment: A Review of the State of the Art*, Michigan State University Rural Development Paper No. 4, East Lansing, Michigan.
Cochran, Thomas C. (1971): 'The Entrepreneur in Economic Change,' in Peter Kilby (ed.), 1971.
Cohen, Alan R. (1967): *Tradition, Values and Inter-role Conflict in Indian Family Business*, (unpublished D.B.A. thesis), Harvard Business School, Harvard.
Cooke, Terry (1982): *Identity, Tradition and Change in Nepal-Tibet Relations*, (unpublished Ph.D. thesis), University of California at Berkeley.
Development Research and Communications Group (DRCG) (1984): *A Study of Non-Agricultural Enterprises in Nepal*, Kathmandu.
Doherty, Victor Sargent (1975): *Kinship and Economic Choice: Modern Adaptations in Western Central Nepal*, (unpublished Ph.D. thesis), University of Wisconsin.
Draper, John N. (1985): *Transcendence and Pragmatism: a Study of Sherpa Religion*, (unpublished M.A. thesis), Australian National University, Canberra.
——— 'The Sherpas: Transformed or Consolidated?' (forthcoming)
Dumont, Louis (1970): *Homo Hierarchicus: the Caste System and its Implications*, University of Chicago Press, Chicago.
Dunlop, David W. (1983): *A Comparative Analysis of Policies and Other Factors which Affect the Role of the Private Sector in Economic Development*, AID Paper No. 20, Washington D.C.
Durkheim, Emile (1964): *The Division of Labour in Society*, cited in Anthony Giddens, 1971.

Fisher, James F. (ed.) (1978): *Himalayan Anthropology*, Mouton Publishers, The Hague.
────── (1986): *Himalayan Traders: Economy, Society and Culture in Northwest Nepal*, University of California Press.
Fox, Richard G. (1973): 'Pariah Capitalism and Traditional Indian Merchants, Past and Present,' in Milton Singer (ed.), 1973.
Fricke, Thomas (1984): *Two Tamang Economies: Incipient Class Formation and its Implications in a North Central Nepali Village*, East-West Population Institute, Honolulu.
Fürer-Haimendorf, Christoph von (1964): *The Sherpas of Nepal: Buddhist Highlanders*, University of California Press, Berkeley.
────── (ed.) (1966): *Caste and Kin in Nepal, India and Ceylon*, Sterling Publishers, New Delhi.
────── (ed.) (1974): *Contributions to the Anthropology of Nepal*, Aris and Phillips, Warminster.
────── (1975): *Himalayan Traders*, John Murray, London.
────── (1978): 'Trans-Himalayan Traders in Transition,' in James Fisher (ed.), 1978.
Gadgil, D.R. (1924): *The Industrial Evolution of India in Recent Times*, Oxford University Press, Oxford.
Gaige, F.H. (1975): *Regionalism and National Unity in Nepal*, University of California Press, Berkeley.
Geertz, Clifford (1962): 'Social Change and Economic Modernization in Two Indonesian Towns: A Case in Point,' in Everett E. Hagen (ed.), 1962.
Giddens, Anthony (1971): *Capitalism and Modern Social Theory: An Analysis of the Writings of Marx, Durkheim and Max Weber*, Cambridge University Press, Cambridge.
Goldstein, Melvyn (1978): 'Ethnogenesis and Resource Competition Among Tibetan Refugees in South India: A New Face to the Indo-Tibetan Interface,' in James F. Fisher (ed.), 1978.
Goodall, Merrill (1975): 'Bureaucracy and Bureaucrats: Some Themes from the Nepal Experience,' *Asian Survey*, October 1975.
Griffin, K.B. and J.L. Enos (1973): 'Policies for Industrialization' in Henry Bernstein (ed.): *Underdevelopment and Development*, Penguin Books, Harmondsworth, Middlesex.
Gumbo, Ugen (1985): *Tibetan Refugees in the Kathmandu Valley: A Study in Socio-Cultural Change and Continuity and the Adaptation of a Population in Exile*, (unpublished Ph.D. thesis), State University of New York, Stony Brook.
Gurung, Naresh Jung (1976): 'An Introduction to the Socio-economic Structure of Manang District,' *Kailash*, Vol. IV, No. 3.
Hageboeck, Molly and Mary Beth Allen (1982): *Private Sector: Ideas and Opportunities* A.I.D. Programme Evaluation Discussion Paper No. 14.

Hagen, Everett E. (ed.) (1962): *On the Theory of Social Change: How Economic Growth Begins*, The Dorsey Press, Homewood, Illinois.
—— (1971): 'How Economic Growth Begins: A Theory of Social Change,' in Peter Kilby (ed.), 1971.
Hamal, L.B. (1972): *Central Banking in Nepal*, Nepali Sahitya Bhawan, Biratnagar, Nepal.
Harris, John R. (1971): 'Nigerian Entrepreneurship in Industry' in Peter Kilby (ed), 1971.
Hoselitz, Bert F. (1964): 'A Sociological Approach to Economic Development' in David E. Novack and Robert Leachman (eds.): *Development and Society*, St. Martin's Press, New York.
Hunter, Guy (1969): *Modernzing Peasant Societies*, Oxford University Press, Oxford.
Ishii, H. (1980): 'Recent Economic Changes in a Newar Village,' *Contributions to Nepalese Studies* 3(1), 157–80.
Jackson, D.P. (1976): 'The Early History of Lo (Mustang) and Nagari,' *Contributions to Nepalese Studies* 4(7).
Kilby, Peter (ed.) (1971): *Entrepreneurship and Economic Development*, The Free Press, New York.
Kolenda, Pauline (1978): *Caste in Contemporary India: Beyond Organic Solidarity*, The Benjamin-Cummings Publishing Company, Redwood City, California.
Kumar, S. (1967): *Rana Polity in Nepal: Origin and Growth*, Asia Publishing House, Bombay.
Lambert, Richard D. (1964): 'The Social and Psychological Determinants of Savings and Investments in Developing Societies,' in Novack and Leachman (eds.), 1964.
Lévi, S. (1905–8) *Le Népal: Etude Historique d'un Royaume Hindou*, (3 Vols.) Leroux, Paris.
Levi-Strauss, Claude (1969): *The Elementary Stucture of Kinship*, Beacon Press, Boston.
Linton, Ralph (1964): 'Cultural and Personality Factors Affecting Economic Growth,' in Novack and Leachman (eds.), 1964.
Lohani, Prakash C. (1973): 'Industrial Policy: The Problem Child of History and Planning in Nepal' in Rana and Malla (eds.), 1973.
McBer et al (1987): *The Identification and Assessment of Competencies and Other Personal Characteristics of Entrepreneurs in Developing Countries*, Washington D.C.
McClelland, David C. and David G. Winters (1969): *Motivating Economic Achievement*, The Free Press, New York.
Manzardo, Andrew E. and Keshar Prasad Sharma (1975): 'Cost cutting, Caste and Community: A Look at Thakali Social Reform in Pokhara,' *Contributions to Nepalese Studies* 2(2), 25–44.

Markham, Clements (1876): *Narratives of the Mission of George Bogle to Tibet and of the Journey of Thomas Manning to Tibet,* Trubner and Co., London.
Marriott, McKim (1976): 'Hindu Transactions: Diversity without Dualism' in Bruce Kapferer (ed.): *Transaction and Meaning: Directions in the Anthropology of Exchange and Symbolic Behaviour,* Institute for the Study of Human Issues, Philadelphia.
Mauss, Marcel (1954): *The Gift: Forms and Functions of Exchange in Archaic Societies,* translated by Ian Cunnison, Cohen and West Ltd.
Mead, Margaret (1964): 'From the Stone Age to the Twentieth Century,' in Novack and Leachman (eds.), 1964.
Medhora, Phiroze (1965): 'Entrepreneurship in India,' *Political Science Quarterly,* Vol. LXXX, No. 4, December 1965.
Messerschmidt, Donald A. (1978): 'Dhikurs: Rotating Credit Associations in Nepal,' in James F. Fisher (ed.) 1978.
────── and N.J. Gurung (1974): 'Parallel Trade and Innovations in Central Nepal: the cases of Gurung and Thakali Subbas Compared,' in C. von Fürer-Haimendorf (ed.), 1974.
Miller, Beatrice D. (1978): 'Tibetan Culture and Personality: Refugee Responses to a Tibetan Culture-Bound TAT,' in James F. Fisher (ed.), 1978.
Mines, Mattison (1973): 'Tamil Muslim Merchants in India's Industrial Development' in Milton Singer (ed.), 1973.
Minturn L. and J.T. Hitchcock (1963): 'The Rajputs of Khalapur, India,' in B.B. Whiting (ed.): *Six Cultures: Studies of Child-rearing,* John Wiley, New York.
Moodey, Richard W. (1978): 'Kinship and Culture in the Himalayan Region,' in James F. Fisher (ed.), 1978.
Morris, M.D. (1973): 'The Emergence of an Industrial Labour Force in India,' in Henry Bernstein (ed.): *Underdevelopment and Development,* Penguin Books, Harmondsworth, Middlesex.
Nafziger, Wayne E. (1971): 'Indian Entrepreneurship: A Survey,' in Peter Kilby (ed.), 1971.
Nandy, Ashis (1973): 'Need Achievement in a Calcutta Suburb,' in Milton Singer (ed.), 1973.
Nepali, Gopal Singh (1965): *The Newars,* States People Press, India.
Nihan, Georges and Robert Jourdain (1978): 'The Modern Informal Sector in Nouachott,' *International Labour Review,* Vol. II, No. 6, Nov–Dec 1978.
Novack, David E. and Robert Leachman (eds.) (1964): *Development and Society,* St. Martin's Press, New York.
Oppitz, Michael (1974): 'Myths and Facts: Reconsidering Some Data Concerning the Clan History of the Sherpas,' in C. von Fürer-Haimendorf (ed.), 1974.
Ortner, Sherry (1970): *Food for Thought: A Key Symbol in Sherpa Culture,* (unpublished Ph.D. thesis), University of Chicago.
────── (1978): *Sherpas Through Their Rituals,* Cambridge University Press, Cambridge.

Owens, Raymond (1971): 'Mahishya Entrepreneurs in Howrah, West Bengal,' in R. and M.J. Beech (eds.): *Bengal: Change and Continuity*, East Lansing, Michingan, 1971.

Papanek, Gustav F. (1971): 'The Development of Entrepreneurship,' in Peter Kilby (ed.), 1971.

Papanek, Hanna (1973): 'Pakistan's New Industrialists and Businessmen: Focus on the Memons,' in Milton Singer (ed.), 1973.

Paul, R.A. (1978): *Sherpas and their Religion* (unpublished Ph.D. thesis), University of Chicago.

————— (1983): *The Tibetan Symbolic World: Psychoanalytic Interpretations*, Chicago University Press, Chicago.

Prabhu, Pandharinath H. (1963): *Hindu Social Organization: A Study in Socio-Psychological and Ideological Foundations* (4th edition), Popular Prakashan, Bombay.

Pradhan, Radhe S. (1984): *Industrialization in Nepal*, N.B.O. Publishing Distributors, New Delhi.

Quigley, D. (1985): 'Household Organization Among Newar Traders,' *Contributions to Nepalese Studies* 12(2), April 1985.

Rana, P.S.J.B. and K.P. Malla (eds.) (1973): *Nepal in Perspective*, CEDA, Kathmandu.

Regmi, Mahesh Chandra (1971): *A Study of Nepali Economic History 1768–1845*, Manjusri Publishing House, New Delhi.

————— (1978): *Thatched Huts and Stucco Palaces: Peasants and Landlords in 19th Century Nepal*, Vikas Publishing House, New Delhi.

————— (undated): *An Economic History of Nepal: 1846–1901* (unpublished draft).

Rose, Leo E. (1971): *Nepal: Strategy for Survival*, University of California Press, Berkeley.

————— and Fisher, M.W. (1970): *The Politics of Nepal: Persistence and Change in an Asian Monarchy*, Cornell University Press, Ithaca.

Rosser, Colin (1966): 'Social Mobility in the Newar Caste System,' in C. von Fürer-Haimendorf (ed.), 1966.

Sadie, J.L. (1964): 'The Social Anthropology of Economic Underdevelopment' in David E. Novack and Rober Leachman (eds.), 1964.

Seddon, J.D. with P.M. Blaikie and J. Cameron (1978): *Peasants and Workers in Nepal: the Condition of the Lower Classes*, Aris and Phillips, Warminster.

Sexton, Donald L. et al (eds.) (1982): *Encyclopaedia of Entrepreneurship*, Prentice-Hall, New Jersey.

Shapero, Albert and Lisa Sokol (1982): 'The Social Dimensions of Entrepreneurship,' in Donald Sexton et al (eds.), 1982.

Sharma, S.V.S. (1979): *Small Entrepreneurial Development in Some Asian Countries: A Comparative Study*, Light and Life Publishers, New Delhi.

Shrestha, Hari Prasad (1985): 'The Marwaris of Nepal,' *Media Nepal*, 1985: 33–37.

Singer, Milton (1972): *When a Great Tradition Modernizes*, Pall Mall Press, London.
———— (ed.) (1973): *Entrepreneurship and Modernization of Occupational Cultures in South Asia*, Duke University (monograph).
Srinivas, M.N. (1962): *Caste in Modern India*, Asia Publishing House, Bombay.
———— (1968): 'Mobility in the Caste System,' in M. Singer and B.S. Cohn (eds.): *Structure and Change in Indian Society*, Aldine, Chicago.
Stiller, Ludwig F. (1973): *The Rise of the House of Gorkha: A Study in the Unification of Nepal 1768–1816*, Manjusri Publishing House, New Delhi.
Suwal, Rajendra (1982): 'Employment Generation: Easier Said Than Done,' in Govind Ram Agarwal (ed.), 1982.
Thapa, Ganesh Bahadur (1982): 'Nepal's Trade Performance: the Use and Abuse of the Engine of Growth,' in Govind Ram Agarwal (ed.) 1982.
Timberg, Timothy (1978): *The Marwaris: From Traders to Industrialists*, Vikas Publishing House, New Delhi.
Toffin, G. (1977): *Pyangaon: une Communauté Newar de la Vallée de Kathmandu*, CNRS, Paris.
Trade Promotion Centre and Nepal Rashtra Bank (1986): *Overseas Trade Statistics*, Kathmandu.
Vindig, Michael (1979–80): 'The Thakali Household and Inheritance System,' *Contributions to Nepalese Studies*, 7 (1 and 2) (December 1979 and June 1980).
Von der Heide, Suzanna (1987): *The Thakalis from North Western Nepal*, Ratna Publishers, Ratna Pushtak Bhandar, Kathmandu.
Wallender, Harvey (1978): *Technology Transfer and Management in the Developing Countries*, Fund for Multinational Management Education, New York.
Weber, Max (1920): *The Religion of India: The Sociology of Hinduism and Buddhism* (English translation by H.H. Gerth and D. Martindale, Glencoe, Illinois, 1958).
———— (1930): *The Protestant Ethic and the Spirit of Capitalism* (English translation), London.
Wiser, William Henricks (1958): *The Hindu Jajmani System: A Socio-Economic System Interrelating Members of a Hindu Village Community in Services*, Lucknow Publishing House, Lucknow.
World Bank (1972): *Industry*, (Section III), IBRD/The World Bank, Washington D.C.
———— (1985): *World Bank Development Report 1985* IBRD/The World Bank, Washington D.C. and Oxford University Press, New Delhi.
Young, Frank W. (1971): 'A Macro-social Interpretation of Entrepreneurship' in Peter Kilby (ed.), 1971.
Zivetz, Laurie (1987): *Training for the Private Sector: The Demand and the Supply*, Management Support Services, Kathmandu.

Index

ADB, *See* Agricultural Development Bank
Acharya, M., 29, 36, 81
Actionaid/Nepal, 219f
Adam Smith, 41
'Adaptive strategies', 112
Adhikari, K.K., 53, 55
Agarwal, G.R., 176, 209, 219
Agarwals, 91
Agrarian societies, 20–1, 38
Agricultural Development Bank (ADB), 162, 191
Aharoni, Y., 43, 133, 189, 221
Allen, M.B., 41
Amatya, U.B., 209, 219
Ashe, J., 41
Ashram, 85, 95
Asia, South (map), 4

Baglung, 75
Bal Bir Serchan, 98
Banian, 62, 85
Banjadi, 25, 31
Bank loans, 217–19
Basa, 85
Bauer, P.T., 11, 30, 36, 38, 211
Bela Belassa, 41
Bennett, L., 29, 36, 81
Berreman, G.D., 23,
Bhairahawa, 86, 100, 169
Bhattarai, M.P., 199
Bhotia, 98
Birgunj Sugar Mill, 168
Bjonnes, I.M., 108
Black market, 41, 61, 88, 122–3, 143, 148, 156, 157
Blaikie, P., 56, 59, 210, 219
Brahmins, 24–5, 67, 127
British firms, 84–5

Brockhaus, R.H., 195
Broehl, W.G., 190–1, 195, 212, 215, 224
Buddhism, 23, 26–9, 127–8; Newari, 74, 75; Sherpa, 105, 108
Burton, R.V., 94
Business ethic, Newari, 81–3; Marwari, 90–1
Bureaucracy, 16, 156–7, 162–4
Butwal, 75

CBS, *see* Central Bureau of Statistics
CCU, 166
CTC, *see* Carpet Trading Corporation
Cameron, J., 68, 69
Candle-making industry, 170–1
Career choices, 192–201, 205–6, 210–12; acquisition of skills, 201–3; family background, 195–201; 'imitative' entrepreneurship, 203
'Caretaker élites', 18–19
Carpet industry, 14, 118–21, 178–81, 228
Carpet Trading Corporation (CTC), 118
Carstairs, G.M., 25
Caste, 9, 23–6, 91, 128
Census (1980), 5, 191, 208–9
Central Bureau of Statistics (CBS), 50, 136, 137, 167, 191
Chakari, 56, 214
Chao, K., 38
Chamaria, Radha Kissen, 86
Chhetris, 52–3, 67, 125, 127
Child-rearing practices, 31–6, 130; Marwari, 94; Newari, 79; Thakali, 101
Chinese invasion of Tibet (1959), 76, 106f, 112
Chuta, E., 42
Cochran, T.C., 20, 31

244 / Index

Cohen, A.R., 93
Colonialism, 17–18, 62–3
'Conscience collective', 21
Construction industry, 228
Cooke, T., 123
Corruption, 6, 156–7, 188
Cottage industries, 60
Cottage Industry Emporium, 60

DCVI, see Department of Cottage and Village Industries
DRCG, 138f, 141, 147, 171, 175, 206, 208, 216, 223
Dalai Lama, 113, 118, 119; Office of, 112
Department of Cottage and Village Industries (DCVI), 152–3
Department of Industries, 66, 67
Desla guthi, 77
Dga-nye, 115
Dharmic dictums, 25, 28
Dharmsala, 113
Dhikuri system, 102–3
Doherty, V.S., 76, 121, 122f
Donor assistance, 230
Draper, J.N., 105, 106, 110
Dumont, L., 24
Dunlop, D., 40–3
Durkheim, E., 19, 21, 133

Employment, 209
Enos, J.L., 41
Enterprise, and entrepreneur, 224; financing, 215–20; labour force, 208–12; management practices, 212–15; marketing, 222–4; role of family, 206–8; technology, 220–2
Entrepreneur, 192–206; acquisition of skills, 201–3; and enterprise, 224; family background, 195–201; 'imitative' entrepreneurship, 203–5; portraits, 47–9
Entrepreneurship, determinants of, 7–45, 124–32; ethnic distribution, 64–72; historical overview, 50–61; Indian and Nepalese compared, 61–4
Entrepreneurial communities, 73–132;

child-rearing, 130; family structure, 128–9; geographical factors, 125; Gurung, 121–2; 'Homelands' (map), 51; Managi (Nyishang), 122–3; Marwari, 83–96; Newar, 73–83; Nyishang, see Managi; religion, 127–8; Sherpa, 103–12; social marginality, 124–5, 131; social organization, 125–7; Thakali, 96–103; Tibetan, 112–21; trading tradition, 130–1; women, 129–30
Equalization of wealth, 21–2
Everest, Mount, 108
Export, carpets, 118, 119, 180; deficit, 142; garments, 181; industries, 151–2

Family and private enterprise, 29–31, 79, 128–30, 195–201, 206–8; Gurung, 121–2; Marwári, 93–4; Sherpa, 111; Thakali, 101; Tibetan, 114
Farming, as career, 210–12; mentality, 14, 211
Five Year Plans, First, 138; Second, 138, 143; Third, 138–9; Fourth, 139; Fifth, 140
Foreign aid, 59
Fox, R.G., 7
Fricke, T., 22
Fürer-Haimendorf, C. von, 14, 28, 97, 98, 100, 104, 106, 107, 109, 110, 111, 130

GDP, 3, 5, 166
GNP, 135–6
GTZ, see German Fund for Technical Assistance
Gaige, F.H., 53, 56, 59, 86, 88, 159, 160, 232
Garment industry, 181–5, 200–1
Geertz, C., 11, 14, 16, 17, 32
Gellner, D., 78f, 80
Geographical factors as a determinant of entrepreneurship, 125
George Bernard Shaw, 189
German Fund for Technical Assistance (GTZ), 158f

Index / 245

Giddens, A., 18
Goldstein, M., 116
Gorkhali (Shah) rule, 54–5, 73, 75
Gorkhapatra Sansthan, 178
Griffin, K.B., 41
Gumbo, U., 112, 113, 114, 115, 116, 117, 120
Gurung, N.J., 122, 98
Gurungs, 121–2
Guthi, 77–8, 82f
Gwali, 78

Hageboeck, M., 41
Hagen, E., 10, 13, 17, 19, 20, 32, 33, 36
Hamal, L.B., 219
Harris, J.R., 14, 195, 204, 216
Himalayan Carpet Export Company, 118, 119
Himalayas, 3
Hinduism, 23–9
Hitchcock, J.T., 32
Hoselitz, B.F., 10, 15, 16
Hunter, G., 22

IDS, 58
ISC, 166
Ijara system, 55, 60, 75
'Impression' management, 109–10
India, and Nepal, 5, 57, 59, 161; immigrants from, 52; industry, 61–41
Indians, business elements 158–60; labour, 176
Indo-Tibetan trading route, 53, 73
Industrial Act, (1974), 139, 142; (1981), 140–2, 149, 157, 165
Industrial sector, 61–4, 135–7, 226–32; basic statistics, 137; classification, 140; Five Year Plans, 138–43; protectionism, 172–7; tax exemption, 141; *also see* Private sector
Industrial Sector Plan Study (1980/81–1990/91), 166
Industrialization in Nepal, 138f
Integrated Rural Development, 158f
Ishii, H., 78

Jackson, D.P., 96
Jagir Khane, 55–6

Jagir system, 60, 75
Jainism, 92
Jajmani system, 24, 53, 198
Jang Bahadur Rana, 57, 86
Jawalakhel, 118, 119f
Jayastiti Malla, 74
Joint family, *see* Family
Jourdain, R., 42, 203
Juddha Shamsher Rana, 86
Jyapoos, 74

Kali Gandaki River Valley (Thak Khola), 96–7, 98
Karma, 20, 25, 26, 28, 108
Kathmandu Valley, 53, 73, 117
Khumbu, 104–5, 228
Kilby, P., 9
Kingsley Davis, 23
Kirana stores, 223–4
Kobang, 96
Kolenda, P., 23, 24, 26, 29
Kot Massacre, 55
Kshatriyas, 24, 25
Kumar, S., 55
Kuta tanne, 162–3
Kyerok Lama, 103–4

Labour, 54, 146, 174–7, 208–12
Lambert, R.D., 14, 15–16, 18–19, 26, 34, 39
Landowners, 13–14, 55–6, 60
Land reform programme (*Mulki Ain*), 58
Levi, S., 74f
Levi-Strauss, C., 21, 22, 131
Lewis, T., 74f, 76
Licensing, 148–9, 152–3, 204
Liedholm, C., 42
Linton, R., 37, 39, 206, 211
Loans, 216–19
Lohani, P.C., 47
Lumbini, 23f

McBer, 192, 201
McClelland, D.C., 17, 32, 33, 34, 203
Mahendra Sugar Mill Private Limited, 169–70
Mahesworis, 91

Malla, K.P., 47, 78f
Malla rulers, 53; King Jayastiti, 74
Management practices, 190, 212–15
Management Support Services, 146
Managis (Nyishang community), 122–3
Manzardo, A.E., 98, 99, 100
Marginality, *see* Social marginality
Marketing, 222–4
Marriott, M., 24
Marwari Sewa Samiti, 95
Marwaris, 83–96; caste, 91f; entrepreneurial origins, 84–5; links with élite, 87–90; Marwari diaspora', 85; philanthropy, 94–5; social organization and internal definition, 90–6; vegetarianism, 91–2
Marx, K., 18, 19, 22, 24
Mauss, M., 21, 22, 131
Mead, Margaret, 39, 211
Medhora, P., 85, 96
Merchants, 13–15
Messerschmidt, D.A., 98, 102, 121
Miller, B.D., 116, 117
Mines, 14
Ministry of Tourism, 72
Minorities, 17f
Minturn, L., 32
Monarchy, 58–9
Money-lenders, 15–16, 22, 115
Mukiya (headman), 98
Mulki Ain (land reform programme), 58

NIDC, *see* Nepal Industrial Development Corporation
Nafziger, W.E., 31
Namche Bazaar, 106, 111
Nandy, A., 11, 16, 26
National Assembly, 58
Nationalism, 64
Nepal Bank, 162
Nepal Industrial Development Corporation (NIDC), 161, 219
Nepal in Crisis, 68
Nepal Textile Association, 151
Nepal-Tibet war (1854–56), 98
Nepal Times, 159
Nepal Trans-Himalayan Traders Association, 68, 70, 179, 180

Nepal Wool Trading Corporation, 180
Nepali, G.S., 74f, 77, 79, 81
Newars, 73–83; business ethic, 81–3; origin and history, 73–7; religion, 74; social structure, 77–81
Nihan, G., 42
Non-Agricultural Enterprises in Nepal, A Study of, 138f, 147
Nyishang community, *see* Managis

Office of the Dalai Lama, 112
Open Generalized License (OGEL) system, 149
Oppitz, M., 104
Ortner, S., 107, 108
Oswals, 91
Owens, R., 30

'Palace capitalism', 6
Panchayat system, 58
Papanek, G., 41
Papanek, H., 11, 14, 17
Policy issues, 40–3, 177–8
Power, 41
Pradhan, R., 138f, 161, 167
Prithvi Narayan Shah, 54
Private sector, donor assistance, 42; élite's control; 59; Indian business elements, 158–60; problems : fluctuating policies and weak co-ordination, 177–8; human resources, 174–7; incentives and loans, 157–65; judicial system, 144; protectionism, 172–4; raw materials, 147–57; relationship with public sector, 165–72, 187–8; *also see* Industrial sector
Production, factors of, 36–40; attitudes to saving in peasant societies, attitude to technology, 39–40; work ethic, 37–9
Protectionism, 41, 172–41
Public sector, performance, 166–7; relationship with private sector, 165–72, 187–8

Quigley, D., 31, 78, 79, 80, 82
Radha Kissen Chamaria, 86
Rana, Juddha Shamsher, 86

Rana, P.S.J.B., 47
Rana rule, 55–8; and Marwaris, 86; and Newaris, 75–6; and Sherpas, 105; and Thakalis, 98–9
Raw materials, 147–57, 170–2
Reciprocity of wealth, 21–2, 131
Refugees, 11–12; Tibetan, 113–14
Regmi, M.C., 54, 55, 56, 57, 75
Religion, 22–9, 127–8
Rising Nepal, The, 166
Rose, L.E., 53
Rosser, C., 75

SATA, *see* Swiss Association for Technical Assistance
Sadie, J.L., 13, 20, 37, 38, 211
Sahuji, 15–16, 199
Salt trade, 98, 99
Salt Trading Corporation, 70–1
Sana guthi, 77
Samiksha Weekly, 159
Sardar, 106
Saving, attitudes to, 37
Seddon, D., 68, 69
Serchen, Bal Bir, 98
Shah (Gorkhali) rule, 54–5, 73, 75
Shakya (artisans), 74
Shapero, A., 216
Sharma, S.V.S., 192, 198, 216
Sharma, K.P., 98, 99, 100
Shaw, G.B., 189
Sherpas, 103–12; accumulation of wealth, 105–8; early history, 104–5; economic organization, 110–11; family and role of women, 111–12; religious and cultural practices, 108–10
Shoe industry, 171–2
Shrestha (merchant and administrative caste), 74
Shrestha, H.P., 84f, 86, 89
Singer, M., 24, 25, 30, 42
Skills, 201–3
Skyid-sdug, 115
'Sleeping' partner, 65
Small Business Promotion Project, 158f
Small industrialists, 25, 128, 191f, 197–201
Smith, Adam, 41

Social marginality, 10–19, 124–5, 131–2; access to ruling élites, 131–2; beyond social marginality, 19–20; geographical factors, 125; groups with entrepreneurial potential, 16–17; immigrants and refugees, 11–12; money-lender, 15–16; the colony, 17–18; traders and merchants, 13–15; traditional élites, 18–19
Social organization, 20–36, 125–7; child-rearing practices, 31–6; joint family, 29–31; reciprocity, and equalization of wealth, 21–2, and internal co-operative system, 131; religion, 22–9, 127–8
Solu, 104–5
Son's role, 35, 207; Marwari, 93; Newari, 79, 81; Sherpa, 111; Tibetan, 114
'Source and force', 60, 61, 144, 148, 162, 184, 185, 217
South Asia (map), 4
Srinivas, M.N., 24
Statistical Handbook (1984), 209; (1986) 137, 167
Statistical Pocketbook (1984), 136; (1986) 50f
'Status withdrawal' theory, 16, 33
Stiller, L.F., 54
Subba, 98–9
Sugar industry, 168–70, 174
Suveida ('necessary facilities'), 138
Suwal, R., 38
Swiss Association for Technical Assistance (SATA), 113, 118, 177f

TGE, *see* Tibetan Government in Exile
TSRO, *see* Thakali Samar Sudhar Sangh
Tamang-Thakalis, 98; *see* Thakalis
Tansen, 75
Taxation: Five Year Plans, 138–41, 151, 152; Garment industry, 184–5; Rana rule, 56
Technology, 121–2, 129–30, 220–2; attitude to, 39–40
Terai, 3, 52, 56, 88; its businesspeople, 159–60

Thak Khola (Kali Gandaki River Valley), 96–7, 98
Thakali Samar Sudhar Sangh (TSRO), 100
Thakalis, 96–103; after the Ranas, 99–100; 'dhikuri' system, 102–3; economic organization, 102; family structure, 101; origins, 96–7; Tamangs, 98; under the Ranas, 98–9; urbanization and dispersion, 103
Thapa, G.B., 143
Thek system, 55
Thouwu, 109
Tibetan Government in Exile (TGE), 113, 116f
Tibetan Women's Association, 115f
Tibetans, 112–21; after the Chinese invasion, 112–14; cultural practices and religious beliefs, 116–17; entrepreneurship in exile (carpet industry), 117–21; family structure, 114; socioeconomic organization, 115–16
Timberg, T., 7, 11, 17, 62, 84, 85, 91, 94
Tiwari, C., 184
Toffin, G., 78
Tourism, Ministry of, 72
Tourist and trekking agencies, 71–2, 204–5
Tourist industry, 107–8, 155, 204–5
Trade and Transit Treaty (1966), 138–9
Trade Promotion Centre, 119, 178, 181, 185
Trade routes, 53
Traders and merchants, 13–15, 130–1
Trans-Himalayan Traders Association, 179
Tribhuvan, King of Nepal, 58

Tshong roo, 123

Underemployment, 209
United Mission to Nepal, 177f
United States, 20
United Tibetan Association, 115f
Uray (business strata), 74, 75, 131

Vaisya caste, 13, 91
Vajracharayas (Buddhist priests), 74
Varna system, 23f
Vegetarianism, 91–92
Village societies, 22, 59
Vindig, M., 101
Von der Heide, S., 98, 99, 100, 103
von Furer-Haimendorf, *see* Fürer-Haimendorf, C. von

Wailender, H., 222
Weber, M., 10, 18, 22, 23, 25, 26f, 27f, 38, 92
Whiting, J.M., 94
Winters, D.G., 32, 34, 203
Wiser, W.H., 24
Women, entrepreneurship, 7f, 33–4, 129–30; Gurung, 121–2; 'Indo-Aryan' and Tibeto-Burman communities, 36; Newari, 81; Sherpa, 111; Thakali, 101
Work ethic, 37–9
World Bank, 57, 139, 142, 153, 180, 188f, 219f
World War II, 1, 57, 138f, 199

Yamey, B.S., 11, 30, 36, 38, 211
Young, F.W., 10

Zivetz, L., 41, 42, 145, 146, 158f, 177f